MANC

Michael Crick has be...
and away since he w...
cated at Manchester...
Oxford, where he edited ~~Oxford~~...
the Union. His previous books about Militant and Arthur
Scargill were acclaimed for being both fair and highly read-
able. He works as the Washington correspondent for ITN's
Channel 4 News.

David Smith first began supporting Manchester United in
the 1950s and since the Munich air disaster in 1958, which
had a profound and lasting effect on him, his whole life has
revolved around the fortunes of the team that rose from the
ashes. On leaving school in 1960 he trained as a commercial
photographer. In 1968 he was elected as committee member
of the newly formed supporters' club and within seven years
became its chairman and travel organiser, working from an
office situated at Old Trafford. In March 1987 he was
advised that both he and his organisation were 'surplus to
requirements' when United's senior management endorsed
the introduction of a commercially orientated club membership scheme to replace the supporters' club.

Michael Crick & David Smith

MANCHESTER UNITED
The Betrayal of a Legend

PAN BOOKS
London, Sydney and Auckland

First published 1989 by Pelham Books/Stephen Greene Press,
of the Penguin Group, London
This edition published 1990 by Pan Books Ltd,
Cavaye Place, London SW10 9PG
9 8 7 6 5 4 3 2 1
© Michael Crick and David Smith 1989
ISBN 0 330 31440 8

Phototypeset by Input Typesetting Ltd, London
Printed and bound in Great Britain by
Clays Ltd, St Ives plc, Bungay, Suffolk

Contents

	page
Acknowledgements	vii
Introduction	1
1 The Beginnings of a Legend	9
2 Into Europe	34
3 The Man who Bought United	52
4 The Search for the Holy Grail	69
5 Decline and Scandal	93
6 The Edwards Family Business	124
7 We'll Support You Evermore	149
8 The Butcher's Boy	168
9 Chief Executive	188
10 The Building of Old Trafford	205
11 Player Politics	223
12 A Different Ball Game	247
13 Selling United	258
14 The Man who didn't buy United	272
Conclusion	302
Postscript	307
Appendix A: Match Attendances 1946–90	311
Appendix B: Player Transfers 1945–90	314
Appendix C: The Edwards Family Tree	322
Bibliography	323
Index	327

Acknowledgements

In the course of research for this book the authors spoke to over a hundred people involved with Manchester United. Many preferred to remain anonymous, but those whom we can thank publicly (in alphabetical order) are: Tommy Appleby, John Aston Junior, John Aston Senior, Ron Atkinson, Alan Ball, Michael Berisford, Alec Bird, Gordon Bishop, Jackie Blanchflower, Alan Brazil, Laurie Brown, Mick Brown, Martin Buchan, Bill Burke, Nigel Burrows, Sir Matt Busby, Mary Carroll, Bobby Charlton, Barry Chaytow, Steve Coppell, Pat Crerand, Jack Crompton, John Crowther, Dick Donald, Ian Donald, Tommy Docherty, Derek Dougan, Tony Dunne, Martin Edwards, Alex Ferguson, John Fletcher, Alan Gowling, Brian Greenhoff, Richard Greenwood, Harry Gregg, Magi Haroun, Sam Holt, Jim Holton, Stewart Houston, David Icke, Brian Kidd, Louis Kilcoyle, Michael Knighton, Denis Law, Lou Macari, John Madeley, John McCabe, Paddy McGrath, Paul McGrath, Danny McGregor, Wilf McGuinness, Andrew McHutchon, Laurie McMenemy, David Murray, Tony Metcalfe, Barry Moorhouse, Willie Morgan, David Murray, Malcolm Musgrove, Frank O'Farrell, John Parncutt, Peter Raymond, Jimmy Rimmer, Dennis Roach, David Sadler, Paul Satinoff, Ron Saunders, Dave Sexton, Eddie Shah, Alex Stepney, Ian Storey-Moore, Rick Taylor and Harvey Wilde Senior.

We are grateful to staff at Companies House; the Football Association; Central Library, Manchester; the *Manchester Evening News*; St Katherine's House and Somerset House for guiding us through our research requests. John Edwards, Chris Ingram and Nick Pitt were extremely helpful in providing detailed information on press coverage of Manchester United for the years 1987–89.

Paul Greengrass, formerly of Granada TV's *World in Action*, kindly lent his extensive research material from the 1980 programme on United. David Sadler, secretary of the Association of Former Manchester United Players, helped us contact many of his members. We would also like to thank Nicholas Mills and Ron Lyle of Cokethorpe School; Michael Fennell of stockbrokers A. J. Bekhor; Graham Endicott of Littlewoods Pools; Stan Royle, the *Manchester Evening News* picture editor; Dave Appleton of Salford City Council; Hugh Adam of Rangers Football Club; and David and Winnie Blakemore of the Warwickshire Supporters' Association. The staff of News Information at ITN were particularly helpful and sympathetic.

Margaret Crick was marvellous in tolerating her husband's behaviour over the past three years during the writing of this book, as were Anne and Gregg Smith who had to endure what was a traumatic period in their family life. Our agent Bill Hamilton saw us through two contracts. We are grateful to Dick Douglas-Boyd at Pelham for accepting the idea originally, and to Roger Houghton and Hilary Foakes for seeing it through its rocky course. John Crick, Margaret Crick, Andrew Curry, Chris Fiddler, Alec Fraser, Nick Pitt, Anne Smith and Nigel Stephenson provided useful comments on various drafts of the text.

Introduction

The fateful summons to see the chairman of Manchester United came at thirteen minutes to five on Thursday, 12 March 1987. David Smith, chairman of the Manchester United Supporters' Club, had been working in his offices below K stand at Old Trafford. It was a brisk three-minute walk – underneath the stand on to the Scoreboard End terraces, along the front of the Panini-sponsored family section and out through the staff entrance, before crossing the concourse to United's modern administration block next to the railway.

The receptionist nodded him through the electronic glass security doors without a thought, for Smith was a regular visitor. Rather than take the private lifts, the supporters' chairman climbed the fifty-one carpeted stairs with their gleaming chrome bannisters. At the top was a luxury suite of offices, rooms that seemed more appropriate to a City merchant banker than the boss of a northern football club.

Martin Edwards put the phone down and seated his visitor in one of the brown swivel chairs at the oblong conference table which stood to one side of the L-shaped room.

'David, it's a bit of a delicate problem I'm going to talk to you about.'

As soon as Edwards mentioned the words 'delicate problem', David Smith knew his instincts had been correct.

'You know this Government guideline where we go for 50 per cent membership?' Edwards continued. 'Well, we're going to go for it.'

The prime minister, Margaret Thatcher, had for some months been arguing for identity cards as a way of tackling football hooliganism. As a first step the Government wanted half of each club stadium to be listed as a 'designated area' for members only. Most clubs had resisted this. Few in football believed that registered members would make any difference to the problem of violence. The fear was, though, that if clubs did not comply with the Government's demands, identity cards would be forced on them by law.

'We could pussyfoot about,' the United chairman went on, 'but I think the more clubs pussyfoot about, eventually the Government might make us do what they say.'

Smith was not surprised. Indeed, he had already written to United suggesting how free identity cards might be distributed to supporters at a future home game. Moreover, he had discussed with Martin Edwards plans for developing the supporters' organisation with a view to it becoming linked more directly with the football club.

The two men who sat talking in the top-floor office that afternoon had much in common. Martin Edwards was forty-one, David Smith fifteen months older. Both had been watching United since they were boys: Edwards had occasionally come to Old Trafford with his parents and sat in the United directors' box; the young David Smith, in contrast, had watched the same '50s team from the terraces of the Stretford End. At the time Martin Edwards joined his father on the United board in 1970, David Smith was already an active official of the Manchester United Supporters' Club. And by the 1980s Manchester United had become a full-time occupation for both of them, as Martin Edwards became one of the first full-time chief executives of a football club, while David Smith was spending most waking hours on work for the club's supporters.

Martin Edwards went on to explain to the supporters' chairman a few details of the membership scheme he now envisaged. It would start the following August, just five months away. But obviously there would be something of a clash between the new official Manchester United membership, and the supporters' club that Smith had run for most of his adult life. It was soon clear that Edwards wanted to swallow up the supporters' body within the official club scheme.

'Now,' Edwards continued, 'this is going to make your role completely surplus to club requirements. I realise you haven't got a contract with the club and, in a way, you're a bit in limbo, but we'll take account of that.'

So, for David Smith, this was the outcome of nearly twenty years' work for the cause of Manchester United. Since the early 1970s, Manchester United had been a full-time job for him, even though he was not actually employed by the club. It had meant fifteen- or sixteen-hour days, often seven days a week. He was not just organising the biggest football supporters' club in the country, but also arranging coach and train trips to away matches. The profits from this travel organisation provided an income to keep him and his family. The work had also involved Smith drawing up measures with United, the Government and the police to combat football hooliganism. And, perhaps in a small way due to those efforts, United fans had, by the end of the '70s, largely lost their reputation as the most troublesome supporters in the land.

Smith was involved in more direct work for the football club too. On Saturday afternoons and weekday evenings, for every first-team match and countless reserve and youth games, he had been down by the touchline, always behind the opposition goalkeeper, taking photographs for the *United Review*. For this work he received no more than an occasional ex-gratia payment. It all meant a lot of effort, and long hours. But Smith had achieved what few people manage – combining a hobby with a job. Manchester United was his whole life. Now, though, he was apparently 'surplus to club requirements'.

'You've given us years of service,' the United chairman admitted, 'which is appreciated, and it's obviously going to come as a blow to you. We realise that, and we will look to compensate you in some way.

'You're not a club employee and you don't work under a contract. Whatever we do, hopefully we're going to be able to give you an ex-gratia payment.'

Edwards talked of making a 'clean break', but of 'cushioning' Smith. The United boss suggested that Smith should go away, think about things and meet him again in a day or two.

In the weeks ahead there were in fact several meetings, all of them in the chairman's suite, and each initiated by Smith. Edwards wanted to get the United membership scheme going before the season ended. He asked for the membership lists from Smith's club, and he was looking for the supporters' club cooperation and goodwill towards the venture. At first David Smith wasn't in principle opposed to Edwards' plans: he felt it was inevitable that some kind of identity card scheme would be brought in. Smith was, of course, upset about the way he was being pushed out, but tried to see if he could maintain a link with the club and protect his family financially. Yet when Edwards tried to discuss money, Smith found it difficult to evaluate the vast amount of work he had done for the club over the years. Nearly all of it had been unpaid.

However, Smith's attitude changed radically when it became clear what kind of membership scheme Martin Edwards was actually planning. One day, while visiting the general office at Old Trafford, he spotted on top of a tray of papers the minutes of a United senior management meeting. These revealed that membership would cost £5 per person. Smith thought that was a bit expensive, but there was far worse to follow. The minutes also revealed an estimated profit of £2.63 per member. In other words he and his club were being sacrificed to make way for a money-making operation. Yet when Martin Edwards announced the scheme at a press conference and later met officials from supporters' club branches, he said that it was 'not designed as a money-making exercise'.

The final showdown came at noon on Thursday, 16 April 1987. This time David Smith, who by now had decided he could not endorse the club's plans, was accompanied by his wife, Anne, herself a founder member and former secretary of the supporters' club. Martin Edwards had his fellow director and club solicitor, Maurice Watkins, at his side. Smith asked whether the club would allow him to continue taking photos for the United programme.

'We didn't visualise that, to be honest,' Edwards replied, and proceeded to ask if Smith would give back the equipment he used as club photographer.

'That is mine, chairman, and there are letters to the club to that effect.'

'Oh, are there?'

Martin Edwards obviously knew very little about the situation. 'Well, what we propose to do is offer you £15,000.'

To Smith the offer only served to confirm that he had made the right decision. He knew the directors had already approved a compensation payment of £20,000. Now Edwards was trying to reduce that by £5,000 because of the photographic equipment which he had not known actually belonged to Smith.

Anne Smith reasoned that surely Edwards could find a job for her husband supervising the membership scheme, saying that he knew best how to deal with all the supporters' branches. Edwards replied that United were worried that several branches had not affiliated to Smith's club, and he wanted to be sure that every branch would accept the new proposals. Privately Smith himself was not too happy about his wife's idea.

After half an hour, David Smith refused to continue the discussion. 'You've broken my life,' he sobbed and stormed from the room.

His wife Anne was left to carry on talking with the United chairman.

David Smith had one further meeting with Edwards, but there was still no chance of being offered further work with the club. The United senior management had vetoed the idea, and seemed determined to get rid of him altogether.

For some months the supporters' chairman had anticipated his demise. Various members of the United staff disliked Smith's independent supporters' operations and saw his work as an obstacle to further commercial expansion. Relations had become difficult a year earlier when Smith helped defend a friend who had been incorrectly accused of fraud within the United Development Association. Smith was also aware of certain malpractices within the Association which had been sanctioned by the United management.

Some weeks before he was finally due to leave Old Trafford, Smith dropped into a room on the first floor of the administration block. Small and without windows, the office was much more spartan than Edwards' large suite situated directly above. Behind the desk sat the man who, more than anyone, was responsible for the legend of Manchester United.

'Boss, I'd just like you to know, before hearing it from anybody else. They've done it, they've got rid of me.'

Sir Matt Busby, the seventy-eight-year-old former United manager, looked puzzled.

'They're kicking me out for the membership scheme,' explained Smith.

The president of Manchester United shook his head in dismay: 'I'm sorry.' Having sat powerless over the years while the club he had built was transformed into a profit-orientated business, Sir Matt understood precisely.

As time passed Smith's initial disappointment turned to fury. He was angry that United supporters were, as he saw it, being exploited by the membership scheme for the benefit of Martin Edwards and his family, who, in salary, bonuses and dividends, were already taking more than £100,000 a year from the club. The supporters' chairman felt that the United legend established by Sir Matt Busby – the great teams of 1948, 1958 and 1968; Duncan Edwards and the Busby Babes who died at Munich; and the family football club – was all being betrayed in the name of profit. Above all he felt the fans, and his members, were being let down by a man who simply wanted to make money from his great club.

Smith gradually cleared the supporters' club files from his office at the ground. Soon the organisers of the official membership scheme would occupy the same rooms. But Martin Edwards never got the membership lists. His £15,000 offer was rejected, and there was certainly no 'goodwill' towards the new scheme. Smith had decided to carry on running the Manchester United Supporters' Club even if it no longer had the football club's backing. He was encouraged by the depth of support he had received, and by the hostility towards Edwards shown in the meeting the United chairman held with branch officials. Being realistic, though, he knew that many of his members would eventually be forced to join the official scheme.

To continue his club, Smith rented a box number from the Post Office with an Old Trafford address. The phone number of the supporters' club office was quickly transferred to an office near Old Trafford lent by a friendly businessman. United were particularly annoyed about that.

David Smith slowly decided that the full story of the Edwards family's betrayal of United now had to be told. Over the years he had, of course, learnt a vast amount about the club. Helping Geoffrey Green in the late 1970s research his history of United had enabled Smith to read United minute books, though the club had stopped Green himself from using much of the material. He had also enjoyed a long friendship with the late United director Denzil Haroun who had taken a close interest in supporters' club activities. In addition, working at the Old Trafford ground every day, in close contact with United players and officials, Smith could not help hearing things the press and the fans never knew. The time had come to tell the true story of life at Old Trafford.

This book is that story. It describes how Matt Busby built Manchester United from the ruins of the Second World War into one of the greatest teams in football history, only to see his ambitions devastated in the snow of Munich airport. It was with the 1958 crash when eight players died, that the legend was born – the extra ingredient that makes Manchester United that bit special.

Yet the week of the Munich crash also saw the entry on to the United scene of Louis Edwards, a Manchester butcher who had been encouraged to join the United board by Matt Busby himself. It was the beginning of the transfer of power from Busby, the man who built the modern United, to the Edwards family who bought it.

A journalist, Michael Crick, happened to visit Martin Edwards' office a few days after Smith's traumatic meeting in March 1987, though he was largely unaware of what was going on. A devoted United supporter since his schooldays in the early 1970s, he was visiting the United chairman while researching a book he also planned about the club. What interested him most was the politics and economics of Britain's most famous football team. His research brought him into contact with David Smith, but it was not until the corrected proofs of Crick's book were about to go back to the publishers that the two agreed to combine their work and his first draft was abandoned.

What follows has the private support of many people involved with the club over the years. It is the work of two United fanatics, whose sincere hope is that the club will be reformed and restored to its former glory; that one day Manchester United will regain its reputation for entertainment rather than money; that lucrative dividends will give way to glittering trophies.

1
The Beginnings of a Legend

'This was a first division club – but, to be frank, in name only.'

Sir Matt Busby on United in 1945.

For the German *Luftwaffe* in the early months of the Second World War, Trafford Park, the large industrial area around the docks at the end of the Manchester Ship Canal, was an obvious target. In the skies of north-west England on the evening of 11 March 1941 there were, according to the *Manchester Guardian*, 'seldom more than a few minutes during which planes could not be heard'. Trafford Park was showered with bombs aimed at the wharves and warehouses, at General Electric, Metro Vickers and the other large works. Some of the bombs went slightly off target and hit a small patch of green next to the great factories, wedged between the Manchester to Liverpool railway and the Bridgewater Canal.

In the local press the following day this particular target got only vague mentions. For security reasons newspapers at the time could not be specific about which particular sites the Germans had hit. 'Slight outbreaks of fire were reported from a football ground,' wrote the *Manchester Guardian*, which could only locate it in an inland town in the North-west. The next day saw a little more detail: 'Incendiaries fell on the main stand, and the dressing rooms were damaged by high explosive.' Yet neither readers of the *Guardian* nor the German *Luftwaffe* were to know until much later that the ground concerned was in fact the famous home of Manchester United.

The stadium that had once staged FA Cup finals and internationals was now in ruins. The main stand next to the railway tracks was reduced to a heap of rubble and twisted metal. So too were the dressing rooms and offices, which meant that many of the club records were destroyed. The pitch upon which United had beaten Bury 7–3 in a wartime game only three days earlier had been scorched by the fire and heat.

Before the war Manchester United's stadium had a more impressive history than its team. It would have been difficult to argue that United were one of the big names in English football. Back in 1888 six Lancashire sides had been among the original twelve founders of the Football League, but Manchester United were not one of them. Nor had United enjoyed the long, consistent successes of historic sides like Arsenal, Everton, Aston Villa, Sunderland and Newcastle United. Manchester United's only significant trophies – two league titles in 1908 and 1911, and the FA Cup in 1909 – had been followed by a long period of mediocrity. Since joining the Football League in 1892 United had spent almost as many seasons in division two as division one.

The German raids over Old Trafford in 1941 – worse than the war damage inflicted at any other league ground – were only the final episode in what had been a wretched decade for Manchester United Football Club. In the early 1930s the club had very nearly gone bankrupt, and, at one point, United had come within a game of being relegated to join clubs like Accrington, New Brighton and Tranmere in the northern section of division three. It would have been so easy for United to go out of existence during these years, and for the city of Manchester today to be sustaining one league soccer club, not two.

The 1931 season had seen United relegated with the club's worst ever record in division one. At the start of

November 1930 the team had not one single league point, after a run of twelve consecutive defeats and forty-nine goals conceded since the start of the campaign. In December 1930 came the club's worst ever loss, 7–0 at Aston Villa. The drop to division two was the inevitable outcome after a league season that saw twenty-seven defeats, 115 goals conceded and just seven victories. The club finished nine points below the safety level.

As early as October 1930 the supporters had been in revolt. Three thousand fans met at Hulme Town Hall, where it was agreed to boycott the next day's game at home to Arsenal. There was then an extraordinary scene where one leader of the supporters' club, a man called Greenhough, stood on a soap-box outside Old Trafford and implored people not to go in. The boycott for that particular game failed – 23,000 went through the turnstiles – but for less attractive visitors in that disastrous season, home gates often fell below 10,000.

Indeed, barely 3,500 came to Old Trafford for United's first home game in division two the following season. In what were depressing times for the economy as a whole, the club was feeling the chill wind of unemployment. Interest payments on the club mortgage were delayed, along with debts to the local council, and income tax was long overdue. A week before Christmas 1931 the club secretary, Walter Crickmer, went to the bank to collect the players' wages. He was refused. Manchester United was £30,000 in debt.

It was at this point that the club was rescued by a wealthy businessman. James W. Gibson, a director of a major local clothing firm, Biggs, Jones and Gibson Ltd, paid the players' wages, and gave the club a further £2,000. But Gibson initially pledged his support for only three weeks, saying further assistance depended on there being sufficient public backing for the team.

The crowd for the next game, on Christmas Day against Wolves, was 33,000, bigger than the gates for the previous four home matches put together, and James Gibson continued his rescue operation. He quickly installed himself as chairman and president of United. The existing directors willingly resigned, and four new men joined Gibson on the board. A public appeal was made for £20,000, earmarked 'solely for transfer fees', and new shares were issued in the company. And, not for the last time in their history, United were aided by their neighbours and rivals, Manchester City, whose chairman urged the public to support Gibson's efforts. In the months ahead Old Trafford attendances did improve a little. Twenty thousand pounds was indeed spent on new players. A promising new manager, Scott Duncan, was appointed. But the results were still not good enough.

In early May 1934 the United team travelled south for the last game of the season, with division three looking an almost certain prospect for the coming autumn. The men who drew up the league fixture list happened, for this final match, to have pitted United against Millwall, the club just a point above them in the table. If the reds won, the London club would go down to the third division instead. A draw would save Millwall.

United won 2–0.

Two years later, in 1936, United returned to division one, having won the second division championship, and after having been unbeaten in the last nineteen games of the season. But the success didn't last long: Manchester United spent just one season in division one before going back down again.

After several unsuccessful months back in division two the manager, Scott Duncan, left to look after Ipswich Town, then a non-league club. From then until 1945 United had no full-time manager. Instead, team matters were looked after by the club secretary, Walter Crickmer, and the long-serving chief scout, Louis Rocca.

Manchester United in the inter-war years had been one of those sides, like Leicester City, Sheffield Wednesday and West Bromwich Albion in the '70s and '80s, who are not quite good enough to be among the elite, but are often too good for the second division. What made the reds' position particularly bleak at that time was that the '20s and '30s era was the heyday of their sky-blue rivals from Maine Road, Manchester City.

The City side of Frank Swift, Sam Cowan, Fred Tilson, Alec Herd and Eric Brook brought the FA Cup back to Manchester in 1934, having been beaten at Wembley by Everton only the previous year. And they carried off the league championship title in 1937, the same season in which United were relegated again. Among the big-name sky-blue footballers, perhaps the leading playing influence was the right-half, a Scot from a Lanarkshire mining family. His name was Matt Busby.

When war broke out in 1939, the league programme was suspended, but there were already signs of how the post-war pattern of Manchester football would be very different. Not only had United bounced back again to division one, but City's run of success had suddenly ended with relegation the very season after they won the title – the only time that has ever occurred. One reason for City's remarkable change of fortune might have been that their Scottish right-half had now moved on, to Liverpool.

At Old Trafford, meanwhile, James Gibson and Walter Crickmer had already taken the first steps in developing a youth programme for United. For years the club had been spending thousands of pounds on transfers, few of which were ever successful. As early as March 1932 Altrincham Football Club agreed to let United use their ground on alternate Saturdays for the reds' new third team, the 'A' side, consisting of teenage players, to play in the Manchester League. Later, soccer clubs in Newton Heath and Denton also allowed United's junior teams to use their grounds.

In February 1938 the board minutes record how the United directors decided that 'with reference to the formation of a Junior Athletic Club for cultivating young players after they leave school, a scheme as submit [sic] was approved, and the matter was left with the Secretary.' So began the famous MUJACs, the players of the Manchester United Junior Athletic Club, an idea of Gibson and

Crickmer. The MUJACs were coached and trained by local teachers, and instructors from Manchester University. According to James Gibson, the club's attitude towards the young boys was not that they would necessarily join United: 'We only tell them that we hope that if as a result of what the club has done they rise to anything like fame they will bear the club in mind.' The United chairman had high ambitions for the junior scheme: 'It is from these unusually comprehensive nurseries that the club hopes an all-Manchester team at some distant period might be produced.' Of the MUJAC's early players, however, only one achieved great success – John Aston.

In these dark years before the outbreak of war, the club were nevertheless gathering together some of the players who would serve them so well in the distant future. Johnny Carey was signed from St James's Gate in Dublin for a fee of £200 in November 1936, after being spotted by Louis Rocca on a trip to watch a different player. He made his United debut a year later, having already played for Ireland. Jack Rowley joined from Bournemouth in 1937, after James Gibson had seen him play during a weekend spent in the south-coast resort. Another young forward, Stan Pearson, came to Old Trafford from local junior soccer. And a young wing-half, Allenby Chilton, arrived from the North-east in 1938.

James Gibson hoped that United's great Old Trafford ground might one day take over from Wembley as the venue for Cup finals, and he talked of extending the stadium to hold 120,000. The FA Cup final had indeed been played at Old Trafford in 1911, a year after the ground opened, and a final replay had taken place there in 1915. During the inter-war years the stadium was a frequent venue for FA Cup semi-finals – 77,000 crammed in to see Wolves beat Grimsby in 1939 – and internationals such as the 1926 England v. Scotland game and England's 7–0 victory over Ireland in 1938. In the late '30s £35,000 was spent on ground improvements, including new roofing over part of the terracing. In 1936 Gibson arranged for a special railway station to be opened alongside the main entrance to the ground.

So, as United faced the Second World War there were glimmers of hope for the future. The reserves won the Central League in 1939 and the first team took the Manchester Senior Cup, a competition contested by league sides in the area.

Yet the club still had no full-time manager; Walter Crickmer carried on looking after playing matters during wartime football. In spite of modest profits in the late '30s, earlier transfer deals had left debts of more than £70,000. And then, suddenly, in 1941 the club no longer had a ground.

Manchester City agreed to lend United their Maine Road stadium for the rest of the war. As for the question of a manager, the chief scout, Louis Rocca, had an idea about a future prospect. In December 1944 he wrote a letter to an old friend, a former City player:

> I don't know if you have considered what you are going to do when the war is over, but I have a great job for you if you are willing to take it on. Will you get in touch with me at the above address and when you do I can explain things to you better.

The recipient, Matthew Busby, was born in May 1909 in Orbiston, a tiny mining village near Motherwell, east of Glasgow. His father was shot dead in the First World War, and for his mother, raising four children in a two-room cottage, times were difficult. The Busbys decided to follow many of their relations to America, and while waiting for a visa the teenage Matt Busby worked as a miner.

Saturdays, however, were spent playing inside-forward in local junior soccer teams. Matt Busby was quickly spotted by a scout for Manchester City, who in 1928 lured him south to England. Ideas of America were abandoned as City persuaded him to go professional, much to the annoyance of his local side, Glasgow Celtic, who also had their eye on him.

Initially things did not go well for Busby at City, since the club was overrun with forward players. 'I feel I am out of my sphere in football,' Busby wrote to Jean, the girl-friend he would eventually marry. 'I actually dreaded the approach of each football season,' he wrote later. Returning to the pits in Scotland was a serious possibility.

The young player stuck things out, however, and indeed at one point was very nearly signed by Manchester United. A United director watched Busby playing for City reserves several times; so did Louis Rocca. A transfer fee of £150, a large sum for a reserve player at that time, was mentioned, but the deal fell through because, Busby says, United could not afford it. Shortly afterwards, Busby was moved to wing-half. There his career progressed rapidly and he became captain of the side. In 1933 he won his only cap for Scotland in peacetime football, though many believe he should have been a Scottish regular.

Busby's move to Liverpool for £7,000 in 1937 marked the final period of his playing career. And indeed, after he had spent the later war years as an instructor in the Army Physical Training Corps, Liverpool was the logical club to return to when hostilities ended. Anfield offered him a five-year contract as a coach. Ayr United thought he would make a good manager. Reading were interested too. Verbally he accepted the job at Anfield, but then came the letter from Louis Rocca.

It led to an interview with James Gibson, who was impressed by Busby's 'ideas and honesty of purpose', and offered him a three-year contract at £750 a year. Busby insisted on five years and Gibson conceded. The Busby family's affection for Manchester, and the fact that they still had many old friends in the city, probably made the difference between Old Trafford and Anfield. The choice had historic consequences.

The nineteenth of February 1945 was the day on which Matt Busby signed for Manchester United. He was still in sergeant-major's uniform and not officially able to start work until October, after he had been demobbed.

The United players soon learnt that Busby's style of management was very different from what they were used to. Before the war football managers had usually been administrators in pin-stripe suits who spent most of the day in their offices, and the former manager Scott Duncan typified this. Matt Busby was still young enough to be playing football himself and was determined to be one of the first tracksuit managers. He would be out training with his players whatever the weather, talking to them and showing by example how he wanted the game played.

The new manager had only taken the Old Trafford job on the understanding that it was on his terms:

> Call it confidence, conceit, arrogance, or ignorance, but I was unequivocal about it. At the advanced age of thirty-five I would accept only if they would let me have all my own way. As the manager I would want to manage. I would be the boss.

Such an attitude, which of course is quite normal today, was highly unusual in 1945. The fact that United had continued since 1937 with the secretary, Walter Crickmer, as the part-time manager was some indication of how the directors saw the job. Team selection was officially the responsibility of the directors, and for many years after Busby's arrival the first item on the weekly board agenda was the selection of club sides for forthcoming fixtures. Indeed, until 1947 Busby would attend board meetings solely to discuss playing matters and then, the minutes often record, 'The manager having conducted his business retired from the meeting.' Only with Busby absent, would the directors discuss the minutes of the previous meeting and the club's financial affairs. Slowly, however, Busby gained power and influence. He was soon present throughout the whole of each board meeting, and while team selections were still mentioned, the item became more of a formality on each week's agenda.

Matt Busby fought several early battles with his board. During one match, for example, while sitting in the directors' box at Maine Road, one board member, Harold Hardman, remarked loudly about Johnny Carey: 'How he can keep picking him, God only knows!'

'Never dare to say anything like that to me when other people can hear you,' Busby blasted when he met Hardman later in the gents. And Busby made his feelings clear at the next board meeting.

Busby says the chairman, James Gibson, could also be difficult to deal with. 'You are always telling me "No",' Gibson complained when Busby had turned down the chairman's latest suggestion of a new player to sign. 'Well, I'm telling you now,' Gibson said, 'go and sign him.'

Busby recalled the occasion:

> 'No,' I said, 'and I will remind you of two things, Mr Gibson. I am here to manage the club and part of management is giving you advice. And the second is that I lived long before I ever saw you.'

Gibson apologised. Busby gained his independence. And Manchester United flourished.

Matt Busby set out to end any divisions among the players, remembering his own unhappy experience at Manchester City:

> As a youngster, I felt that there was too much class distinction at Maine Road, and in most other clubs as well, too large a gap between the established first-team players and the rest of the playing staff. Team spirit and pride in the club – two most valuable assets – suffered accordingly. . . . I learned a lesson at Maine Road – the lesson that team snobbery has no place in a happy club; and what unhappy club could possibly enjoy any consistent run of success?

Busby also decided to try to emulate some of the better practices he had seen during his brief stay at Liverpool. The Merseyside club, he says, 'treated everyone on the staff as human beings should be treated, with kindness, consideration and understanding . . . Liverpool were always prepared to reward good service, even when they could so easily have evaded their obligations to players whose first XI days were ended.' He was particularly impressed by the way in which Liverpool had given one of their former star players, Jimmy McDougal, full pay long after he had been dropped from the first team.

For the first four years after the war United carried on playing at Maine Road, and by now bushes were growing through what was left of the Old Trafford stand. In the post-war reconstruction, a football stadium was not a priority for a building licence and permission was needed even for exterior painting work. City and United played home league games on alternate Saturdays and all their reserve matches at United's training ground, The Cliff, in Salford. The club's administration had been moved to one of James Gibson's business premises, the Cornbrook Cold Stores, about a mile from Old Trafford. One small office was occupied by Walter Crickmer, his teenage clerk, Les Olive, and a typist loaned by Gibson from his firm. It also hosted weekly board meetings.

The players would often train on a patch of concrete at the back of Old Trafford, while any medical treatment or indoor practice was carried out in a small second-hand Nissen hut bought by Walter Crickmer for £85 in 1947.

If the club lacked many basic resources, at least Busby had inherited several promising players. Along with Carey, Pearson, Rowley, Aston and Chilton, who had all joined the club before fighting began, several others had been recruited by Crickmer and Rocca during the war. Left-winger Charlie Mitten joined the staff in 1940; wing-halves Henry Cockburn and John Anderson arrived as junior players in 1944. Forward Johnny Morris and goalkeeper Jack Crompton had also been spotted in Manchester youth teams. While nearly all the important ingredients were already there when the new manager arrived, it was left to Busby to devise the right recipe for success.

His club captain, Johnny Carey, is widely regarded as one of the greatest players Ireland has ever produced, and indeed he appeared regularly for both Irish international teams – on one occasion within the space of three days. Carey could play in any position, and during his time at United he wore every shirt except number eleven, including the goalkeeper's jersey for one whole match. Calm, thoughtful and with a perfect understanding of the game, Carey was the obvious team leader. Before the war the Irishman had usually played at inside-forward, but, in a typically inspired move, Busby moved him further back and mainly played him at right-back. There he organised the defence brilliantly.

Carey was just one example of the way Busby experimented with players in new positions, remembering how he himself had been successful at Manchester City only after moving from inside-forward to wing-half. A second change involved John Aston, the former MUJACs player, who was switched from the forward line to left-back. The two ball-playing forwards-turned-defenders created a new phenomenon in football – attacking, creative full-backs.

The post-war Manchester United side is best remembered for its forward line – Delaney, Morris, Rowley, Pearson and Mitten. Jimmy Delaney was the only major player whom Busby bought for United in those years. A fast Scottish right-winger, Delaney had already won a Scottish Cup medal with Celtic in 1937. When Busby bought him for £4,000, many observers considered him to be past his best and injury-prone. They were totally wrong: Delaney went on to play nearly 200 games for United and was recalled by Scotland.

Johnny Morris, at inside-right, was known for his individual touches and nutmegging – putting the ball through an opponent's legs. The centre-forward, Jack Rowley, was known as 'the Gunner' for his powerful shot, and could be depended on for goals – in five of the six post-war seasons he scored more than twenty in the league alone. Stan Pearson also hit the net regularly, while Charlie Mitten, at outside-left, who was skilled at crossing, hit the ball hard and rarely failed with a penalty.

In the half-back line Henry Cockburn was still working five days a week in a Lancashire mill when he won his first England cap in 1946, after just six league games for the reds. The 6-foot Allenby Chilton was switched from wing-half to the centre of defence.

It has been said that Matt Busby inherited his first great team. Players like Johnny Carey and Stan Pearson disagree. 'He had some talent,' says Pearson, 'but it definitely needed sorting out.' That was certainly what he did.

'Every good general needs good lieutenants,' Busby, the former army PT instructor, argued. Shrewdly he chose as his main assistant a Welshman with an Irish name, Jimmy Murphy, who joined United in 1946. Busby had known Murphy through his playing days, and when they met again in the summer of 1945 Busby asked him to come to Old Trafford. A cheerful, smiling character, yet firm, Murphy was Busby's first and perhaps most important signing. Like many successful partners they rarely mixed socially. Murphy would be much tougher with the players than the manager himself, and often kept them from bothering Busby.

> It could be that what either Jimmy Murphy or I lacked the other had. He would always give a straight-forward opinion. He was no yes-man. But once having made a point he would accept that mine was the decision. He was forthright with never a suggestion of usurping my position. In fact he turned down many managerial jobs offered him at other clubs. If he judged a player I found that his judgements almost always confirmed mine. He was invaluable in handling boys but his value did not rest there. He could tackle the established players with the same conviction and enthusiasm.

Below Busby and Murphy, everyday training sessions were run by Bert Whalley, a former United centre-half who had been forced to retire early through injury. The other trainer, Tom Curry, was an old-fashioned sponge man who had been with United before the war. He would never allow swearing in the dressing room and protected the players like his own children.

On Sunday mornings Matt Busby, the coaching staff and players would come to the ground for a regular ritual – some after they had been to church. It was a chance for treatment, to discuss what had happened the day before, and for a light kick-about. One morning two first-team players were in a bad state after the previous night, and as Busby was arriving Curry hid them in the toilets. Busby was not fooled. He carried on as normal, apparently oblivious to their absence. But as he passed Curry on his way out of the changing rooms he said quietly, 'You can tell those two to come out of the toilets now.' He had the ability to know when something was going on behind his back and to handle it without making a great fuss.

Louis Rocca carried on looking for new players right up until his death in 1950. As successor to his great friend, Busby appointed as his main scout Joe Armstrong, a GPO engineer who had previously scouted for Manchester City. Armstrong had spent all his spare time scouring park and schools pitches before becoming United's chief scout full-time. When other scouts were knocking on a youngster's front door, it was said, Armstrong would be there in the kitchen, drinking tea with his parents, having already struck a deal. Armstrong was assisted by three superb Irish scouts, Bob Bishop and Bob Harper in Northern Ireland and Billy Behan in Dublin. Together they served the club for several decades and found dozens of stars for United and the two Irish international sides.

The highly efficient Walter Crickmer continued as club secretary behind the scenes. He was 'a wise little man', says Busby, who gave 'invaluable' advice about procedures. Crickmer was prepared to recognise, however, who was now in charge of the club.

Matt Busby's philosophy was a simple one. Les Olive, a United servant for more than forty years, recalls that 'Matt was a great example to anybody by the way he treated people he met. He always used to tell me that if you can't say a good word about anybody then don't say anything.'

It was this attitude, as much as Busby's knowledge of the game, that endeared him not only to those he dealt with every day, but also to complete strangers. Never one to seek the limelight or personal glory, he was always quick to praise the assistance of others. He possessed the knack of never forgetting people, and many who had met him just once found that Busby would remember their names or faces many years later.

When league football resumed in August 1946 United got off to a brilliant start with five wins in five games. In spite of having to play at Maine Road the fans flocked to see them, as indeed they turned up everywhere in those post-war boom years for soccer. United were soon attracting bigger attendances than City, their second-division hosts. City did not mind much at first: United were paying £5,000 a year rent as well as a percentage of each gate.

United came second in the league in 1946–47, just a point behind the champions, Liverpool: it was their highest position since winning the title in 1911. The 1947–48 season saw them runners-up again, and even playing home games at City's ground they chalked up one of their highest-ever attendance figures. An average of 54,890 went through the turnstiles.

Soon Busby's team had some silverware to reward their followers. United's 1948 FA Cup run must be one of the most impressive of all time. In every round the reds beat top-ranking first-division opponents – Aston Villa, Liverpool, Charlton Athletic, Preston North End, Derby County and Blackpool. Every tie was won by a margin of at least two goals, without any replays. And, of course, every game had to be played away from home: because of City's own Cup run even Maine Road was available on only one occasion, and other 'home' matches had to be played at Goodison Park and Huddersfield.

One of the most remarkable games in United's history occurred at the start of that Cup run, in front of 65,000 at

Villa Park in January 1948. The Birmingham side were ahead within fourteen seconds, with a goal direct from the kick-off. Yet by half-time Morris with two goals and Pearson, Rowley and Delaney with one each had put United 5–1 up. Surely the tie was now beyond doubt. Bit by bit, through the second half Villa chipped away at the Manchester lead: 5–2, 5–3 and then Villa made it 5–4 with still nine minutes left in which to grab what everybody must have thought would be the inevitable equaliser. It was not to be. Two minutes from the end, Stan Pearson put the game beyond doubt and United returned home with a remarkable 6–4 scoreline.

The final against Blackpool at Wembley that April was almost as dramatic – indeed it is regarded by many as the finest Cup final of all time, a masterful display of attacking football. Blackpool may have languished in divisions three and four in modern times, but they were then a major force in English soccer, boasting both Stan Mortensen and the great Stanley Matthews. The seaside club took the lead with a controversial penalty. Rowley equalised, but Blackpool went in at half-time 2–1 ahead of Mortensen. It was only in the sixty-ninth minute, after a long period of pressure from Blackpool, that United could equalise again, when Rowley headed in Morris's free kick. Then John Anderson, who until recently had been in the reserves, set up a goal for Pearson, and later scored himself from 30 yards to make the final result 4–2.

The players shared out a bonus of £550 for their Cup success, and a further £440 for coming second in the league. Today such successes would earn players thousands of pounds each – a vast increase, even allowing for inflation.

The debts United had inherited from the dismal pre-war and wartime years were quickly wiped out by Busby's run of success. With vast crowds bringing in the cash, and United restricted first by FA rules in the wages they could pay players, and second by the Government's refusal to grant a building licence, annual profits piled up: £10,215 in 1946; £13,393 in 1947; £22,329 in 1948 and £50,810 in

1949. By the end of the decade the club's bank balance was more than £50,000 in credit.

In spite of the Cup success, the league championship would still elude Matt Busby's side. The reds came second for a third successive year in 1949, this time five points behind Portsmouth. But the crowds continued to pour on to the high Maine Road terraces. Eighty-two thousand nine hundred and fifty saw the reds draw 1–1 with the champions Arsenal on New Year's Day 1949 – the all-time record gate for a league match – while 81,500 turned up to see non-league giant-killers Yeovil beaten 8–0 in the fifth round of the FA Cup.

United were enjoying the most successful period in the club's history and Matt Busby's work was well rewarded. In October 1947 his salary was increased from £750 to £1,750, and for the 1948 Cup win he got a bonus of another £1,750. In March 1949 the directors gave him a three-year contract on an annual salary of £3,250, a vast amount at that time. It was more than five times the maximum earnings for players, who received £12 a week in the playing season and £10 in summer, and more than four times Busby's starting salary in 1945. No wonder Busby turned down an offer from Spurs of £3,000 a year, and an approach to return to Manchester City.

There are few players who speak ill of United's, and arguably football's, greatest manager. Even those who departed Old Trafford under protest retain the greatest respect for the man they still refer to as 'Boss'.

Busby was determined to develop a family atmosphere around him. At Christmas the team members were each given National Savings certificates. The players would be taken to fights at Belle Vue or to the theatre. There were annual summer outings for both players and staff to Blackpool or Colwyn Bay. And on one occasion Busby organised a trip to see England in a mid-week match at Wembley when three United players were included in the side. A large party went, from first-team players down to the third team.

In August 1949 United at last returned to Old Trafford, marking the first game back with a 3–0 win over Bolton. City had long been making it clear that United could not go on sharing their ground forever, and finally, in November 1948, served notice to quit at the end of the season. 'My board feel that your directors will appreciate that existing conditions cannot be expected to continue indefinitely,' wrote the City chairman. This put United in a bit of difficulty, since they had hardly been able to carry out any repairs at Old Trafford since the 1941 blitz. It was not lack of money, but simply that successive applications to the Ministry of Works, including a delegation to London, had failed. A building licence was eventually issued in January 1949, but when Old Trafford reopened, the main stand still had no roof, and even the directors had to sit without cover, hoping it would not rain.

Back at Old Trafford crowds were in fact smaller than they had been at Maine Road, and the move failed to give the extra push the club needed to win the league. They dropped to fourth in 1950 before coming second once again in 1951, for the fourth time in five years.

After further five-figure profits – £35,604 in 1950 and £22,677 in 1951 – the club finally wiped out the last of the debts hanging over from the inter-war years. The chairman since 1931, James Gibson, had for many months been absent from board meetings through illness. He did, however, live just long enough to hear the news that the club had returned to the black. Gibson, the man who rescued United, was replaced as chairman by Harold Hardman, who had sat on the board almost continuously since 1912. Small in stature, Hardman was a Manchester solicitor, yet unlike Gibson, was not particularly wealthy. He had once played football himself, for Everton, England and United briefly, after winning an Olympic medal in 1908 as an amateur player for Great Britain.

In spite of the successful results on both pitch and balance sheet, things did not always go smoothly for Busby. The players briefly went on strike after the 1948 Cup final, while Johnny Morris was transferred to Derby County after clashing with Busby on a matter of principle. As in recent times, United crowds had become accustomed to a high level of entertaining football, yet were impatient for the ultimate success of trophies. In January 1951, after three successive defeats, and not having won at Old Trafford for three months, there was even talk of Busby going.

'I'm not getting the sack,' Busby told the magazine *All Football*:

> Let me scotch first those rumours which, I am told, go the rounds – I am not resigning. I am not being sacked and there is neither trouble nor panic in our camp.
>
> These rumours seem to have started because we are not quite the glamour team we used to be. Maybe we are not. You cannot stay on top all the time and we had a longer run than usual. . . . There is nothing to panic about. Before long you will see Manchester United back on top, beating the best.

Fifteen months later, when United met Arsenal at Old Trafford in the last game of the 1951–52 season, they finally made it to the summit. The 6–1 victory over the Londoners, their nearest rivals, secured the first of Matt Busby's five league titles. United's success had not been a foregone conclusion, however. No fewer than six different clubs headed the table at one point or another, but for much of the campaign Arsenal themselves had looked the most likely title winners, having been unbeaten from the end of December until late April.

Seven members of the 1952 championship side – Carey, Cockburn, Chilton, Pearson, Rowley, Aston and Crompton – had helped lift the FA Cup in 1948, but an era was drawing to a close. It was clear that new blood would have to be injected. Busby was keen on continuing the youth policies developed by James Gibson and Walter Crickmer in the 1930s. The transfer market would only be used as a last resort. 'Jerry builders' Busby called those clubs who sank all their cash into expensive, glamorous first teams: 'Costly imports of temperamental stars, and the acquisition of expensive cast-offs from other clubs, did not fit in with my plans.' What Busby proposed was quite natural today, yet pioneering at the time.

> In 1946 it was revolutionary even to think about getting boys straight from school. Get them early enough, I thought, and they would be trained according to some sort of pattern: in my case, the pattern I was trying constantly to create at Manchester United, in the first team and any other team, was that if a boy came through as far as his ability, courage, speed and character were concerned, he would fit into the pattern without feeling like a stranger among people, painting pretty pictures he did not understand and had never seen before.

Manchester United's pre-war junior scheme, the MUJACs, had been closed down in 1941, and it was not until 1947 that Busby was able to get it going again. Joe Armstrong, together with no more than seven or so other paid scouts, was sent off to discover the Manchester United players of tomorrow. Busby himself was also closely involved in the work:

> With a railway timetable my constant companion, I travelled the length and breadth of the British Isles to watch school teams, youth teams, works teams, and even Water Board teams. As soon as a tip arrived from one of my scouts, I followed it up regardless of the distance involved or the inconvenience suffered. . . . Yes, the hunt was on – and I was first in the field, knowing that before long the competition would become fiercer, and well aware that you cannot discover footballers if you sit in the manager's chair all day.

As other clubs began to copy United, there were stories of boys' parents being offered illegal payments to clinch their signatures. Five hundred pounds or £1,000 might be handed over in banknotes. Alternatively, the father of a promising young player might be employed as a part-time scout, though of course he was not expected to do anything for this. But such inducements were rarely the deciding factor in joining United. The club's growing prestige was more important.

Once taken on as apprentices the teenage boys were housed with the club's special team of landladies, and they were sent on training courses and fixed up with part-time jobs in case they never made it as footballers. Their previous junior clubs would be given grants in gratitude. The minutes in March 1949 record, for instance, how Ryder Brow, the north Manchester junior club that had just provided United with a young player called Roger Byrne, were sent a cheque for £25. 'It has never been my entire and complete aim to build a Manchester United team capable of winning the League or the Cup,' Busby wrote, 'but rather to concentrate on a system which will produce a number of first-class Manchester United teams, from fifteen-year-olds upwards.'

Buying players through transfers was only the 'last resort' for Matt Busby. 'If my club decide to buy a player, we do so only because every other method of filling a place in the United team has failed,' he said. Between 1951 and 1958 the United manager acquired only one player through the transfer market. And through careful sales the United transfer account remained in healthy surplus from his arrival in 1945 until 1958.

Within a few months of the 1952 title win United had fallen to fourth from bottom of the first division, only just above Manchester City. They had lost six of the opening eleven matches. When the shareholders began asking questions at the Annual General Meeting, Busby promised that there was '£200,000 worth of skill in the youth and reserve sides . . . in another couple of years we shall have wonderful young material when it is needed most.' His estimate would be the equivalent of £12 million worth of talent today. And Busby was right. Within twelve months several of these young players would be brought into action.

Busby's promising teenagers soon distinguished themselves in the Football Association's new knockout competition for club youth sides, the FA Youth Cup. It was a measure of the excitement generated by the young players that more than 20,000 turned up on a Monday afternoon in May 1953 to see them beat Wolves 7–1 in the first leg of the final. Eddie Colman, Duncan Edwards, Billy Whelan, David Pegg and Albert Scanlon helped the reds win 9–3 on aggregate.

Duncan Edwards had been spotted in Dudley, under the eye of the local Wolves scouts – recommended by the former Arsenal captain and future City manager, Joe Mercer. The deciding factor was that Edwards wanted to play for Manchester United more than any other club. In his brief career in football Edwards achieved a reputation as one of the greatest players the world has ever known. There was little on which he could be faulted. Physically he was large and powerful, but he was also fast and tireless. He was strong with either foot, a good header of the ball, and accurate passer, a keen tackler and a superb defender, yet he regularly scored goals too and had a powerful shot. No one could agree on whether it was best to play him in defence, midfield or attack. One interesting side point is that, strangely, Edwards rarely kicked the ball with the inside of the foot but nearly always with the instep, whether he was passing or shooting.

Eddie Colman was another exciting prospect, snapped up from local Salford football. He had superb ball control and was known for his swerving hips and for sending even his own players the wrong way. In time he formed a brilliant wing-half partnership with Edwards.

The youth team's triumph made up for the stumblings of the first team who, having finished the 1952–53 season in eighth place, by far their lowest position since the war, began the following campaign without a victory in the first eight matches. For a midweek friendly game at Kilmarnock in October 1953 Busby decided to experiment with some of the talent he was nurturing. Stan Pearson and Jack Rowley made way for Irish centre-half Jackie Blanchflower and the forward Dennis Viollet, and half-way through the first half Henry Cockburn went off injured and was replaced by the seventeen-year old Duncan Edwards.

It seemed to work. Kilmarnock were beaten 3–0 and Busby decided to keep the changes for the following league match at Huddersfield. Viollet, Blanchflower and Edwards kept their places for the rest of the season. Stan Pearson never played for United again.

The Kilmarnock and Huddersfield games have gone down in United's history as the beginning of the 'Busby Babes', though the process of bringing in the new blood was in fact a very gradual one. Blanchflower had actually made his debut eighteen months before, and both Viollet and Edwards had played odd first-team games at the end of the previous season. Duncan Edwards' first appearance had been against Cardiff that spring, at the age of sixteen.

Other changes had already occurred. Johnny Carey had left to become manager of Blackburn in the summer of 1953, having turned down a coaching job under Busby. In March 1953 the United manager had crossed the Pennines to sign Barnsley's young centre-forward, Tommy Taylor, for £29,999. He and Jimmy Murphy spent four days in a local hotel waiting to pounce, and the final pound had been knocked off to prevent the record fee going to the player's head. Another forward, Johnny Berry, had been signed from Birmingham in 1951.

Slowly the pieces of Busby's new team were being gathered together. Left-back Roger Byrne had been in the side continuously since 1951, while two other 'Babes', Mark Jones and Bill Foulkes, had made their first-team debuts in 1950 and 1952. It was a while, however, before the new blend matured sufficiently. In 1954 and 1955 the reds had to be content with fourth and then fifth in the league table.

The youth team had turned into a conveyor belt of talent, and could not be faulted. A further victory over Wolves

secured a second Youth Cup in 1954. Playing at centre-
forward was another hot prospect, Bobby Charlton, who
had been spotted in the North-east. This time 28,651
turned up for United's win in the second leg at Molyneux,
a crowd Wolves would rarely expect for first-team games
nowadays. West Bromwich Albion were the beaten finalists
as the youths claimed their third Cup victory in 1955, this
time winning 7–1 on aggregate.

The stream of young players progressing to the first team
was soon attracting the international selectors. Tommy
Taylor first appeared for England in 1953; the two full-
backs, Roger Byrne and Bill Foulkes, made their England
debuts in 1954, and though Foulkes never appeared again,
Byrne went on to win thirty-three consecutive caps. Taylor
and Byrne were joined against Scotland in 1955 by the
eighteen-year-old Duncan Edwards; he was the youngest
man ever to play for England and was rarely out of the
national team thereafter.

Everything was now in place for the 1955–56 season. It
was to be the most outstanding league campaign in United's
history. At Old Trafford the team went unbeaten, winning
eighteen matches and drawing the remaining three. The
championship was clinched with a 2–1 win at home to
Blackpool on 7 April.

For a championship-winning team Matt Busby used a
remarkably high number of players during the course of
the season – twenty-four. Tommy Taylor was out through
injury early in the year, but it was also an indication of
how many good players there were to choose from. The
team got off to a poor start, but once a settled side had
been chosen, round about November, they lost only three
times between then and the end of the season. The side's
youth has often been exaggerated: the average age was
actually twenty-three, but it was one of the youngest championship teams in history.

Ray Wood, a goalkeeper signed from Darlington for
£5,000, was said to live on a diet of tea and cigarettes. Bill
Foulkes and Roger Byrne worked successfully at full-back.

Eddie Colman, Mark Jones and Duncan Edwards filled the half-back positions. Johnny Berry and the speedy David Pegg were the outside-forwards; Billy Whelan, a player said to be like oil because of the way he slipped past opponents, shared the inside-right shirt with Jackie Blanchflower and Johnny Doherty; Tommy Taylor was centre-forward and Dennis Viollet, with his lightning pace and superb dribbling ability, played at inside-left.

Roger Byrne and Johnny Berry were all that remained from the team that had won the title four years earlier. Only three of the players had cost the club transfer fees. 'One of the secrets of Manchester United's success,' said Roger Byrne, 'is that nearly all of us grew up together as boy footballers. We were knitted into a football family. Apart from Johnny Berry – formerly with Birmingham City, Tommy Taylor and Ray Wood, who quickly fitted into the Old Trafford set-up – the Manchester United way is the only way we know.'

The great collection of players in reserve had also won the Central League title for the first time since 1947. Largely through his clever youth policies, and with only selective use of the cheque book, Matt Busby had produced his second great side. Now the Busby Babes would look for those wider horizons that in such tragic circumstances would establish the United legend.

2
Into Europe

'I asked a nurse which hospital we should go to next, to see the other lads. She looked puzzled. I asked again where the other people were, and she said there were no others. She said the only survivors were in the hospital in which we were standing. That was when the whole thing really hit me.'

Bill Foulkes on the day of Munich.

When United's directors met at Old Trafford on 22 May 1956 for their regular board meeting, they had in front of them a letter from Sir Stanley Rous, Secretary of the Football Association. He invited the club to take part in the new European Champion Clubs Cup Competition, United having qualified by winning the Football League Championship. The European Cup, as it became known, had been initiated only the year before by the French sports magazine *L'Equipe*. The idea of a competition for the top European sides had first been mooted before the war, but had only been made a realistic possibility by the advent of floodlights and regular air travel. Just sixteen teams had taken part in the first year, though not all of them had been national champions. For the first final, which at the time of Rous' letter was yet to take place, Real Madrid were due to play the French side, Stade de Rheims.

The three United directors present at the board meeting

unanimously agreed to enter the 1956–57 contest. It was a
momentous decision in the history of the club, one that in
time would bring both disaster and triumph, and transform
Manchester United, a successful English football club, into
a world legend.

Matt Busby was extremely keen on entering the new
competition. Always a pioneer, he believed that the contact
with foreign club sides could only help British football.
The 1950s had been a dismal period for the English national
side. The first World Cup that England entered, in 1950,
after boycotting the competition in the 1930s, led to humiliating defeat by the United States. Then came an even
greater upset to national pride – the Hungarians' surprise
6–3 defeat of England at Wembley in 1953. The following
spring England's inferiority was confirmed when the Hungarians won 7–1 in Budapest. Busby was among those who
believed that the nation which had invented football would
never overcome its two recent World Cup failures if it
remained isolated. 'Prestige alone demanded that the Continental challenge should be met, not avoided,' he stated.

The United manager also felt the experience of competition against the best clubs in Europe would be invaluable
to his young players. And it would boost the United bank
balance with money from television rights as well as gate
receipts.

Taking part in the European Cup was not an easy
decision, though. Chelsea, the 1955 league champions, had
been persuaded to withdraw from the previous contest by
the League Management Committee, who argued that the
club would not be able to cope with the extra fixtures on
top of the English league and FA Cup competitions. More
cynical observers suggested that the football authorities
were frightened that crowds would be impressed by Continental skills and demand higher standards at home. It was
thus left to the Scottish club, Hibernian, to defend British
interests in the first year of the European Cup. They
reached the semi-finals and made £25,000 in the process.

Matt Busby accepted that the League's arguments against

entering the Cup might have carried some weight for some
sides. Participation would mean fifty or sixty first-team
matches over a nine-month season:

> An 'ordinary' club, boasting no more than thirteen or
> fourteen players of the required first team strength,
> would most certainly find the European Cup a burden;
> I have thought for a long time that, without consider-
> ing such distractions, the League programme is
> already too congested for comfort. At Old Trafford,
> however, I have at least eighteen players, maybe
> twenty, who could be played in the first team in the
> place of the regulars without any noticeable reduction
> in the strength of the team as a whole. Other man-
> agers, no doubt, have similar ideas about their
> reserves, but how many of them would feel confident
> about playing seven or eight members of the reserve
> side in the first XI? . . . Many clubs have the quan-
> tity, but few the quality.

However, only a few weeks after United had accepted the
FA's invitation, the Football League, the lower authority,
were expressing doubts. In August 1956 their objections
grew louder. They wrote to say that United's 'participation
was not in the best interests of the League, having regard
to the possible effect on League match attendances', and
they asked the board to reconsider.

By now United had been drawn against the Belgian champions, Anderlecht, in the first round, and the opening game
was only three weeks away. The Old Trafford directors
stuck to their decision, but to placate the League they
decided to pay the usual 4 per cent levy normally paid on
league match receipts, for European cup games too. The
era of English clubs playing in Europe had begun. 'Some
people called me a visionary,' said Busby of this venture
on to the Continent, 'others a reactionary, while a few called
me awkward and stubborn.'

Yet there was another problem. European Cup matches
were played in the middle of the week, and United had not

yet installed floodlights at Old Trafford. They could never expect high attendances if games were played on Wednesday afternoons, while local employers would be angry about people taking the afternoon off work. The General Electric Company told the club that there would be an eight-to-fourteen-month delay for the delivery of steel for the towers on which the lights would be mounted. So Matt Busby approached Manchester City to see if they would again let United use Maine Road, which already had lights. The City chairman, though, was not convinced that United's venture would be worthwhile, and predicted no more than 10,000 would come to the first home game. City's terms – £300 or 15 per cent of the gate – reflected his pessimism.

Many observers regarded United's opening tie against Anderlecht as an easy one since the Brussels side consisted of amateurs and part-timers. Yet their opponents had been Belgian champions seven times in the previous ten years, and in 1953 had beaten the league champions Arsenal at Highbury.

In the first leg, in Brussels, the Belgians hit a penalty against the post, before Viollet and Taylor gave United a 2–0 lead for the return trip to Manchester. Matt Busby told shareholders at the AGM the following week that he was keen to win the European Cup and thought the team had a 'very good chance'.

A crowd of 43,635 assembled at Maine Road for the second game, fourteen days after the first. It was many more than the City chairman had expected, though not an unusual attendance by any means – but then Manchester did suffer torrential rain and the overall result of the tie already looked beyond much doubt. However, those wise enough to go that night were treated to an extraordinary spectacle amid the pools of water, possibly the greatest game in United's distinguished history.

Anderlecht had made several changes in the team that lost in Brussels and suffered for them. United were ahead after nine minutes with a header from Tommy Taylor. He toe-poked a second goal shortly afterwards. Then Taylor's scoring partner, Dennis Viollet, got in on the act with a hat-trick before half-time. Two of these goals were the results of mistakes by the Anderlecht defence; the third a powerful shot from the edge of the penalty area. United went in 5–0 ahead at the interval, 7–0 up on aggregate.

In such a position most sides would enjoy their lead and relax, yet the second period proved just as exciting. A goalmouth scramble allowed Taylor to complete his hat-trick. Whelan made it 7–0 and Byrne passed to Viollet for his fourth goal and the reds' eighth. Johnny Berry got the ninth and Whelan scored a second to create United's all-time record score – 10–0. It might have been even higher had not the players been trying desperately to get a goal for David Pegg; he had made five of the goals, but was the only member of the forward line not to score himself.

Over the years many sides achieved double-figure scores in European competitions, but invariably against much weaker sides from countries such as Iceland, Malta, Norway and Luxembourg. United had marked their first European game on English soil by beating a top Continental team. 'Why don't they pick this team for England?' the Anderlecht captain wanted to know. Matt Busby called it 'the finest exhibition of teamwork I had ever seen from any side either at club or international level'.

No wonder 75,598 turned up for the next European game United played at Maine Road, against the West German champions, Borussia Dortmund. At first United seemed to be carrying on where they had finished only three weeks before, with another brilliant display of precise, zestful, entertaining, attacking football. Dennis Viollet's two goals, and an own goal by the Germans, sent the reds in 3–0 up at the interval. But then United became cocky. The Germans meanwhile raised their game considerably, fought back fiercely and scored two goals in reply.

After Borussia's second-half performance in Manchester, the 3–2 lead the reds took to Germany looked precarious. But it proved sufficent as, on a hard, frosty pitch United held out in the second game, urged on by several thousand British servicemen stationed near by, to draw 0–0.

Before the next round in the New Year, United asked the Football League for permission to increase bonus payments for European games. They turned the request down, but the League secretary, Alan Hardaker, did say that if United progressed further in the competition they might look upon the request more favourably.

The club's next opponents looked like being the toughest so far. Atletico Bilbao had won both the Spanish Championship and the Spanish Cup in spite of their rivals, the European champions Real Madrid. Moreover, in the previous round Bilbao had defeated the great Hungarian side Honved. First, though, United had to get to Spain.

The club had decided to go by aeroplane to the away games of the European ties. There was simply no alternative if United were not going to disrupt the normal league match programme. Most European venues were too distant for the team to contemplate travelling by boat and train. Air travel, of course, did involve greater risks. In 1949 the great Italian side Torino, winners of four successive Italian championships, had been completely wiped out in an air crash on the Superga mountainside outside Turin. And indeed, when United had visited the United States the following year, the club's directors had insisted that the players should not travel by air in America.

The two planes that took the United party to Bilbao went through some terrible weather, and had to stop at Bordeaux to refuel. Then on arrival, Bill Foulkes recalled, it was far from sunny Spain:

We evidently circled over Bilbao for some time, and because the clouds rolled back from time to time I could see that there was snow on the ground below. I wondered why we did not go in to land, and I soon found out. The steward . . . asked us to keep our eyes skinned, and to let him know if we saw an airport . . . Imagine the scene, as the Manchester United party

glued their heads to the windows to look for Bilbao
airport. Every time someone spotted a wide road they
would sing out – there it is – but eventually the pilot
got us down on a deserted field. There were no airport
buildings, just a landing strip and an old shed where
the customs men lurked.

In fact it had not been until the British assistant consul
heard the Dakota circling overhead that he had rushed off
to get the airfield reopened!

Bilbao's ground was just as unwelcoming. It had suffered
heavy rain for several days and then a snowstorm just before
United arrived. The reds conceded three goals before half-
time. Taylor and Viollet got two back within eight minutes
of the second half, before Bilbao scored two more to make
it 5–2. Finally, five minutes from time, Billy Whelan took
the ball more than half the length of the field, through the
mud, past several Spanish players before placing it in the
top corner of the net. Most of those who witnessed the goal
regard it as one of the best they have ever seen. Having
lost 5–3, United were only two goals down, and had some
faint hope for the game in Manchester.

Meanwhile United had a league match at Sheffield Wednesday the following Saturday. The pressure was on the
party to get home quickly from what was their longest
European journey so far. 'In view of the League's suggestion that United should have nothing to do with the European Cup,' Busby commented later, 'I could well imagine
the repercussions if we failed to turn up at Hillsborough.'
But Bilbao was still under a snowstorm. The next day at
the airfield, players, officials, supporters and journalists all
had to help clear the snow and ice from the wings of the
plane.

Then, according to Bill Foulkes, it was another rough
journey back to England:

When the crew condescended to fly us home, the trip
became every bit as ghastly as the outward journey

had been. This time we were tossed about in a fearsome gale.

As we came to land at Jersey airport, which was on a cliff top, the plane dipped below the cliff, and then shot over the top to bounce in on the runway. Taking off again, the plane seemed to be whisked 60 feet into the air, bumped down again, and then we were away.

Manchester United had certainly learnt about the hazards of winter air travel in Europe. Yet it was typical of the attitude of the club in that era that a few days afterwards the United directors presented the pilot with an inscribed silver cigar box, and his navigator with a pen set, in appreciation of the 'skilful and safe handling of the private aircraft . . . in very difficult weather conditions'.

The team did get to Hillsborough but, with exactly the same side that had played in Spain, not surprisingly they lost 2–1.

By now the European Cup had truly captured public interest. In the second leg at Maine Road, Bilbao understandably went on the defensive. United missed several good chances before Dennis Viollet made it 1–0 at half-time. Two United goals were disallowed for offside before Tommy Taylor made it 2–0 with nineteen minutes to go. Taylor's cross to Berry five minutes from the end gave United the tie 6–5 on aggregate. In three European ties Maine Road had enjoyed three superb displays of football. Even the Football League had to acknowledge United's achievement, and it now granted permission for United to pay the players bonuses.

Great games and great goals against great sides had put United through to the semi-finals, where they had the biggest challenge of all, the European champions Real Madrid. Fortunately the away game was not due to take place until April, by which time Spain would be rather sunnier. By then the team was on target to perform a remarkable football treble – the European Cup, the league championship and the FA Cup. No team since Preston

North End and Aston Villa in the late nineteenth century
had achieved the double of the League and FA Cup. Now
Manchester United were on the way to adding the European
trophy as well.

In the FA Cup, the third round had taken them to third-
division Hartlepool on the north-east coast. United threw
away a three-goal lead, but a late winner saved any embarrassment. Wrexham were easier opponents in the fourth
round, with the reds triumphing 5–0. Everton were
defeated 1–0 at Old Trafford, and the sixth round provided
the most difficult opposition so far. Third-division Bournemouth had already slain two giants, Wolves and Spurs. By
half-time at Dean Court, a third looked to be in deep
trouble: the home side were 1–0 ahead and Mark Jones had
gone off injured. Two goals by Johnny Berry, however,
ensured United's place in the semi-final against Birmingham
City. The match at Hillsborough was a fairly easy game.
United scored two early goals from Berry and Bobby
Charlton, who was that day making his debut in the FA
Cup. United were at Wembley for the first time since 1948.
The treble was getting closer.

United's second journey to Spain was somewhat easier
than the first, and snow had given way to sun. But the
match itself was so much harder. One hundred and thirty-
four thousand people filled Madrid's vast Bernabeu stadium, almost certainly the largest crowd ever to watch
Manchester United. For Matt Busby this was the big test.
He had already travelled to France to see the Madrid side
beat Nice, and by all accounts came back somewhat in awe
of them and particularly of their Argentine centre-forward,
Di Stefano.

The 3–1 defeat in Spain was not a disastrous score – the
Bilboa matches had proved that it was possible to wipe out
a two-goal lead. United's attack had been ragged and below
form, while Madrid had not looked invincible in defence,
and Di Stefano had been dogged by Jackie Blanchflower
and Eddie Colman. Back in Manchester new floodlights at
Old Trafford meant United could now play on their own

pitch, and the new local ITV station, Granada, paid £2,500 for transmission rights.

Though the score was 2–2 this time, Real Madrid's superiority was obvious. The Spaniards first let United exhaust themselves, then took a two-goal lead through Kopa and Di Stefano. Charlton and Taylor scored two in reply but the Spaniards deservedly went through 5–3 on aggregate. In Busby's words: 'A great, experienced side will always triumph over a great, inexperienced side.' Yet coming back from two goals down to draw the match was some achievement, and towards the end Real Madrid had anxiously been kicking the ball out of play.

The treble was now out of United's grasp, but the rare FA Cup and league double looked almost certain. United had clinched a second successive league championship with a 4–0 win over Sunderland five days before the Madrid game. The points total, sixty-four, was the best since Arsenal's sixty-six in 1931, and the second highest of all time, yet had been achieved after the busiest fixture list yet tackled by an English club. The runners-up, Spurs, were eight points behind, and few thought United could lose against Aston Villa in the final. Matt Busby felt certain of victory. Yet, as so often in cup finals, form was cast aside. Manchester's chances were gravely reduced when the goalkeeper, Ray Wood, was charged by Villa's Peter MacParland. Wood went off with a broken jaw. Jackie Blanchflower took over in goal and did well. But Villa went on to win 2–1.

Busby had now gathered around him almost enough players to field two top-class sides. Though the team was so young, seven of them – Byrne, Berry, Edwards, Foulkes, Pegg, Taylor and Wood – had played for England, while Blanchflower, Webster and Whelan had also won international caps. To the players who had won the league the year before had been added a nineteen-year-old inside-forward, Bobby Charlton, who scored ten goals in just fourteen games – half of them, appropriately, in two games against Charlton Athletic!

Matt Busby's ambition of three league championships in a row, emulating Huddersfield and Arsenal in the inter-war years, got off to a good start in 1957, with five wins and twenty-two goals in the first six matches. But then several players hit bad form, and the side suffered too many silly defeats. Meanwhile Stan Cullis' emerging Wolves side quickly raced ahead and by January their lead over United was six points. The reds were confident of catching them but, as it turned out, to have done so would have required winning every game from mid-January until the end of the season.

Hopes were still alive in the cup competitions, however. Perhaps this year his more experienced side would achieve glory in the tournament that Busby told the 1957 AGM had made United 'a household word throughout the universe'. In preparation Busby had played two games in Copenhagen the previous May, and then in Berlin and Hanover before the new season started. The preliminary round draw was kind to United. The reds triumphed 6–0 over Shamrock Rovers in Dublin, though the second leg at Old Trafford was a much more embarrassing affair, with United winning, perhaps rather fortunately, 3–2. The Czech champions, Dukla Prague, were United's next opponents. A 3–0 victory in Manchester in November was more than enough to allow for a 1–0 defeat in Prague in the second leg.

Again United experienced the problems of winter air travel. The players were due to play at Birmingham City the following Saturday, but fog in Britain meant that United could not catch their intended flight. A new route was worked out. The team flew back via Amsterdam and made the rest of the journey to Manchester by boat and coach. The press did not get home until the Friday. Jimmy Murphy wrote later:

How we wished there was more elasticity to give an

English club more breathing space to go into Europe and win the European Cup as a gigantic boost to the prestige of British football. That's what we were hoping to do. But always there was this mad dash to leave England on a Monday after a hard league match the previous Saturday: a European Cup game in mid-week, then another hectic scramble to get home, usually on the Thursday, so that the lads could be in trim for another tough league match on the Saturday.

For the quarter-finals United again met East European opposition – Red Star Belgrade. The first match was at Old Trafford in mid-January. Though they deserved to win, United were sloppy and the final score was only 2–1.

Before setting off for Yugoslavia the Busby Babes were to give what was perhaps their greatest ever performance against an English side. A massive crowd of 63,578 crammed into Highbury on 1 February 1958. Exploiting a frail Arsenal defence, United had shot into a 3–0 lead before half-time, with goals from Edwards, Charlton and Taylor. In the dressing room at the interval the players were euphoric, but Johnny Berry warned that the game was not over yet. And, sure enough, in a remarkable three-minute spell fifteen minutes into the second half, Arsenal scored three times to level the scores. While most sides might have been destroyed by such a sudden setback, the babes remained calm and continued playing as before. Soon Viollet and Taylor pushed the reds into the lead again. A late Arsenal strike narrowed United's lead to one goal, but the Londoners were unable to pull off another comeback. Five of the United team – Byrne, Colman, Jones, Edwards and Taylor – would never play on English soil again.

For the trip to Yugoslavia United had chartered their own special plane so as to avoid any problems with scheduled flights. But the trip from Ringway to Belgrade was another troublesome winter journey. Fog in Manchester had made it doubtful whether the plane would ever take off in the first place. Munich in southern Germany was just over half-way on the 1,150-mile journey and a logical spot for the Elizabethan aircraft, *Lord Burghley*, to refuel. By the time the party reached Yugoslavia, it was snowing.

The match in Belgrade was yet another of those dramatic European Cup games. Just as at Highbury, United were 3–0 ahead by half-time. And just as at Highbury the three-goal lead was thrown away. Taking advantage of United's injuries, the Yugoslavs struck back to make the final result 3–3. The reds, however, were through to the semi-finals again by virtue of the victory in Manchester. Again the result was 5–4, though this time over two matches.

The Elizabethan began the long journey back to Manchester the following morning. Once again there was pressure to get home. United had a home league match on the Saturday, and their opponents were Wolves who were six points ahead of United at the top of the table. So a victory was vital if United were to maintain their ambitions of three successive championships, and Busby hoped to get back for a day's rest on the Friday.

The plane's departure from Belgrade was delayed by an hour when Johnny Berry mislaid his passport. Then the Elizabethan stopped again to refuel in Munich. It was wet and cold in the Bavarian capital, but United had overcome bad flying conditions before. The players settled into their seats and began their usual card schools. Twice the aircraft tried to take off. Twice it sped along the runway, twice it could not get off the ground, and twice the pilot quickly brought it to a halt and taxied back to the start. The party went back to the airport building while checks were made, then quickly returned to the aircraft. For a third time the plane raced through the snow down the runway. It took off slightly, but hit a house at the end of the runway and crashed.

There had been one important absentee from the plane. Jimmy Murphy, who had been appointed manager of the Welsh national team the year before, had gone to Cardiff instead, for a World Cup qualifying match against Israel on the Tuesday night. Murphy had arrived back at Old

Trafford just before 4 p.m. on the afternoon of 6 February.
Matt Busby's secretary told him the news.

> The numbing horror of that moment will live with
> me till I die. I dashed into my office and picked up
> the phone . . . and put calls through to the police . . .
> newspapers . . . BBC, asking for news. Then it
> started to come in.
> Roger Byrne . . . Eddie Colman . . . Mark
> Jones . . . Tommy Taylor . . . Billy Whelan . . .
> Geoff Bent . . . and David Pegg were dead, killed in
> a snowstorm at Munich airport. So was Bert Whalley,
> one of my closest friends and one of the greatest soccer
> coaches I ever met. Tom Curry, dear patient Tom, the
> club trainer, and the club secretary, Walter Crickmer,
> they too had been killed and Matt Busby was fighting
> for his life.

Eleven more had died too – eight journalists and three other
passengers.

The airline, BEA, flew relatives of the survivors out to
Munich, and Jimmy Murphy joined them on the plane.
Busby's wife Jean and his children Sandy and Sheena were
in the hospital when a priest gave him the last rites. Duncan
Edwards also lay dangerously ill near by, with injuries that
meant he would never play again even if he lived. Busby
beckoned Murphy to his side with a slight flicker of his
hand. 'Keep the flag flying, Jimmy,' he murmured.

Slowly the United manager recovered. Another of the
injured Johnny Berry, came to Busby's bedside, complaining how his best friend Tommy Taylor had not been to see
him yet. Berry did not know Taylor was dead. It was
Busby's lowest point.

United's league match at home to Wolves was, of course,
postponed. So too was the following week's FA Cup tie
against Sheffield Wednesday, but Murphy, with no other
coaching staff to help, would eventually have to come to
terms with the club's crisis. United boasted strength in
reserve. But in addition to the seven dead, eight other

players were injured, three of whom would never play again.

The Football Association gave United special consideration, and agreed to suspend the rule whereby players could only appear for one club in the FA Cup competition in one year. This eased Murphy's problems only slightly. It was impossible to know how much the survivors had really recovered from the crash, and how the injuries and trauma would affect their game in the long term.

United had great reserves of wealth but, though people were sympathetic, clubs would not sell their players at bargain prices. Only Liverpool and Nottingham Forest came forward to offer players. When Murphy looked down the list of remaining fit staff at Old Trafford, he was in despair: 'It read like a team of schoolboys. There was plenty of talent which might – and indeed did – show itself in two, three or four years' time. But I needed players, top-class players with first-division experience, immediately.'

A week after the crash Jimmy Murphy reported to the directors on his search for new talent. He had thought of two Swansea players from his own Welsh side. Mel Charles, the versatile wing-half, was 'not available', while the Welsh club wanted £35,000 for their winger, Cliff Jones. Murphy thought that was too much, and Spurs snapped up Jones instead. Ernie Taylor of Blackpool was coming for an interview. Jimmy Murphy was considering several other players, though few were up to United's usual standards – Bobby Mitchell, the Newcastle winger; Sunderland's Colin Grainger and Billy Elliott; Jim Iley of Spurs; Joe Haverty of Arsenal; Preston's forward, Bob Foster; Laurie Hughes of Liverpool and Brian Pilkington of Burnley. The board minutes record the acting manager's plight: 'The following team was chosen provisionally for the match *v.* Sheffield Wednesday: Gregg or Gaskell, Foulkes, Greaves or P. Jones, Goodwin, Cope, –, Webster, Taylor, Dawson, Pearson, –.' Possible players from other clubs to fill the blanks would be watched on the coming Saturday.

The Sheffield Wednesday match was rearranged for Wednesday, 19 February, thirteen days after the crash. When the programme went to press the final selection was so uncertain that every place in the United line-up was left blank in what became probably the most historic English football programme of all time.

In the end Murphy bought only two major players. Ernie Taylor, the tiny inside forward who had won the FA Cup with both Newcastle and Blackpool, came to United with the help of Paddy McGrath, a United supporter who owned nightclubs in Blackpool and Manchester and who was a close friend of both Busby and Murphy. Stan Crowther, a tough-tackling player who had helped Aston Villa beat United at Wembley the year before, signed just an hour before the kick-off against Wednesday.

Of those who had played against Red Star Belgrade, only Gregg and Foulkes lined up for the game. Taylor and Crowther made their debuts, but the rest of the side had just ninety-one league appearances between them. Ian Greaves, Ron Cope, Freddie Goodwin, Colin Webster and Alex Dawson had all played for the first team before but were more accustomed to the reserve and youth sides. Mark Pearson, at inside-left, was making his debut. So too was the new outside-left, Shay Brennan, a midfield player who had been plucked from the A team.

Poor Sheffield Wednesday did not stand a chance. There were officially 59,848 inside the United ground that night. It was 7,000 below the capacity, but only because many of those with tickets could not get in because of the tens of thousands of mourning supporters who packed the streets all around Old Trafford. The patched-together red side was carried along by the noise and emotion. Shay Brennan's corner was helped into the goal by the Sheffield goalkeeper, and he scored a second later. Alex Dawson made it three with five minutes left.

Remarkably, after scoring twice on his debut, Shay Brennan got only four more goals in 356 more games for the reds, though most of them were at full-back.

Ian Greaves, replacing Roger Byrne at left-back, recalled

later: 'It was an electrifying night but there was no cheering in the dressing room afterwards – we were all sad. I felt in a way that I shouldn't have been there, that I was stepping into someone else's shoes.'

Two days after the Sheffield Wednesday game, Duncan Edwards died.

Slowly, the survivors of Munich returned to the side – Bobby Charlton, Ray Wood, Albert Scanlon, Ken Morgans and Dennis Viollet – though two players, Jackie Blanch-flower and Johnny Berry, were injured so badly that they would never play again. Perhaps not surprisingly, United's league form went to pieces. Of the fourteen league games left to play, United lost eight and won only one. They finally finished ninth. But the stirring Cup performances continued.

In the sixth round United visited West Bromwich and led 2–1 until four minutes from the end, but had to settle for a 2–2 draw and a replay. At Old Trafford the Bir-mingham side had the better of much of the play, but Colin Webster's goal in the final minute saw United through to the semi-finals. That the Cup competition had drawn that special spirit out of the players was shown by the fact that West Bromwich Albion beat United 4–0 at Old Trafford in the league only three days after the replay.

United were fortunate to draw the easiest of the semi-final qualifiers, second-division Fulham. Once again the fans were treated to two great matches. The first at Villa Park produced a 2–2 draw, while London welcomed United again for what proved to be another historic and high-scoring visit to Highbury, transmitted live on television.

Twice United went ahead and twice Fulham equalised. But in the second half United's superiority was established. Alex Dawson scored a hat-trick and Charlton's goal in the last minute made it 5–3. Incredibly, United were back at Wembley.

Matt Busby, now out of hospital, was able to go to the final as a spectator, hobbling on crutches, though Jimmy Murphy was still in charge of the side – a point acknowledged in typical style by Busby when, only minutes before kick-off, he said to the players: 'Good luck lads. Just go out and follow Jimmy's instructions.' Dennis Viollet had at last recovered from his injuries and was brought into the final team even though he had played only two games since Munich. Two of the youngsters brought in from the reserves, Mark Pearson and Shay Brennan, had lost their places.

Every neutral wanted United to win, of course. But by now the spell over United's remarkable FA Cup run was broken. Their opponents, Bolton Wanderers, were only a middle-ranking first-division side, but they easily over-powered United. Bolton took an early lead through Nat Lofthouse; Bobby Charlton hit a post, but Bolton made it 2–0 when Lofthouse charged Harry Gregg into the goal.

Hundreds of thousands welcomed the losing side back to Manchester, many more than saw the FA Cup taken back to Bolton. At Wembley the United players had worn special badges on their shirts depicting the phoenix, the mythical bird that rose from the ashes. United had indeed risen again, for the third time in thirty years.

That summer the England team suffered in the World Cup in Sweden. Before Munich, with Roger Byrne, Duncan Edwards and Tommy Taylor regularly in the side, England had been unbeaten for three years against foreign opposition and the United trio had contributed seventeen goals in the previous twelve games. The Munich crash destroyed any hopes that England might recover from the humiliations of the early 1950s. It would be another eight years before Alf Ramsay's World Cup side restored national pride. By then Matt Busby had built his third team and embarked on a further chapter of glory for Manchester United. But from 1958 onwards the Manchester United over which he presided was no longer an ordinary football club.

3
The Man who Bought United

'The welfare and continued progress and success of Manchester United are now my life ambition.'

Louis Edwards, 1962.

On the afternoon of the day after Munich the United board met at the home in Bowdon, Cheshire, of Alan Gibson, son of the late United chairman, James Gibson. It was one of the odd aspects of the Munich disaster that none of the club board had flown with the team to Belgrade. On nearly all United's previous journeys at least one director had gone with the players. This time, however, Harold Hardman had not been well enough to fly, while Alan Gibson himself was recovering from a broken leg.

The brief hand-written minutes from that historic board meeting gave only stark details, and fail to reflect the full tragedy of the circumstances in which they met. Indeed, the first item on the agenda was not about Munich at all, but the death five days earlier of the director, George Whittaker, whose funeral Harold Hardman had attended that morning. Whittaker had died in a hotel in London on the morning of United's historic 5–4 victory at Arsenal.

The three remaining directors then heard reports on the news from Munich. They extended 'their sympathy and condolences to the families of the deceased and injured', and were told that relatives had been flown out to Germany.

Walter Crickmer, the club secretary, had been among the dead. The directors appointed his assistant, Les Olive, as acting secretary, and authorisation was sent to the bank for him to sign cheques. The board then took a decision that was to have far-reaching effects. 'It was proposed, seconded and carried unanimously,' the minutes recorded, 'that Mr Louis Charles Edwards of "Caudebec", Alderley Edge, Cheshire, be and is hereby appointed and co-opted as an additional Director of the Company.'

That Louis Edwards should have been elected to the United board the very day after Munich was pure coincidence and nothing to do with the tragedy. According to Louis Edwards' son Martin, his father had in fact been considered for election a few weeks earlier, but had been vetoed by George Whittaker, though there is no record of this in the club minutes. Now, with Whittaker's death, the opposition to Edwards had been removed. Yet had Whittaker not opposed the appointment initially, Martin Edwards suggests that, as a director, his father would almost certainly have flown to Belgrade with the official party, and might easily have perished in the Munich crash.

It would be several weeks, of course, before Matt Busby, fighting for his life in the Rechts der Isar hospital in Munich, would get to hear of Louis Edwards' election. When the news was finally given to him, he must have been delighted. United's board, in his view, would now be in safe hands for the difficult rebuilding that lay ahead. Busby had long worried that the board members were nearly all getting on in years, and was anxious about what would happen when the present directors passed away. The United manager saw Louis Edwards as a future chairman, and had been pushing him in that direction since first meeting him socially in Manchester a decade earlier.

For a generation after the Second World War the Manchester Opera House in Quay Street was to the city's showbusiness life what Old Trafford was to football. There Tommy Appleby, one of Britain's top post-war provincial theatre-managers, presided over a different show every week, with a stream of stars from all over the world. On Mondays, after the week's opening night, Appleby would hold a party for his performers, who over the years included names such as Noël Coward, Stewart Grainger and Laurence Olivier. He would invite his own personal guests along to swell the numbers. Usually the party would move on to eat at a restaurant, often Arturo's in Portland Street. Throughout the North-west Tommy Appleby's first-night parties were renowned as great social occasions, at which many of the area's most influential figures would regularly be seen.

From 1947 onwards Matt Busby's wife Jean and his daughter Sheena frequently went to drama and ballet performances at the Opera House. Busby himself did not always share their enthusiasm – perhaps the weekly drama at United was sufficient. So while the ladies were watching a performance, Busby would often wait and chat in Tommy Appleby's office ready to take them home afterwards. And, of course, as the distinguished manager of the successful local football team, Busby was an obvious guest for Appleby to invite to the Monday-night celebrations.

Busby found the parties a rare chance to get away from the problems of football, problems which were not always confined to team matters. Busby had sometimes found relations difficult with his first two chairmen, James Gibson and Harold Hardman. The United manager was always insistent that it should be he, not the directors, who ran the club. In the early 1950s it was obvious that Hardman, who was then over seventy, would not be around for ever. Three other directors, George Whittaker, William Petherbridge and Dr McLean were all beyond retirement age. Only Alan Gibson, the biggest shareholder, added any youth to the board. But Gibson had never been well enough to hold a full-time job, was not a forceful character, and admitted he had never been that much of a football fan. There was really no obvious successor as chairman.

Moreover, Busby feared that the club might easily be

taken over by certain unsavoury local businessmen, the shady types who hover on the fringes of any top football club. To prevent this, and to ensure that there were more understanding, sympathetic directors in future, the United manager was hoping to influence who joined the board. And Tommy Appleby was able to bring him into contact with more suitable candidates.

Louis Edwards was a local meat trader, co-owner, with his brother Douglas, of Louis C. Edwards and Sons (Manchester) Ltd. He and his wife Muriel, together with Douglas and his wife Emmeline, were keen theatre-goers and often went to the Opera House together. They would frequently rely on Appleby to fix up last-minute tickets. A large, roly-poly, ebullient character, Edwards enjoyed fat cigars, fine food and champagne – in later years he became know as 'Champagne Louis'. But he suffered from a slight stammer, which gave him some insecurity on public occasions. He claimed to have supported Manchester United, the local football team, since his childhood in Salford. Louis Edwards could also boast a family connection with one of the great historic figures of Manchester United Football Club.

After Matt Busby, it could be argued that the most important name in the club's history was Louis Rocca, the man who wrote the letter that brought Busby to Old Trafford. Rocca never played for the club or served as manager, secretary or chairman, but, by all accounts, he enjoyed a leading role in United's affairs throughout the first half of the twentieth century. He had arrived as a tea-boy in the 1890s, during the time when the club was still known as Newton Heath. During the 1920s, '30s and '40s, Rocca served as assistant manager and chief scout, and was responsible for finding many of the players whom Busby inherited, including Johnny Carey. He boasted a network of Catholic priests looking for new young talent, and perhaps more than anyone, Louis Rocca's influence gave United the reputation for being a Roman Catholic club. According to Geoffrey Green's history of the club, Louis Rocca also claimed credit for suggesting the very name Manchester United, though as he was only nineteen at the time when the change occurred in April 1902, this seems rather surprising.

Like the Edwards family, and like so many Italian immigrants, the Roccas were in the food trade, and ran a confectionery business on the Rochdale Road. In 1926 Louis Rocca's younger cousin, Joe, married Beatrice Edwards, Louis Edwards' eldest sister.

In view of the family connection with Louis Rocca, it is perhaps surprising that Louis Edwards did not meet Matt Busby until Appleby introduced them to each other at one of his Opera House parties. Appleby, who has now retired and lives in Sale, reckons that it must have been around 1950. Until 1988 Appleby had two seats in the United directors' box, where Sir Matt Busby used to pull his leg about the historic introduction, forty years ago. With hindsight Busby probably wishes it had never happened.

After meeting Matt Busby, the meat trader was soon taking a keen interest in the club. Martin Edwards remembers going with his parents to watch his first match at Old Trafford in 1952. Louis and Muriel Edwards were guests of Matt Busby in the directors' box.

Two former United players, Jackie Blanchflower and John Aston Senior, both remember encountering Louis Edwards for the first time on a tour to the United States in the summer of 1952. Aston recalls that, one night on the *Queen Mary*, the players were invited into the first-class restaurant and treated to champagne by a large man beaming at them from his table on the balcony above. Officially Louis Edwards had gone to America on business, but had arranged his itinerary carefully to be in New York and Chicago when United were playing there, and to ensure that his outward and return sea crossings coincided with the team's sailings. It is also said that when Louis Edwards discovered that Matt Busby was a strong Roman Catholic, he rediscovered his own Catholic upbringing and background, and began attending dinners of the Catholic Sportsmen's Club.

Another important Manchester businessman whom Busby met through Tommy Appleby was Willie Satinoff, whose family ran a clothing company, Alligator Rainwear. Satinoff was a keen race-goer and owned several racehorses, one of which, Red Alligator, included both his company's title and his allegiance to United in its name. Satinoff would often get Appleby to bring show-business guests along to his private box at Aintree, and after meeting him, Busby sometimes joined them at the races. Occasionally all three men would fly to a racecourse in a private plane. As a keen Manchester United fan Satinoff used to go to nearly every away match.

Willie Satinoff was by far the stronger of the two candidates whom Busby might have had in mind for the United board. He had been even more successful in business than Edwards. Unlike the rather hesitant meat-man, he was a good public performer. Satinoff dressed immaculately and was extremely popular with everyone. And in contrast to the 17-stone Louis Edwards, Willie Satinoff was slim; he played five-a-side daily at the YMCA and rarely drank. People also say he understood football far better then Louis Edwards and that he was just as close to Busby. 'For many years,' according to the *Manchester Guardian*, 'a deep attachment existed between Satinoff and Busby. Satinoff became almost an honorary member of the Manchester United football team and followed them wherever they went.' Those words, however, were written in his obituary.

The honorary member's fervour for United had cost him his life. Unlike the United directors, Willie Satinoff had gone with the official party to Belgrade in February 1958. He died at Munich.

Many who knew him, including Busby's close friend Paddy McGrath, believed that, had he lived, Willie Satinoff would have been the obvious successor to Harold Hardman as United chairman. They argue that certainly he would have been elected to the club board in due course. There, by all accounts, he would have been a formidable force, and perhaps an obstacle to the ambitions of Busby's other

close businessman friend, Louis Edwards. It is unlikely
that, had Willie Satinoff lived, whether as a United director
or simply as dedicated supporter, Louis Edwards would
have been allowed to get away with the clever plan he was
to carry out over the next seven years.

Shortly after Louis Edwards' election to the United
board, the club issued ten shares to him in order to comply
with rules requiring directors to have a nominal shareholding. They would have cost Edwards just £1 each, the face
value, but with more than 4,000 shares issued altogether
Edwards' ten were only a tiny fraction of the equity. To be
certain of achieving his next target – the chairmanship –
Edwards would require a majority holding of more than
2,000 shares.

In the years immediately after his election Louis Edwards
quickly immersed himself in the club's affairs. He soon
became by far the most active of the four directors. He
represented the club at many of the funerals of the Munich
victims, and for many at United this was the first time they
had met him. He went to the Football Association memorial
service at St Martin-in-the-Fields in London, and in late
February attended Duncan Edwards' burial in Dudley.

Louis Edwards became involved in negotiations over the
Munich insurance and held consultations with a QC. Discussions over catering at Old Trafford were also left to
Edwards at one stage. And, when Matt Busby signed Albert
Quixall from Sheffield Wednesday in September 1958 for
a record fee of £45,000, Louis Edwards was the only director to accompany him across the Pennines to complete the
deal. Three years later Edwards helped Matt Busby in
another record signing – Denis Law from Torino for
£115,000.

In 1961 the board set up a three-man sub-committee to
deal with financial matters comprising the three youngest
directors – Edwards, Alan Gibson and a newly co-opted
board member, Bill Young, who was a close friend of
Gibson. Harold Hardman had decided not to serve on the
finance committee and Louis Edwards was elected its chair-

man. By 1962 the two directors' signatures on the annual accounts were those of the club chairman Harold Hardman and Edwards.

It was only after more than four years on the United board, however, that Louis Edwards set about acquiring a shareholding to accompany his commitment in terms of activity. At that time Manchester United Football Club Limited was a private company. Most of its 4,132 ordinary £1 shares had been issued before the First World War, though more equity had been issued after James Gibson saved the club in 1932. Many of the original shareholders had, of course, died, and in most cases their equity had passed to their heirs. It was rare that shares were sold by one person to another, since any such transaction had to be approved by the board of directors. A fair proportion of such requests was turned down. As well as the ordinary shares, there were 1,725 preference shares. These had priority when it came to dividend payments, but only a tenth of the voting power of the ordinary shares. Preference shares can therefore largely be ignored when considering questions of voting power.

Sometimes shareholders who wanted to sell would offer their stock to the board and this would be divided among the directors who paid the face value of £1 for each share. In this way, between 1958 and 1961, Louis Edwards acquired seven ordinary shares to add to his original ten. But overall his holding was still insignificant: less than one per cent of the company's capital.

Of the 142 shareholders at the time of the company's annual return in 1962, none had a majority of the 4,132 ordinary shares in the company. The highest stake was held by the Gibson family. Anne Gibson, wife of the late chairman, James Gibson, held 894, and their son, the United director Alan Gibson, owned 832. So between them Alan Gibson and his mother could command 1,726 shares, 41.8 per cent of the equity. The next biggest shareholder, with 468, was Mabel Whittaker, the wife of George

Whittaker, the director who died five days before Munich. Only five other people had more than 100 ordinary shares.

Over the next fifteen months, however, between October 1962 and January 1964, the whole spread of shares in Manchester United Football Club Ltd was transformed in favour of Louis Charles Edwards.

With a copy of the 1962 share register, Edwards drew up a list of those stockholders whom he thought might conceivably be interested in selling their shares. One by one they were approached. To carry out the mundane task of actually knocking on shareholders' doors, Edwards called on the services of a corrupt Manchester Conservative councillor called Frank Farrington. Alderman Farrington had often carried out small chores for Edwards in the past and helped him get meat contracts. In the post-war years Farrington had earned a reputation in Manchester business and political circles as 'the Kingmaker'. As a member of the council since 1927, he had never enjoyed high political office, but held influential positions, such as being on the board of the Manchester Ship Canal Company. The alderman was not very wealthy and lived in a council flat, but through his political and personal connections in Manchester he could 'fix' things.

As a boy, Frank Farrington had helped to clear stones and glass from the pitch in the days before 1910 when Manchester United played on their old ground at Clayton. Now he was being asked to go out and use his contacts to prepare the ground for his friend, Louis Edwards.

On an autumn evening, totally unexpectedly, a shareholder would receive a knock at the door. One such visit was to Norman and Alice Rowbotham at their terraced home in Ilkley Street, which happened to be in Farrington's council ward. Rowbotham had inherited 100 shares from his uncle Albert who had bought them when United were in trouble in the 1930s. Mrs Rowbotham and her two small children were asked to leave the room, and Farrington insisted on secrecy and urgency. It was a matter of 'take it or leave it'. Norman Rowbotham did not earn much from his job at a local ICI factory, and with Christmas on the way they accepted Farrington's offer of £500 – £5 for each share.

Two days later Farrington picked Rowbotham up and took him to New Street, Miles Platting, where Louis Edwards personally handed the money over in the Edwards' company boardroom. Afterwards Farrington demanded £50 from Rowbotham, as his cut of the deal. A few days later Edwards sent the Rowbothams a few chops and ¾lb beef.

Another seller, Nat Rose, had arranged to meet Farrington, whom he already happened to know, for a drink in a hotel off Albert Square. Once a deal was agreed, the councillor took Rose to the meat factory where Edwards handed over the cash in £1 and £5 notes. Rose and his wife used the money to pay for a two-week holiday in Majorca and put the rest in trust for their son when he reached twenty-one. They were sent a turkey for Christmas and a joint of meat.

After Farrington had trudged the streets of Manchester for a while, Edwards decided that it might be simpler to make his approaches by post. He sent out dozens of letters to shareholders in the autumn of 1962 and winter of 1963. Each, it seems, had an almost identical text. 'You will be aware that I am a Director of Manchester United F. C. Ltd.,' Edwards began, 'having been appointed to the Board just after the Munich air crash in February 1958.' Edwards proceeded to claim that United was now his life ambition, and told each recipient how he wanted to bolster his shareholding in the club. Those who received the letters were offered £15 a share – well above the market value, Edwards claimed, but a sign, he said, of his 'unstinted and sincere devotion' to United. 'If you are interested will you please write to me at my office address, a suitably addressed envelope being enclosed for your use. I am sure that the Chairman and my colleagues on the Board would approve the transfer of shares.'

Once shareholders had replied to Edwards' standard letter, much of the day-to-day administration of the operation was then carried out by Thomas McKeown, the secretary of the Edwards' meat company. McKeown sent out subsequent letters to shareholders, stockbrokers, solicitors and to Les Olive, the company secretary at Old Trafford. The work was done from the firm's offices in Miles Platting.

Ironically, among the first shareholders to give a favourable reply, in December 1962, was Mabel Whittaker, widow of George Whittaker, the director who according to Martin Edwards had originally vetoed Edwards in 1958. Mrs Whittaker was offered only £12 for each of her 443 shares – less than other people – but was delighted to accept since she was rather hard up and living on a meagre pension. The transaction meant that Edwards was now the club's third largest shareholder. Her late husband would not have been pleased.

Each transaction had to be agreed by the United directors. The first two deals, for 120 shares, were agreed by the board at a meeting on 16 October 1962. Mabel Whittaker's sale went through in early December, and later in the month four more transfers, totalling 300 shares to Louis Edwards, were agreed. The directors had never known so much share activity before. Normally they were asked to approve only a few transfers every year. Now, in the space of just a few weeks, Louis Edwards had become the company's largest shareholder, with a bigger stake than either Alan Gibson or his mother. It must have been obvious what Edwards was doing.

When, at the first meeting in the New Year, the board were asked to approve three more transfers, for 155 shares, they gave their approval but with a condition. In future, it was agreed, no transfers to Anne Gibson, Alan Gibson or Louis Edwards 'would be registered if it would cause any changes in the present balance of holdings'. But transfers to other individuals would be permitted.

The share-buying stopped – at least for a while. Then, rather than try to buy shares himself, which was no longer allowed, Louis Edwards brought in his brother, Douglas, the co-chairman of the meat company, and Denzil Haroun,

a Manchester businessman of Syrian ancestry involved in
the textile trade. Haroun was married to Edwards' sister
Peggy, a distinguished amateur golfer.

In March 1963 the approaches to shareholders restarted,
with Thomas McKeown again responsible for the administration. Copies of the following standard letter were sent
out to many different targets:

Dear Mr X

May I introduce myself to you as a regular and ardent
supporter of Manchester United. I am in the fortunate
position of being a regular guest in the Directors'
Box through the invitations of my brother-in-law, Mr
Louis Edwards, who, you will be aware, is a Director
of Manchester United F. C. Ltd. I also travel to away
games whenever possible.

I would like to extend my interest in the club by
becoming a shareholder and I notice from the Annual
List that you do hold xx Ordinary shares. I should
be very grateful indeed if you would consider selling
your shares to me. I am willing to pay £15 (fifteen
pounds) for each Ordinary share. This price is far
higher than the commercial or economic value of the
shares but it represents an earnest desire to support
my devotion and interest in the club with a fair sized
shareholding. I can give you my personal assurance
that if you did transfer your shares to me they would
be held very securely in my family and would, therefore, be valued very carefully by persons who had the
best interests of the club at heart.

If you are interested in selling will you please write
to me, a suitably addressed envelope to my business
address being enclosed for your use.

Yours faithfully,

D. D. Haroun

Virtually the same letter was sent out by Douglas Edwards, with the personal details suitably changed and with variations in the offer price. In May 1963 Haroun secured the largest remaining holding apart from the Gibsons' – 160 shares from Richard Shaw at £15 each. The sale was agreed by the board.

In July the United directors approved eight different transactions to Douglas Edwards, involving 81 shares. It was an extraordinary decision in view of their previous decision on Louis Edwards' sharebuying, and they cannot have been unaware who Douglas Edwards was. In October came another nineteen transfers to Douglas Edwards representing 147 shares.

Many shareholders seem to have been delighted by Edwards' approaches. A widow said that her husband had originally bought the shares in 1913 and that selling them was a hard decision. However, she reached it because, as she explained, 'I'm middle-aged and in the course of time [the shares] will go to some relative who maybe is not [as] interested as you are.'

Most had retained their holdings for years without realising what they were worth. One holder of a single ordinary share had acquired it back in 1924, while he was social secretary of the supporters' club in order, he said, to attend shareholders' meetings. Those who sold their shares to Louis Edwards sometimes expected favours in return, such as match tickets or priority in the queue for season tickets. In some cases Edwards obliged. Others found that they had asked too late, after their deal had gone through, and were told that there was nothing the United director could do.

Occasionally the transactions involved famous names from United's history. Two hundred pounds, for instance, was paid for eight shares from Winifred Meredith. She was the daughter of Billy Meredith, the great Welsh winger who played for United between 1907 and 1921, and had inherited them on her father's death in 1958. Douglas Edwards visited her personally. Another attracted by the Edwards' offer was Clarence Hilditch, a United player from the 1920s, who was also briefly player-manager at one point. He received £500 for his twenty shares.

At one point Edwards also expressed some interest in buying shares in Manchester City – for what reason is not entirely clear; perhaps it was to bargain with City supporters who held United shares and were prepared to swap.

Over the months the price that the Edwards family were prepared to pay for shares gradually rose – from £5 at the start to £12.50, £15, £20 and then finally to £25. It seems that few people tried to bargain over the price. For many the offer was far greater than what they had thought the shares were worth. 'I have had several requests for this share,' wrote a lady who held just one, 'but not until I received your letter was anyone prepared to say what they were prepared to pay for it and being financially embarrassed just now I felt it time to take your offer.'

However, it was clear that while deals for small amounts of shares from obscure shareholders might gradually build up Edwards' stake, it might never be possible to secure a majority of the equity without acquiring some of the Gibson family's large holding. The deal that effectively clinched control for Louis Edwards came in September 1963, when Alan Gibson agreed to sell 500 of his shares at £25 each, or £12,500 in all.

At this point the United directors seemed to give in, acknowledging that now Louis Edwards could not be stopped. If the second largest shareholder, Alan Gibson, was willing to sell to Edwards, there seemed little reason to preserve the share balance between Edwards and the Gibson family any longer. On 8 October 1963 Harold Hardman proposed, and Alan Gibson's friend, Bill Young, seconded, that the directors should rescind their previous decision which in theory prevented Louis Edwards buying any more shares, and the deal with Alan Gibson was allowed to go through. At the same meeting it was announced that Denzil Haroun had been nominated to the board for the coming AGM. And when Haroun secured election by the shareholders, the man who nominated him was Douglas Edwards.

Louis Edwards had 1,835 ordinary shares which, together with the 642 preference shares he had bought, gave him 1,899 of the company's votes – or 44 per cent. But the shares which had been acquired that summer by Douglas Edwards and Denzil Haroun meant that he and his relations now had a majority.

An interesting side point is that United's company share register sometimes records the share selling price as £1 per share, when in fact Edwards and his relations had paid more than that. At that time United had a rule that shares only be sold at face value – £1 each. Indeed, the board had vetoed several other proposed share transactions because they were at more than face value.

On 14 January 1964, to tidy matters up and to make sure of an absolute majority, Louis Edwards bought 238 shares from his brother Douglas and 150 from his brother-in-law Denzil Haroun. Louis Edwards now owned Manchester United. In December 1964 the meat trader's powerful position on the board was acknowledged when he was proposed by Alan Gibson as vice-chairman of the club and elected. Six months later, in June 1965, Harold Hardman died. He was eighty-three and had served more than fifty years as a director and fourteen years as chairman. Now there was only one possible successor. Louis Edwards was duly elected unopposed.

It had proved a remarkably cheap exercise for the Manchester butcher. Louis Edwards' total bill worked out at somewhere between £31,000 and £41,000, a sum he could easily afford following the flotation of his meat company on the Stock Exchange in 1962. In return for that money he had bought control of one of Britain's wealthiest and most popular football clubs.

Some indication of how inexpensive his purchase had been may partly be gauged by the fact that gate receipts for the 1963–64 season, for instance, were £172,000 – five or six times what Edwards had spent. The year before,

United had broken the British transfer record by buying Denis Law from Torino for £115,000. Law's fee was roughly three times what it cost Louis Edwards to buy control of the whole club.

It was so simple, and had been carried out with little fuss. No doubt dozens of businessmen, in Manchester and beyond, would have been delighted to pay £35,000 or so at that time to secure the effective ownership of one of Britain's top soccer clubs. Yet, had an outsider tried to do what Edwards did, he would have been stopped by the board who would have refused to authorise the transaction. Even small share transfers were often rejected by the board. In 1965, for instance, David Meek, the *Manchester Evening News* reporter, was stopped from buying a single share.

Edwards only succeeded in his takeover because the United board acquiesced in the process. No director had the wealth or will to stop him. Alan Gibson, the only man with the share-power to stand in Edwards' way, was not strong enough. The chairman, Harold Hardman, dreaded that Edwards would get the chairmanship, but knew it was unavoidable after his death. He even offered to sell his seventy-one shares to a wealthy builder, the father-in-law of the then United goalkeeper, Harry Gregg, if it might prevent the inevitable. Hardman had at one time earmarked as his successor a local Football League referee, Gordon Gibson, who often joined the players' Sunday morning get-togethers. But Gibson had neither the necessary shares nor money. By the time he was in his eighties Hardman was no longer strong enough to stop the new man. And, of course, the real force at Old Trafford, Matt Busby, was not to realise the long term implications. As manager he was happy to support Edwards' plans, which, it must be said, involved ambitious developments for United.

Investing in a football club was even less of a serious financial proposition in the 1960s than it is nowadays. The dividend was limited to five per cent of the face value of the shares – little more than £100 a year for Edwards, even if a dividend was awarded. But the immediate return on

Edwards' investment was prestige in Manchester business circles. He was now chairman of one of the most famous and glamorous football clubs in the world. And the potential value of the club – measured largely in terms of the goodwill of the citizens of Manchester to follow United week in, week out – must have been several hundred thousand pounds, even in 1964. However, it would be many years before Louis Edwards and his family realised any great financial return on his shrewd but simple investment.

4

The Search for the Holy Grail

'Frankly, ever since my wife, Jean, had told me in the Munich hospital that she felt sure the lads who had died would have wanted me to carry on, I had become increasingly obsessed about United winning the European Cup. It was almost as if this glittering trophy were the Holy Grail.'

Matt Busby on the European Cup.

It took months for Matt Busby to recover from Munich. Indeed, in some ways he was never really the same again. Although Busby was at Wembley for the 1958 FA Cup final, it was not until after a long convalescence that summer at Interlaken that he was ready to return to Old Trafford.

The United manager had in fact been very close to death. Inside an oxygen tent, he had a collapsed lung, and twice a priest administered the last rites. When Busby began to regain consciousness and learned the terrible news, he blamed himself for what had happened. After all, he had taken the Manchester United team into Europe against the advice of the Football League. 'I will never go back into football,' he vowed.

But his wife Jean persuaded him to reconsider. 'I don't think you are being fair to the people who have lost their loved ones,' Busby recalls her saying. 'And I am sure those who have gone, too, would have wanted you to carry on.'

The spirit which pushed the hastily rebuilt United side through three more rounds of the FA Cup to the 1958 final was not enough, however, to make further progress in the European Cup. To help United, the European Football Association, UEFA, had paired them against the team left in the competition for whom the away leg would provide the easiest journey by boat and train – AC Milan. United beat the Italian champions 2–1 in the first leg of the semifinal, after being 1–0 down. They did so, moreover, without Bobby Charlton. The FA, in an insensitive decision, had insisted that the United forward should play for England in a friendly match against Portugal the night before. Charlton was also called away by England for the second leg, played a few days after the disappointment of the FA Cup final. The Italian champions overwhelmed United 4–0.

Matt Busby was made a CBE, and the United board increased his salary to £5,000 a year. He knew that any European ambition would have to be forgotten for the time being. But in the long term the goal was to win the European champions' trophy in memory and in honour of those who died.

The European football authorities at that time had rather more of a human face than their English counterparts. As a gesture of sympathy, UEFA actually invited Manchester United to compete in the European Cup the season after Munich, 1958–59 – in addition, of course, to the new English league champions, Wolves. They were even drawn in the qualifying round against Young Boys Berne, the Swiss champions.

Arguments went on all summer, and only a few days before the first match was due to take place the Football League, after much debate, forced United to withdraw on the grounds that they were not league champions. The Football Association, the superior body, went along with the League's decision, though initially the FA had been quite happy for United to compete. It was a mean, heartless decision by the English authorities, especially since in those early years other sides had competed in the European Cup without being national champions. United played the Young Boys fixtures as friendlies, winning 3–2 on aggregate, but the Swiss team went on to the European Cup semi-finals. The reds, had they been allowed to compete, might have done even better. Who knows? Matt Busby's new team did well enough in the league championship the season after Munich to be runners-up to Wolves, who retained their title, and the reds remained in contention almost until the very end.

The rebuilt side seemed to be carried along by a tide of post-Munich emotion in the 1958–59 season. The average home gate at Old Trafford, 53,258, was the highest in Britain, and the second highest in United's history. Away from Manchester, gates were locked at many grounds as the public paid homage to the team that had risen from the ashes. Crowds of more than 60,000 were recorded at Newcastle, Manchester City, Everton and Arsenal.

Despite prolific scoring by Bobby Charlton, who got twenty-nine league goals – his best ever season – and a record 103 league goals for the team as a whole, Matt Busby knew that the team were not really good enough. Of the side that had lost to Bolton at Wembley in 1958 only three – Gregg, Foulkes and Charlton – would stay long at Old Trafford. By January 1962 the other eight had all left for new clubs.

The production line of great players from the youth sides seemed to dry up. Of the team that won United's fifth successive Youth Cup in 1957, only David Gaskell enjoyed a long first-team career with the club. Three survivors of Munich, Ray Wood, Albert Scanlon and Ken Morgans, never seemed to be the same again, and Jimmy Murphy feels that this was also true of Dennis Viollet, though he carried on scoring frequently. Some of the young reserve replacements may have been called on too early in the emergency situation after Munich. At the same time other clubs, such as Wolves, were copying United's youth programme and getting more of the best young players.

The club had been badly under-insured at Munich, and

Busby could not simply buy a new team with the compensation money. A cheque for £112,000 arrived from the insurance company, and it was split equally between the club and the dependents of the dead players. It meant that these relations were badly provided for, living without pensions. This would be a source of some ill-feeling in later years.

Another £10,000 compensation arrived for the two players who were unable to play any more – Jackie Blanchflower and Johnny Berry – and again it was divided 50–50. The airline, BEA, were sued by the club, and after five years of negotiation United finally received £35,000 in January 1963. So, in all, the club itself ended up with around £100,000 to compensate for the loss of ten great players who, even at 1958 prices, would have been worth much more on the transfer market.

Between 1949 and 1958 Busby had bought only five significant players – Ray Wood, Reg Allen, Johnny Berry, Tommy Taylor and Harry Gregg – and three of them were goalkeepers. In his thirteen years at United Busby had a trading surplus on transfers of more than £50,000. Now, in spite of the meagre insurance money, he felt he had no option but to spend as best he could, abandoning his reliance on the youth sides, if United were to remain a leading team. He was only too aware of how Torino had declined after the Superga disaster wiped out their team in 1949. 'I was determined to keep the name of Manchester United on people's lips,' he said later. 'We always had to look as if we were doing something. Having been the greatest, we could not settle for anything else.'

The first new transfer, in September 1958, was the England forward, Albert Quixall, who cost Busby a then English record fee of £45,000 from Sheffield Wednesday. Quixall was never a great success at Old Trafford, however, and failed to win back his England place.

Further transfer activity failed to stop the slide over the coming seasons. Maurice Setters joined from West Bromwich Albion for £30,000 in 1960 as a replacement for Wilf

McGuinness who had been forced to retire through injury. Noel Cantwell cost £29,000 from West Ham the same year. In between, a left-back, Tony Dunne, was signed from Shelbourne for just £6,000. Dennis Viollet, who in 1959–60 had created a club record of thirty-two league goals in a season, was replaced by David Herd, who cost £35,000 from Arsenal in 1961.

For five years United did not do well enough to qualify for European competition, though later the runners-up spot achieved in 1959 would have given them a UEFA Cup place. Yet as Busby tried to rebuild his side, buying many more players than he would have liked in normal circumstances, experimenting with different combinations, bringing young players up from the youth teams, the goal of winning the European Cup one day became all important. In fact it was the only thing Busby cared about. It became an obsession which permeated the whole club.

Players who went to Old Trafford in the early '60s remember the powerful, overriding importance the European trophy had acquired. 'Almost from when I joined,' says David Sadler, who arrived in 1962, 'everything was geared towards winning that cup.' Pat Crerand, who joined a few months later, agrees: 'When I came in 1963 there was this great underlying wish to win the European Cup. I think that was the aim all the time I was here.'

In those years United developed a close relationship with Real Madrid. In 1958 the Spanish champions had offered to pay for the Munich survivors to have free holidays in Spain. At one point Matt Busby was even offered the manager's job at Real Madrid by the club president, Santiago Bernabeu. 'Their actual words were: "We'll make it heaven and earth for you," and I know they would.' In Spain he could probably have won the European Cup not once but several times. Busby thought about the offer for a week, but decided his heaven and earth were in Manchester. He knew the boys who died at Munich could be commemorated only by the team they had once played for.

During what was a wilderness period for United after

Munich, Busby prepared for the eventual return to European competition with regular friendly games against the very best sides that Europe could offer. In 1959 he flew to Spain to persuade Real Madrid to come to Old Trafford.

> Real Madrid at that time were commanding about £12,000 to visit any club for a match, an enormous sum then. I said the crash had ruined us financially as well as physically and I would be grateful if they would take this into consideration. Mr Bernabeu turned to the business manager and said: 'We must treat Matt and Manchester United generously.' They did, and Real Madrid came at less than half price.

The club that won the European Cup five times between 1956 and 1960 actually visited Manchester three years in succession, 1959, 1960 and 1961, though they were guaranteed a share of gate receipts, worth around £10,000, for the later trips. These friendlies were treated as grand occasions, with big dinners at hotels and exchanges of gifts. When United went over to Madrid in 1959, Les Olive was allocated £40 to spend on 'fishing tackle' as a present for Santiago Bernabeu.

Equally, the players were expected to treat the games as if they were full competitive matches. Before meeting the Spaniards at Old Trafford in December 1961, the team was sent to the Norbreck Hydro hotel in Blackpool, a treat normally reserved only for big cup games. The sea air perhaps contributed to United's 3–1 victory.

Benfica of Portugal were another team to come to Manchester, in 1962, shortly after winning the European Cup for the second time. Other visitors were First Vienna and Bayern Munich. In turn United played twice at Real Madrid and also visited the Dutch side Feyenoord, Rapid Vienna, Torino, Valencia, Juventus, Roma and Hamburg. They played three times in Munich too. More often than not, United would beat these top Continental teams, but much more important than winning was the experience gained for the time when the assault on Everest – the European Cup – could be mounted again.

Busby's transfer dealings failed initially to build a side good enough even to qualify for one of the three European competitions that now existed. It was not until two Scottish internationals were brought to the club that United really began to click again. In the summer of 1962, after long negotiations, Matt Busby parted with another record sum, £115,000, to Torino for the exciting inside-forward, Denis Law. Law was paid £100 a week on a two-year contract. Before Munich the United manager had once offered Huddersfield £10,000 for the young Law. As Scotland manager he had also awarded him his first cap, again while the player was still only in his teens.

Denis Law's presence, however, was not enough to stop the threat of relegation in the cold winter of 1962–63, and it was not really until a second player arrived, from Glasgow Celtic, that Law began to score with his customary regularity. Busby saw Pat Crerand as the midfield distributor who would deliver the ball to his expensive new marksman in a combination that had already worked successfully for Scotland. Some say that, of all the players Busby ever managed, Crerand was the one who came nearest to the kind of role he himself once played in the Manchester City side.

While the league campaign of 1962–63 was a fight against the second division which was only resolved successfully in the closing matches, the FA Cup was more encouraging. Three home wins against Huddersfield, Aston Villa and Chelsea, all played within fifteen days because of the winter freeze, followed by victories at Coventry and over Southampton in the semi-final at Hillsborough, put the reds back at Wembley. Leicester City began favourites, but were overwhelmed by the new United side. The Crerand–Law combination produced an opening goal and two more from David Herd secured the club's first trophy since Munich. United were back.

Busby inherited and remoulded his 1948 side and created

his 1958 Munich team. Seven of the 1963 cup winners, in
contrast, had been bought – Dunne, Cantwell, Crerand,
Setters, Quixall, Herd and Law – and all except Tony
Dunne had cost large sums. Only the two Munich survivors, Bill Foulkes and Bobby Charlton, along with David
Gaskell and Johnny Giles, were products of United's
famous youth programme. That year the United board
increased Busby's salary to £6,000 a year and extended his
contract to a further seven years.

The 1963 FA Cup victory signalled the beginning of
Busby's third burst of success and ultimately the most
triumphant team of them all. It was the start of the decade
associated with three world stars – Bobby Charlton, Denis
Law and the Irish genius who made his debut the following
September, George Best. And as confirmation that the club
had finally emerged from the dark post-Munich period, in
1964 George Best helped the youth team secure the FA
Youth Cup once again.

Winning the FA Cup put United back into Europe for
the first time since 1958, if only in the European Cup-
Winners Cup. The next five years saw almost non-stop
involvement in European competition, as United's attacking team went in search of glory both at home and abroad.

After Munich Matt Busby had adopted a rather different
style of management. The United manager continued to
suffer back pain from the crash, and he had had trouble
with his legs even before Munich. In the winter of 1961 he
was in hospital for several weeks for an operation. His poor
health meant that he could no longer spend much time in
his tracksuit out on the practice pitch. Jack Crompton, the
former goalkeeper, had come to the club from Luton to
look after the training sessions, while John Aston Senior
also joined the coaching staff. In recognition of his poor
state of health, Busby was given a paid holiday every year
by the directors, and £5 a day expenses, to help him recover
after each arduous season.

Though the nature of Matt Busby's leadership changed
in some respects, he was just the same father-figure, protect-

ing and guiding his United family. Just after the players had made their first air journey since Munich, one of the crash survivors, Bill Foulkes, went to phone his wife to say that he had arrived safely, only to find Busby had called her first. 'He is not only worried about the team winning but that individual players should do well for themselves,' said Denis Law. 'It is the league side which is his bread and butter, but he will go out of his way to explain to a boy why he has been left out of the sixth team. He knows how hurt that lad could be by failing to find his name listed on the notice-board.'

Busby would rarely raise his voice, and instead remained content simply to puff on his pipe. He would always find time to chat to members of the Old Trafford staff. The United manager was not always able to keep the house in order, though. In 1961, while at the Norbreck Hotel in Blackpool, rumours that several United players were involved in fixing matches were investigated by newspaper reporters. Lack of concrete evidence meant the story was never published, but it was a matter of great concern at the time.

The board minutes show how Busby was becoming more and more involved in the administrative side of running a large football club. For instance, he drew up the directors' rota for attending Central League matches; he had talks with a QC over the claim against BEA over Munich. Other responsibilities shouldered by Busby included talking to a local brewery over ground advertising and negotiations with the FA over plans to stage World Cup games at Old Trafford.

The year 1964 saw Busby's side finish runners-up in the league, four points behind Bill Shankly's Liverpool. They reached the semi-finals of the FA Cup for the third time in three years only to lose to West Ham, and reached the quarter-finals of the European Cup-winners Cup competition. The reds won 4–1 in the first leg of the quarter-final against Sporting Lisbon in Manchester and another European semi-final seemed certain, only for the side to fall

to pieces in Portugal and lose 5–0. The normally calm Matt
Busby felt so angry about the way the team had thrown it
away that, totally out of character, he unleashed his rage
on to the players. 'What was going to happen to us when
we got back to Manchester was nobody's business,' recalls
Pat Crerand. 'He told us our performance was an insult to
the people of Manchester.'

Yet the Lisbon debacle was typical of United's legendary
inconsistency. Bobby Charlton recalls:

> They were remarkable years because we could never
> guarantee to play well. Brilliant one week, exasperat-
> ingly poor the next, and that was part of the fasci-
> nation. I had a friend who never missed a match,
> going to quite extraordinary lengths to ensure that he
> was always there, simply because he didn't want to
> miss the incomparable performance of which he was
> convinced we were capable.

In 1965 United won the league for the first time in eight
years, though it was a much closer race than Busby's previous success. Chelsea and Leeds United both led the table
for long periods, and in the end success was only achieved
on a goal average margin of 0.686 over Don Revie's new
Leeds United. The forwards Busby had bought were now
piling up the goals – Law got thirty-nine in all competitions,
David Herd twenty-eight and John Connelly, the England
winger bought from Burnley, nineteen. Busby's home-
grown stars Bobby Charlton and George Best contributed
eighteen and twelve goals respectively. As his reward Matt
Busby got a £4,000 bonus, and the board allotted him 500
shares, though it was six years before Busby took them up.

A campaign in the Inter-Cities Fairs Cup that year led
to a narrow defeat by the Hungarian side, Ferencvaros, in
a replay in the semi-finals. But the club's latest European
setback was compensated by the fact that the championship
qualified United for the European Cup for the first time
since the fatal year of 1958. At last they were back at base
camp.

It was perhaps fortunate for Matt Busby that, since United's previous appearance in the European Cup, no other English qualifier had won the trophy. Wolves, Burnley, Spurs, Ipswich, Everton and Liverpool had all failed even to get beyond the semi-finals. In view of England's 1966 World Cup win and English clubs' domination of the competition in the late 1970s and early 1980s, it is perhaps surprising that not even the great Spurs double-winners, nor Bill Shankly's Liverpool, reached the European final. At that time the tournament was dominated by the great Mediterranean clubs from Spain, Italy and Portugal. It looked almost as if English clubs had a gentleman's agreement among themselves that, after Munich, United should be allowed to win the competition first! Spurs and West Ham, however, did achieve success in the Cup-Winners Cup.

United stormed through the European champions' competition in the 1965–66 season, with every forward grabbing goals. The Finnish amateur team HJK Helsingin were beaten 9–2 on aggregate and ASK Vorwaerts of East Germany went out 5–1, but the most remarkable achievement came in the quarter-finals against Benfica, the team that had twice won the European Cup.

The 3–2 scoreline from the first leg at Old Trafford left United in a precarious position for the second leg in Lisbon. The Portuguese champions had played eighteen home matches in Europe since 1960 and won every single one of them, regularly scoring five goals or more. But United fans need not have worried. In front of 75,000 people the reds, and George Best in particular, turned on a magnificent display that established Best's name in world football. Matt Busby said United's 5–1 victory that night was the club's best performance since 1945. In effect, Manchester United had already proved themselves the top team in Europe and worthy successors to Real Madrid and Benfica. But perhaps through the pressure of also going for the FA Cup and league title, the most glittering prize of all would elude them again.

Typically, United threw it away in the semi-final. Partizan Belgrade were seen as a much less worrying proposition than the Portuguese champions had been. But a 2–0 defeat in Belgrade saw United lose George Best with a leg injury, and in the home leg Partizan closed down defensively and the reds managed to win only 1–0. For the third time United had been eliminated at the semi-final stage. The effort of chasing the league title, the FA Cup and the European Cup all in one season had proved too much and, as so often happens, they had ended up with nothing. Liverpool had become league champions and England's next representatives in the competition. After United had beaten Benfica so comprehensively in Portugal, it all seemed so unfair. For Matt Busby the European Cup looked as distant as ever:

> I was at my lowest ebb since the Munich air crash, and it was in my mind to turn my back on football altogether. It seemed the fates had conspired against the club and myself, and I remember telling Paddy Crerand: 'We'll never win the European Cup now.'

Crerand reassured his boss that the team would win the league again the following season and finally clinch the European trophy the year after.

Many believe, though, that the 1960s Manchester United side was at its best in 1965 and 1966. Most of the players – Paddy Crerand, Bobby Charlton, Nobby Stiles, Denis Law and George Best among them – seemed to be in the prime of their career. Real Madrid beat Partizan 2–1 in the 1966 European Cup final, but if United had been given the chance, the odds are they would have defeated the Spanish champions, who were nothing like the Real Madrid of old.

Yet winning the league championship once again, simply to get to base camp, might take years with so many other good teams in contention – Liverpool, Everton, West Ham and the emerging Leeds United and Chelsea sides. Matt Busby, now fifty-seven, seriously considered retirement.

But he was again persuaded by his wife Jean that those who died at Munich would have insisted that he try again.

Had Manchester United won the European Cup in 1966, as a prelude to England's World Cup, it might have given Matt Busby the chance to retire then, and a new manager could have rebuilt the side while it was still at its peak. Alternatively Busby could have begun the necessary rebuilding himself. But with another league title needed as soon as possible, and the European Cup still to win after that, it was best not to disrupt what was still a good side. So when Blackburn's centre-half, Mike England, and Blackpool's midfield player, Alan Ball, were available for transfer, Busby allowed them to move to Spurs and Everton respectively. He did actually make Blackburn an offer of £85,000 for England in June 1966, but did not want to get into an auction with Spurs, the club England eventually joined for the same sum. Busby preferred his previous method of relying on the club's young players, some of whom, such as John Aston, David Sadler and Bobby Noble, were already following George Best from the 1964 Youth Cup side. Between buying the two Burnley wingers, John Connelly in April 1964 and Willie Morgan in October 1968, Busby bought only one other player, goalkeeper Alex Stepney, though he proved an excellent buy.

At times Busby came under fire for the way in which his players went about their task. United in the 1960s were frequently criticised for being a rough, dirty side. Critics would point to the number of players who had been sent off. Indeed, more United players were dismissed in the 1960s than in the '70s or '80s when referees have been much more prepared to send players from the field. Often though, especially with Pat Crerand, Denis Law and George Best, it was a case of lost tempers and retaliation.

On the first Saturday in May 1967, Manchester United fans in their thousands flocked to the home of West Ham United at Upton Park in the East End of London. By one o'clock the gates were closed with 38,000 people inside. It was the climax to a season in which United players had

devoted everything to giving Matt Busby another go at the
ultimate trophy. For once other competitions had taken
second place. Fourth position in the league the previous
season had not been good enough to qualify for the European Inter-Cities Fairs Cup. Blackpool had knocked United
out of the League Cup by a surprise 5–1 score at Bloomfield
Road, while the FA Cup United lost at home to second
division Norwich City. Yet the reds marched steadily
towards the league title. Since the New Year the formula
of winning at home and drawing away had been applied
religiously in all sixteen league matches. If United improved
on the formula and clinched two points that day in East
London, the title was theirs.

Within ten minutes West Ham had conceded three goals.
By the end they had let in three more to lose 6–1. As far
as the European Cup was concerned, Busby was at base
camp for the fourth time. He could not afford to slip up
again. Recognising this, the United board decided that no
players could be released to play in testimonial or benefit
matches over the coming year.

The story of how United progressed up that mountain
the following season has been told many times. Hibernians
of Malta, Sarajevo from Yugoslavia, and Gornik of Poland
were all eliminated before a clash with Real Madrid in the
semi-final that, if the United story were a work of fiction,
would have been made the final. The reds pulled back from
being 3–1 down in the second leg to draw 3–3 and go
through to their first European Cup final, 4–3 on aggregate.
And, appropriately, a rare goal from Bill Foulkes, one of
the two Munich survivors playing, proved to be the winner.

Yet United's famous 1968 victory over Benfica at Wembley could so easily have gone badly wrong. The apparently
comfortable 4–1 scoreline was only achieved in extra time,
and then after Alex Stepney pulled off a miraculous save
from Eusebio in the dying minutes of normal time when
the score was 1–1. Had Eusebio not tried to make it a
spectacular goal, Benfica might have taken the trophy back
to Portugal. Had United failed in that attempt on the Euro-

pean Cup, Matt Busby probably would not have been given
a further opportunity. 'Without being disrespectful to the
players involved, the 1968 team was not our best,' Bobby
Charlton said recently. 'Manchester City had won the
league and we had faded. A lot of us were past our peak.
I knew I wasn't going to get another chance and about half
the team were in the same boat.'

Perhaps it was that knowledge which made the difference, with extra-time goals from George Best, Brian Kidd
and a second goal from Charlton himself. Matt Busby wept
with his players on the Wembley turf that night. The eight
players who died at Munich had their memorial at last.
'The moment when Bobby took the Cup,' said Busby many
years later, 'it cleansed me. It eased the pain of the guilt
of going into Europe. It was my justification.' Young John
Aston, son of the 1948 left-back, had a brilliant game on
the left wing. Today he remembers the post-match banquet
as a rather 'strange' affair. It was not the normal kind of
noisy, wild football celebration after a Wembley triumph.
There was more of a sense of relief, he says, of a job being
completed, particularly for those who had actually been at
Munich – Matt Busby, Bill Foulkes and Bobby Charlton.
The parents of many of those who had died, and some of
the survivors, had also been invited along. Indeed, for one
survivor of the crash, Bobby Charlton, the night was so
emotional that he could not bring himself to attend the
dinner but retired to his hotel room. 'He couldn't take it,'
explained his wife Norma, 'with complete strangers coming
up and slapping him on the back and telling him what a
wonderful night it is. . . . He's remembering the lads who
can't be here tonight.'

That summer the Queen knighted the United manager.
Manchester had already given him the freedom of the city.
For their part the club directors had always rewarded Busby
generously over the years. Since February 1967 he had been
on £10,000 a year and a ten-year contract, and substantial
annual bonuses had been transformed into large pension
contributions. In July 1968 Busby's Rover car was replaced

by a Mercedes. But rather than grant Busby a testimonial match, as happens with most successful long-serving players and managers, the United directors agreed in September 1968 to what appeared to be a much smaller recognition of the manager's achievements.

A year earlier, in August 1967, Manchester United had opened a small souvenir shop in a hut by the main entrance to the ground to cater for the growing interest in the club. The board had lent the enterprise £1,000 to get going. Now it was agreed that the Red Devils Souvenir Shop would be sold to Matt Busby for £2,000 on a twenty-one-year lease at a rental of £5 per week. At the time the directors had little idea of the true value of the shop, and in later years it would enjoy long queues outside the entrance from 1.30 on Saturday afternoons, as the new generation of football supporters demanded a greater variety of articles bearing the name and colours of their beloved club. In time, also, Busby voluntarily offered to pay more than the initial £5 a week rent.

Eight months after the famous Wembley victory, football reporters were summoned overnight to a 'special press conference' at Old Trafford. What was about to happen had been predicted by some of them in that morning's newspapers. Before the television lights, the stills cameras and reporters with notebooks, Sir Matt Busby, having served as manager of Manchester United for twenty-four years, announced that he would retire from team affairs at the end of the season. But he would not stop working for the club; he would just be taking more of a back-seat, administrative role.

Sir Matt had told the United directors of his decision more than two weeks earlier, just as 1968 was drawing to its close. The board begged him to stay as manager. He turned down their appeals, feeling that the football duties of managing such a major club had become too much on top of his other tasks. 'I could hardly see over the top of the pile of correspondence on my desk every morning,' he said.

After their triumph in the European Cup the previous spring, the 1968–69 season had been an anti-climax. United were sixth from bottom of the league table on the day Busby made his announcement. They had won only one away match so far that season and that was at Queen's Park Rangers who were later relegated with a record low number of points.

United's position that winter was only highlighting the fact that for Sir Matt there was really nothing else to achieve. United had become the first English team to win the European Cup. No matter what happened now, nobody could every take that achievement away, and defeat by AC Milan in the 1969 semi-final did not seem that serious. The attempt to go one better and win the unofficial World Club Championship against the Argentine side Estudiantes had failed. But the violence and acrimony that accompanied both games, with three men sent off, led many to conclude that the contest was not worth playing.

'Manchester United have become rather more than a football club,' Busby told journalists at the January press conference. 'They are now an institution.' And everybody in the room knew that just one man, almost single-handed, was responsible for making it an institution and creating the United legend – Sir Matt Busby himself.

His team's victory against Benfica at Wembley the previous May had provided such an obvious closing chapter to the Busby story. Winning the European Cup at United's fourth attempt, twelve years after first entering the competition, had partly made up for all the setbacks and nightmares of the previous years. The Holy Grail had been found.

Twenty-three years after arriving at that mediocre club next to Trafford Park, with a bombsite for a ground, Busby had finally built United into one of the greatest football clubs in the world. It was an obvious end to a remarkable career. But as things turned out it was not quite the end.

To many outsiders Sir Matt's successor, Wilf McGuinness, was an unexpected choice. Yet United's policy of keeping things in the family had worked well over the years – the trainer, Jack Crompton, the chief coach, John Aston Senior, and even the secretary, Les Olive, had all once worn United shirts. Even for Wilf McGuinness it was a genuine surprise. 'Someone in the office suggested I ought to come with a tie on the next day,' he remembers. There had been no preparation for the job; McGuinness had barely worked with the first team, though he had coached most of the players at some point in the reserves.

McGuinness would start simply as chief coach under Sir Matt, who would become general manager. 'He has a bit of experience to pick up yet in management,' explained Busby, 'I think it's a question of starting this way. I think he will have enough to bite on without taking on other things which could come later.' The plan was that McGuinness would eventually become team manager.

As a United player, McGuinness' early career had been highly promising, yet sadly short. One of the Busby Babes, he played eighty-three games and won a league championship medal in 1957, but injury ensured that he did not make the fatal flight to Belgrade. He even won two England caps in 1959 before his career was suddenly ended by a broken leg. In the family tradition, United kept McGuinness on the staff – training the youth team and the reserves. He also helped coach the 1966 England World Cup team, and the under–23 side.

His selection in 1969 as chief coach and future manager was popular with younger players, but the more senior professionals were less enthusiastic. Bill Foulkes, Shay Brennan and Bobby Charlton were all older than McGuinness and had achieved far more in football.

'For one reason or another, whether inexperience or slight immaturity,' Busby says, '[he] did not get the response I had hoped he would get from the players.' Sir Matt feels McGuinness mishandled the older men: 'He was probably too close to them. He had played with most of them and knew their habits and this they resented. Disharmony developed and team discipline waned.'

McGuinness had an atrocious start in August 1969 with home defeats by Everton (0–2) and then Southampton (1–4). Losing to Everton was perhaps forgivable – they became league champions – but the Southampton result was different. Three times Southampton winger John Sydenham beat Shay Brennan to deliver a perfect cross for Ron Davies; three times Davies headed past Bill Foulkes to score.

For United's fourth game, against Everton at Goodison Park, McGuinness went much further than dropping the obvious offenders, and caused a minor sensation by also leaving out Bobby Charlton and Denis Law. McGuinness admits now that an away game at Everton was not the time to drop experienced players. United lost 3–0 this time and as a result were second from bottom. Charlton returned for the following game, but Law played only eight more league games that season; and Shay Brennan had only nine more matches. Bill Foulkes never represented United again. The manner of Southampton's 4–1 victory had shown how badly Manchester United needed a new centre-half and full-back.

The axings undermined McGuinness from the very beginning. 'Wilf's manner of telling players that they were dropped often rubbed them up the wrong way,' complained Charlton. 'The way he did it meant that he lost their confidence.'

'Not everyone, sadly, would play for Wilf,' said David Sadler later. 'The side as a whole did not give 100 per cent effort for him. It was as simple as that.' One senior player even went to Louis Edwards' home to complain.

Denis Law, though, rejects the accusation that senior players would not play for McGuinness:

> I believe that the real reason he failed was that he tried to introduce an approach to the game which was totally alien to the players who had earned United their years of success. . . . One of the most significant changes brought about by Wilf was his use of blackboard coaching at team talks. Matt Busby had used

the blackboard only occasionally. . . . Wilf had it out
all the time. . . . Instead of going out to play football,
as they had been accustomed to doing, players were
going out with their minds stuffed with plans and
tactics.

Alex Stepney says McGuinness 'was not strong. He had
moments of frightening indecision. He could not stand up
and administer the kind of discipline that would gain him
respect – adult discipline. Something was missing in his
make-up. Perhaps it was simply experience.'

Bobby Charlton and McGuinness had been great pals,
but Charlton complained that McGuinness as a superior
did not know how to talk to him. A famous incident
occurred one morning at The Cliff. Bobby Charlton had
finished training early to go to London for an engagement.
He returned to the changing room, showered and put on
his suit. Then McGuinness demanded that all the players
gather on the pitch for a team talk. As it was drizzling and
pretty cold, Charlton suggested they meet under the stand
by the pitch rather than out in the middle. McGuinness
said no. As the rain got heavier Charlton turned up his
collar and put his hands in his pockets.

'Right, Bobby Charlton, twenty press-ups,' shouted
McGuinness, referring to the traditional penance for anybody caught with his hands in his pockets. Charlton replied
that McGuinness had to be joking if he expected him to do
twenty press-ups in his suit and shoes out on a muddy
pitch. McGuinness insisted he was not joking, and so, in
front of everybody, the world-famous star performed his
punishment. McGuinness' reputation was the one which
suffered, though, not Charlton's.

McGuinness says the incident was misinterpreted, and
that it was all in a humorous spirit. When Alex Stepney
told the story in his autobiography, McGuinness threatened
him with a writ, but several players recall the event as
Stepney does and say that the manager was serious. Whatever the spirit in which it happened, the story provided

ammunition for those players who felt that McGuinness was not up to the job.

The squad which McGuinness took charge of included several ageing stars, but there was young blood too: it was not quite as decrepit as some have since made out. Alex Stepney, aged twenty-four, had not even reached his peak, and kept United's goal for another nine years. Tony Dunne, twenty-seven, would play first-division football for another decade. George Best, twenty-three, Brian Kidd, twenty, John Aston, twenty-one, and David Sadler, twenty-three, were still young, and the latest signing, Willie Morgan, was only twenty-four. Nobby Stiles was twenty-seven, Pat Crerand thirty, and even Bobby Charlton, at thirty-one, would play in the 1970 World Cup. Denis Law, twenty-nine, would play for Scotland in the World Cup five years on. Only Bill Foulkes, thirty-seven, and Shay Brennan, thirty-two, were past their best in 1969. It would be four years before United replaced either player adequately.

After the dismal start in 1969 United bought Arsenal's Scottish centre-half, Ian Ure, for £80,000. He was in fact Busby's choice, selected in spite of unfavourable reports from scouts, and McGuinness was only too pleased to accept the deal. At nearly thirty-one, Ure was only a temporary stop-gap, but he made an immediate impact and United went unbeaten for ten games. McGuinness wanted to buy other players but says he was not allowed to. Among those he would have liked were Colin Todd, the Sunderland defender, Malcolm Macdonald, the Luton centre-forward, and Mick Mills of Ipswich. Another target, particularly after the problems he had caused United, was Ron Davies, but the board decided in April 1970 that Southampton's £200,000 price was too high.

The rest of the 1969–70 season went fairly well. In the league the team finished only eighth, but cup campaigns were more successful, with semi-final places in both domestic competitions. But United's position was made worse by the sudden burst of success at Maine Road. After the league in 1968 and the FA Cup in 1969, City won two trophies in 1970 – the European Cup-Winners Cup and the League Cup. Yet United could so easily have taken the latter trophy. In the semi-final United lost 4–3 on aggregate after Alex Stepney had instinctively parried the ball as it sailed into the net from a City indirect free kick.

Similarly United might have contested the FA Cup final rather than Leeds United. The semi-final went to a third game after goalless draws at Hillsborough and Villa Park, where United might have won. Denis Law missed a good chance, while George Best seemed to have his mind on other things. Heading for goal, Best trod on the ball and fell flat in the mud. He had spent the afternoon trying to evade McGuinness to make love to a woman he had met at the team hotel.

Best was becoming a major problem. Some of the team resented the way the Irishman got away with such behaviour before an important game, and criticised McGuinness for apparently being powerless to stop him. 'If I had been manager of Manchester United, George would not have played that match,' says Alex Stepney.

However, Best's brilliance often let the rest of the team off the hook. The United star was still in his early twenties, and these were his best years. Yet the decline of the team around him is partly, Best thinks, why he went off the rails and resorted to drink:

> My goals became all-important because others weren't scoring them so frequently. Instead of revolving around me, the team now depended on me and I lacked the maturity to handle it. I began to drink more heavily, and on the field my list of bookings grew longer as my temper grew shorter.

In the summer of 1970 McGuinness was officially promoted to team manager, though he still did not enjoy the status of every other post-war manager in being invited to board meetings. The first part of the following campaign ensured his dismissal. By Christmas United were fifth from bottom, having won only five games. The sole consolation was another League Cup run, and facing third-division Aston Villa in the semi-final this time, Wembley seemed assured.

Over the twelve days before Christmas things went badly wrong, however. In three successive home games United lost 4–1 to City, scrambled a 1–1 draw in the first leg against Villa, and lost 3–1 to Arsenal. Then United went out of the League Cup 2–1 at Villa Park.

On Tuesday, 29 December 1970, after eighteen months as chief coach and team manager, Wilf McGuinness was dismissed with half of his contract to go. Busby originally suggested that to avoid humiliation, McGuinness should ask to return to his old job of reserve trainer. He accepted at first, but later said that the board would have to sack him. So they did.

Sir Matt agreed to take over again to allow time for a new manager to be chosen. 'I feel sorry for Wilf,' Busby said. 'He might have been a wee bit raw.' Privately he had seen early on that McGuinness was not going to work, but compassion prevented him from doing anything. McGuinness seemed so happy. He was assuming that he would be manager for good. Private schooling had been fixed up for his children.

McGuinness had been put in charge of several players nearing the ends of their careers who had managerial ambitions of their own. It was easy for them to mutter how they could have done things better. The close contact that some kept with Sir Matt – Denis Law, Pat Crerand and Willie Morgan, for instance – on the golf course or in restaurants on Saturday nights, maintained a channel for discontent, perhaps more imagined than real. 'I didn't mind other players going behind my back,' McGuinness said recently. 'What I did mind was that he accepted their side of the story rather than mine.'

Pat Crerand believes that McGuinness would have succeeded as manager had he been given the job several years later, 'when Bobby, Denis and I had retired'. He shares the view that Sir Matt Busby's decision to appoint a manager from within the 'family' was correct in principle, only that McGuinness was too inexperienced, unable to stop the joking and laughing and become a figure of authority. Yet the failure probably turned United against further inside appointments when that may have been just what was needed to ensure long-term continuity in the Busby way of running the club.

Wilf McGuinness was shocked by his sacking and went around almost in a daze. He harboured mixed feelings, partly wanting to get his own back and yet not wanting to harm the club he loved. He had expected to have longer to prove himself. United believed in loyalty, didn't they? They were not a club to sack loyal employees.

Sir Matt brought back several players dropped by Mc-Guinness – Alex Stepney, Pat Crerand, Willie Morgan and Alan Gowling – and form improved quickly. Busby had only done what he had always done: motivate players, the prime requirement of a successful manager. He might have exercised better discipline than McGuinness, but underneath the tensions between United's fading stars remained and would trouble his successor.

Wilf McGuinness spent two months with the reserves, then left to run Aris Salonika in Greece. He later managed York City, with little success, and is now physiotherapist at Bury. It is downhill after Old Trafford, as so many have found.

'He came as a boy and left as an old man,' says Tony Dunne. In Greece, McGuinness' hair started falling out. Then it grew back, but white and wispy, before disappearing again. The doctors said it may have been delayed shock. Today he is totally bald, and looks almost unrecognisable from his United days. He is in popular demand as an after-dinner speaker and often involved in get-togethers of former United players. And he has regained his jovial outlook on life, cultivating a new 'Kojak' image.

'When you look like I do,' he says, 'you have to laugh at things.'

5

Decline and Scandal

'We cheat, we tell lies, we con people. Any manager who says we don't do that isn't being honest. That's the only way to survive. It's the law of the land.'

Tommy Docherty on football managers, 1979.

The two men met secretly late one Wednesday night in April 1971. They had chosen a petrol station near Haydock, at the point where the East Lancs Road crosses junction 23 of the M6. Both men had just been to see Leeds United record a historic 1–0 victory over Liverpool in the Inter-Cities Fairs Cup semi-final at Anfield. But what they wanted to discuss was too delicate a matter for the Liverpool directors' box.

The younger of the two Scots, who was driving with his son back to Glasgow, was the first to arrive. A few minutes later the older man turned up. His journey was much shorter – just 40 miles back to Chorlton-cum-Hardy in Manchester. For about three-quarters of an hour the manager of Celtic, Jock Stein, sat in Sir Matt Busby's Mercedes and discussed the possibility of his coming to Manchester United. They parted with a hand-shake, and it looked as though there was a deal.

After the failure of his own first choice for United manager, Wilf McGuinness, Sir Matt felt relieved that his club

would now be in capable hands. The two men came from
very similar backgrounds in the Lanarkshire coalfield. Both
had a similar approach to football – allowing freedom of
expression, attacking play and building up a family atmosphere within their clubs. Stein had proved himself a good
manager with more than one team. He had transformed
little Dunfermline Athletic to the extent that they won the
Scottish Cup in 1961. Now Jock Stein's Glasgow Celtic
were unchallenged in Scottish football and just about to
win their sixth successive league championship. Moreover,
in 1967, Stein had actually gone one better than Busby
himself when Celtic became the first British club to win the
European Cup.

For Sir Matt it had been a risky, secretive process luring
the new man in, and extremely difficult to avoid publicity.
The first approach had been made by one of the United
players Busby was close to, Pat Crerand. This had been
after another European game – the second leg of Celtic's
European Cup quarter-final against Ajax in Glasgow a few
weeks earlier. Crerand had once played for Stein at Celtic,
and during a small party at the manager's home after the
match Crerand took him upstairs and told him that Busby
wanted to know if he was interested in United. He certainly
was. A meeting with Busby and Louis Edwards in the
Manchester area followed, and then that late-night secret
encounter at the petrol station.

A few days later, though, Jock Stein rang Busby to say
he had changed his mind. He would not be coming to Old
Trafford after all.

The Celtic manager said later that his family had persuaded him to say no: his son George was due to go to
Manchester as a student anyway, but Stein's wife Jean did
not like the idea of leaving all her friends. Stein also felt a
sense of loyalty to Celtic. Some believe, however, that he
had simply used the United offer to get a bigger pay rise
out of Celtic.

There was also another reason to turn Manchester United

down. His son George explained in the recent biography by Ken Gallacher:

> He had always insisted in every job he had that he was in complete control of the playing side. He would not take a job under any other circumstances. Basically he wondered if he would be allowed to be his own man. He was insisting that he wanted to bring in his own backroom staff so that he had his own people round him. But Sir Matt had his own loyalties, and he wanted this one kept on and the next one kept on, and he was suggesting that maybe this bit of business should be handled in this way, and so on. The conversation in that car at the petrol station went through all of this. Dad did want Sir Matt to be there. He knew that he would need to have him around the place when he needed advice about the club – but he wanted to be his own man and he agonised over whether that would be possible or not.

Ironically, in wanting to be his own man, Jock Stein was taking exactly the same attitude that Sir Matt himself had shown on arriving at Old Trafford a generation earlier.

In later years Stein regretted his decision not to take on United. In spite of his continued success with Celtic, the Glasgow club treated him badly and eventually pushed him aside. Stein's only period in English football was forty-four days with Leeds United in 1978 before he became manager of Scotland. But Manchester United probably suffered from Jock Stein's decision even more than he did. Had the Celtic manager taken over in 1971, United might well have avoided the decline and scandal that were to follow in the 1970s.

The Chelsea manager, Dave Sexton, also turned the United job down after seeing Busby in Manchester when the London side played Manchester City in the European Cup-Winners Cup semi-final. Eventually, in June 1971, six months after Wilf McGuinness had been sacked, another secret motorway rendezvous, just off the M1 near Coalville, led to Frank O'Farrell, the Leicester City manager, taking the job.

Busby explained to O'Farrell that he himself would have nothing more to do with team matters. O'Farrell said a few days later:

> I didn't have to ask about full control. He had made it all very clear, and to have pressed it further would have been insulting. I don't think enough people have realised what this must have cost him. This is his club, these are his players. Cutting himself adrift like that must be almost like walking out on a family. He must believe it's the best thing, but I still think it was the action of a great man.

Sir Matt had originally intended to carry on as United's general manager, in charge of administrative affairs, but he gave the job up after a few months. He was appointed to the United board and took up the 500 shares which had been allotted to him six years before.

Once the new league season started, United hit top form. Frank O'Farrell was only using the players left to him by Busby, but the crucial difference was how he deployed them. Because Pat Crerand was suspended for the opening two matches, O'Farrell played Alan Gowling in midfield instead, and Willie Morgan was brought back from the forward line to play alongside Gowling and Bobby Charlton in a 4–3–3 formation. Crerand never played again. By mid-December United had built up a five-point lead – the equivalent of seven points today. The star forwards were scoring regularly once more – by Christmas Best had seventeen goals and Denis Law eleven.

The bookmakers made United odds-on favourites for the championship. Closer observers were more sceptical, arguing that United had been lucky, that the team's defence was weak and that the side depended too much on George Best. Results in the New Year showed just how justified such scepticism was. United lost seven league matches in a row and slipped from the top spot.

The frailty of United's early-season dominance was most cruelly exposed at Elland Road in February 1972 when, with no goals at half-time, Leeds United scored five times in the second half to win 5–1. Towards the end of the game Leeds men were simply passing the ball from player to player, taunting United to come and get it, egged on by a home crowd who cheered every pass and each failed tackle with increasing intensity. Some observers see that afternoon at Leeds as marking the real end of United's post-war period of greatness. It was the day when exciting red gave way to clinical dull white, when Leeds United's hard, methodical game began to dominate British football. And the board were quickly losing faith in the new Manchester United manager.

So long as the men he had inherited from Sir Matt were doing well, O'Farrell saw little point in buying new talent. When the slide began, however, O'Farrell was slow to react. Perhaps O'Farrell's biggest missed opportunity was not buying the England World Cup midfield player Alan Ball from Everton. In Christmas week 1971 Ball joined Arsenal instead for a record £220,000. Yet Ball might have been ideal for United. He lived in Bolton, was friendly with many of the players, often watched United games and sometimes wore a United scarf. 'I made it quite common knowledge,' Ball says, 'that if I'd had the chance to join United I would have jumped at it.' His father, Alan Ball Senior, was a frequent visitor to Old Trafford and kept begging United officials to sign his son. On the morning it was announced that Ball was about to sign for Arsenal, O'Farrell and his coach Malcolm Musgrove made frantic efforts to contact him. They tried to work out what train he was on, and left messages for Ball to contact Old Trafford, but it was too late.

In the meantime O'Farrell also faced increasing difficulties with George Best. After his brilliant form in the autumn, Best's play had slumped dramatically, especially after a threat to his life before a game at Newcastle in October. Observers say that to avoid any gunmen in the crowd, Best never stopped moving that day at St James's Park. With his Irish background, the threats had to be taken seriously. A police guard was put on his home and he withdrew from an international in Belfast. The anxiety only increased when Best's sister was shot in the leg after leaving a Belfast dance hall.

The troubles in Ireland also caused Best to worry about his parents. He was seeing them less often than before, and at one point he seriously discussed the idea of United arranging to move his mother and father over to Manchester for safety and so that he could be close to them.

The Irishman's business interests were also worrying him. At that time the rag trade was going through a bad spell and Best's Manchester clothes boutiques were proving not to be the money-spinners that people believed they were.

The first week in January 1972 Best failed to turn up for training on every single day. The other players insisted that he should not be included in the team, but because Best had played such an important role in United's early-season success, O'Farrell desperately needed him. When United had been through this before, in January 1971, Busby had suspended Best, but O'Farrell argued that doing so this time was not in the best interests of the club. Instead, he fined Best two weeks' salary, ordered him to do extra training and told him to leave his modern £30,000 house and return to his former landlady, Mrs Fullaway, until the end of the season. However, the second requirement was largely ignored and in reality there was nothing O'Farrell could do to stop Best's life of late-night drinking, gambling and seemingly non-stop sex, as described so graphically in the book he wrote later with Michael Parkinson.

It was probably too late to stop the sad demise of one of football's greatest players, a decline coinciding almost exactly with the fall of one of its greatest clubs. George Best argues that both were closely linked:

When the bad times started I couldn't bear the

thought of going out on the pitch. I used to drink, so I didn't have to think about it. Which came first? The bad times then the drinking or the drinking then the bad times? I'm still sure it was the thought of playing in a bad team, of not winning anything, of not having a chance to play in Europe that drove me to it. All right, you could say that if I'd trained and lived properly, United might have stood a better chance of doing well. That's true, but I just couldn't see myself doing it single-handed.

With Denis Law and Bobby Charlton approaching the end of their careers and Pat Crerand already retired, Best was the last relic of the club's greatness. United felt a need to cling on to him – at no matter what cost, it seemed. He was still only twenty-six, yet no one realised that by 1972 he was beyond reform, that the great days of George Best would never return.

Frank O'Farrell did not spend much time with the players. He might give a friendly team talk at the start of training on Monday, praising the good points from Saturday and drawing attention to weak spots, but it was rare to see him in a tracksuit on the training pitch, and indeed on some days he might not meet the players once. His coach, Malcolm Musgrove, handled the day-to-day running of the team.

Yet it was not until late February 1972 that O'Farrell forked out any money to improve the side. Martin Buchan, Aberdeen's young defender, cost £125,000, while the Nottingham Forest winger Ian Storey-Moore was bought for £180,000 after an embarrassing public tussle with Brian Clough at Derby. Despite these two deals, United had bought only four new players in the four years since winning the European Cup.

Then came George Best's sudden announcement that summer, from a beach in Spain, that he was retiring from football. Nobody really believed it, and after several weeks Best returned to Manchester and agreed to play on.

O'Farrell demanded that he go and live at Pat Crerand's house in the hope that Crerand would be able to keep him from the bottle. In fact Best spent no more than a week with the Crerands. He was even sent to a psychiatrist.

In the 1972–73 season United's goal-scoring skills almost totally deserted the star-studded midfield and forward line-up of Morgan, Best, Kidd, Charlton, Law and Storey-Moore. By late September, nine months after holding top spot, they were bottom, having lost five games and drawn four. As results got worse so did relations between the players. Malcolm Musgrove drew lots to decide which of them would share rooms at a hotel in an effort to break up the old alliances. 'The big three, Denis Law, Bobby Charlton and George Best, were at loggerheads,' according to Stepney. 'There were long days when they simply did not speak to each other.'

Charlton felt that 'there was no feeling of fun in the club any more'. At one point he was so annoyed about Best's behaviour, and O'Farrell's failure to deal with it, that he thought of leaving the club. Charlton had long ago been annoyed by what he felt was Best's selfishness on the pitch. (George Best would never take up golf, it was joked, because he hated parting with the ball.) Now, as club captain, Charlton felt it was his job to pass on the players' complaints about Best's behaviour to Sir Matt. 'It seemed at times that Best was the club. The atmosphere was terrible.'

George Best himself felt that Charlton should have retired. Their rift was most public when Best declined to play in Charlton's testimonial match. The Irishman said that to do so would be hypocritical. He spent the night drinking instead.

Some of the players resented what they felt was Charlton's superior attitude. Charlton's low opinion of some of his famous colleagues at that time is exemplified by a comment made in 1973, just before he retired. 'I may be thought odd, but when I think of United,' he told the *Sunday Telegraph*, 'I think of Roger Byrne, Duncan Edwards and Eddie Colman before the [Munich] crash, and

Harry Gregg, Bill Foulkes and Nobby Stiles afterwards. Those like Best, Law and Crerand, they were replaceable somehow, they weren't the heart of the team.'

When O'Farrell acted to strengthen his squad, he went for goal-scorers. First he paid £60,000 for Wyn Davies from Manchester City, then parted with another £200,000 for Bournemouth's prolific forward, Ted MacDougall. Yet O'Farrell failed to find any good defenders. Peter Shilton could not be persuaded to leave Leicester, while a good opportunity was missed when Don Revie briefly put right-back Paul Reaney on the transfer list at Leeds. O'Farrell went for another Leicester player, David Nish, but would not match Derby's £225,000 offer, which he thought was too much for a left-back.

Impressive victories over Derby and Liverpool were out-numbered early in the 1972–73 season by poor defeats, often by mediocre sides, and third-division Bristol Rovers knocked United out of the League Cup at Old Trafford. Tottenham visited Manchester in late October after nine successive league defeats at United's ground. Their 4–1 victory, in which Martin Peters scored all four goals, summed up United's demoralisation.

It was soon clear that Frank O'Farrell had lost the confidence of the United directors, particularly after an extra-ordinary incident involving the *Manchester Evening News* reporter, David Meek. On the Monday after the Spurs defeat, Meek wrote an article calling for more support for the United manager, who had received a mauling in the national press. Under the headline 'Be Fair to Frank', Meek argued that responsibility for the club's troubles should be shared with O'Farrell by the players and directors. 'I would like to see dynamic leadership from the board to counter hypothetical questions about O'Farrell's future at Old Trafford,' he wrote. The United manager privately thanked Meek for writing it.

Others at Manchester United, however, were not so happy about the article and three days later the *Evening News* sports editor received a letter from United saying that

Meek was 'no longer welcome' to travel on team coaches and trains to away matches, as he had been doing for the previous fourteen years. The ban quickly became known, and most journalists and supporters realised that Meek had touched on a sensitive subject – the directors now had serious doubts about O'Farrell.

The atmosphere among the players grew progressively worse. George Best admitted publicly that there was a possibility that United might be relegated. 'If that happens I will ask for a transfer. If United said no, then I would quit.' Ted MacDougall, meanwhile, found the other players hostile. 'I was regarded as nothing more than a third-division upstart,' he said afterwards. Of Bobby Charlton, MacDougall said later, 'I once asked him the best way to United's training ground and I'm still waiting for an answer. If he didn't feel like it, Bobby just wouldn't bother to reply.'

The George Best situation grew worse. In November he began to miss training again. The player made it clear that he wanted to talk to the directors, not the manager, and in despair O'Farrell asked the board to see him. So the United directors stepped in, suspended Best and put him on the transfer list.

Perhaps embarrassed by the lack of interest, Louis Edwards and Sir Matt Busby met George Best again a week later and tried to persuade him back into the fold. O'Farrell was not even consulted about this meeting. Best agreed to resume training and, when questioned, Louis Edwards admitted that Best was now off the transfer list.

O'Farrell was furious at the way in which Busby and the directors had taken over responsibility for Best behind his back, though it had been his original decision to let Best meet them. What little authority he still had with the players was being publicly chipped away, while George Best was being allowed to behave as he wanted. Had this state of affairs continued much longer, O'Farrell might have resigned. But results overtook him.

O'Farrell's career at United effectively came to an end

two Saturdays before Christmas 1972 at Crystal Palace's ground in South London. The 5–0 defeat was perhaps United's worse performance in post-war football. Palace were one of the worst teams in the first division, in bottom place when the match began. They were relegated to division two at the end of the season, and to division three a year afterwards.

Two evenings later, at Bobby Charlton's testimonial dinner, the United manager was denied a place at the top table. First the Meek business, then the Best matter, now the dinner placings – the public signals about Frank O'Farrell's reduced standing were as clear as Politburo positions on the Lenin mausoleum.

The following day, Tuesday, 19 December 1972, was mild for the time of year. That afternoon Frank O'Farrell, Malcolm Musgrove and the chief scout, John Aston Senior, were summoned before the board at Old Trafford. 'A nice day for an execution,' O'Farrell remarked as Aston arrived to give him a lift to the ground.

There they were officially dismissed. On the same day the United board announced, by mutual agreement, the end of George Best's career at United.

Frank O'Farrell believed his overriding problem, as it had partly been for Wilf McGuinness, was Sir Matt Busby's continued presence and status within the club. Relations had gone badly almost from the very first day when Busby had shown O'Farrell round Old Trafford. O'Farrell was taken to what Sir Matt intended should be the new man's office, which was being fitted out down the corridor from Busby's bigger room. O'Farrell insisted that, as the man in charge of team affairs, he should have the main office and that Busby should move.

That was the kind of small thing that irritated O'Farrell but which others might hardly notice. As a director Sir Matt also had the right to draw whatever expenses he wanted without being held accountable for them, whereas O'Farrell was allowed to claim only £40 a month without saying what the money was for. O'Farrell resented this too.

A short way into the 1971–72 season, when United had been doing well, Busby was quoted as saying that he regarded O'Farrell as his 'last great signing, possibly the greatest of the lot'. To most people that would be a compliment, but not to O'Farrell. He felt Busby was trying to steal his glory, and was so angry about the comment that he has kept the newspaper cutting ever since.

Moreover, Busby's personal relations with the players were still a problem. They referred to Sir Matt as 'big boss' and O'Farrell as 'little boss', while in team talks the older members of the team would mention how they liked to do it 'Matt's way'. O'Farrell particularly disliked the fact that Busby would socialise with the older players, though it probably did not happen as often as he feared.

Frank O'Farrell found his dismissal hard to accept. He was unemployed for the first time in his career. At the last minute, he and his wife had to buy their own Christmas turkey – the one promised by Louis Edwards never arrived!

Initially, the United directors promised to honour O'Farrell's five-year contract in full, but he took legal action to recover other income he felt he had lost. Eventually a £45,000 payment was negotiated, but only in return for O'Farrell promising not to talk publicly about his time at the club. O'Farrell felt that the agreement was nullified by critical comments in Busby's book, *Soccer at the Top*, published in 1973, and some years later he wrote his own book with James Lawton of the *Daily Express* entitled *Nice Day for an Execution*. Extracts were due to be serialised in the *Sunday Mirror*, but then, only a few days before publication, O'Farrell withdrew them on legal advice and the book was never published.

Sitting in the directors' box that dismal December afternoon at Crystal Palace was the Scotland manager Tommy Docherty. As the players left the pitch after the final whistle, Docherty remarked to Sir Matt Busby that the 5–0 scoreline could easily have been 10–0. 'If anything happens over the weekend,' Busby asked, 'are you interested in coming to Old Trafford?'

The following Wednesday Sir Matt Busby was playing golf with Willie Morgan at Mere golf club in Cheshire. Despite the conversation with Tommy Docherty at Selhurst Park the previous Saturday, the United director did not have Docherty's home telephone number, and he asked Morgan if he could give it to him. Morgan said that Docherty would be an ideal manager for United and added that he had been most impressed with him while playing for Scotland during the 'mini-World Cup' tournament in Brazil the previous summer. Another Scotland player, Denis Law, expressed the same view when asked by Busby. The tempestuous, loud-mouthed Tommy Docherty of old was now a reformed character, they argued. Docherty had restored the international career of both players, but Law and Morgan would later regret those testimonials bitterly.

Louis Edwards and Tommy Docherty shook hands in Edwards' silver Rolls-Royce on its way from Manchester airport. And so, three days before Christmas 1972, there was installed in the manager's office at Old Trafford one of the most complex and interesting characters to appear in this long and twisted tale.

The more one talks to people who know him, the more one is forced to conclude that Thomas Henderson Docherty is two characters, not one. Every individual has good and bad characteristics; Tommy Docherty had them in extremes. The attractive Tommy Docherty is immensely generous, friendly, down-to-earth and a great motivator of players – qualities which have helped bring success. The unpleasant Tommy Docherty can be totally unreliable, cruel and callous – traits which led to his undoing at United and at many of the other clubs with which he has been involved.

Docherty plunged into the transfer market as he had so often done before. His first target was George Graham, who cost £120,000 from Arsenal. Scotland full-back Alex Forsyth arrived from Partick Thistle the following day for

£100,000. Three weeks later Lou Macari was bought from
Celtic for £190,000. No fewer than six of the players who
had represented Scotland in the Brazil 'mini-World Cup'
were now at Old Trafford – Forsyth, Buchan, Morgan,
Graham, Law and Macari.

A much less well-known (and uncapped) Scottish player,
Jim Holton, was signed from third-division Shrewsbury
Town. Docherty himself had never seen Holton play, but
the rugged, young centre-half probably made the most
immediate impact of all Docherty's signings at that time.
Harry Gregg, the former Shrewsbury manager, had originally recommended him to Docherty when he was manager
of Scotland. Within just a couple of weeks of Docherty
taking over at United, Jimmy Murphy and Docherty's
assistant, Pat Crerand, watched Holton and backed Gregg's
tip.

Yet Docherty believed he had been brought to Old Trafford to perform the unpleasant task Busby, McGuinness
and O'Farrell had all failed to do: get rid of players – the
'dead wood', as he called them. 'I sussed it out very quickly.
I knew I'd been called in to do the dirty work,' he wrote
some years later. 'I would have suffered . . . if I hadn't
gone "Chop, chop, chop . . ." and been ruthless and firm.'
It was a policy he followed at many clubs he managed.

The first man to find himself out of favour, and almost
straight away, was Ted MacDougall. Docherty felt that
MacDougall did not have any technical ability. He dropped
him almost immediately. By the end of February MacDougall was transferred to West Ham for £170,000 – £30,000
less than United had paid Bournemouth five months before.
(The transfer later led to a court case. Bournemouth successfully argued that they were entitled to an extra £25,000
which United had promised to pay when MacDougall
scored twenty goals, since he never had the chance to score
that number.)

Some argue that O'Farrell's other striker, Wyn Davies,
was also discarded prematurely. He played only four

matches under Docherty before moving on to Blackpool in the summer.

In just three months Docherty bought seven players, as many as Busby, McGuinness and O'Farrell had brought to Old Trafford in the previous six and a half years. A revolution was under way. 'A club riddled with cancer,' is the dramatic way in which Docherty has described the United he found in those early, hectic months: 'Old players, skivers, players who were more concerned with getting rid of the next manager, whoever he may be. . . . Not all the players had a bad attitude, I hasten to add. Just a section. They had virtually taken over. It was like a canker.'

In Docherty's first season United gathered enough points to remain in the first division without really playing well. The young Jim Holton at centre-half made a tremendous difference, and United fans immediately took to a player who clearly gave his best in every game. 'Six foot two, eyes of blue, big Jim Holton's after you,' chanted the Stretford End, though Holton's eyes were in fact brown! To many observers Holton was the hard kind of central defender United had lacked since Bill Foulkes retired in 1969. He missed little in the air, tackled well and frightened opposition forwards.

After George Best's second retirement at Christmas 1972, the summer of 1973 saw the departure of the two other superstars – Bobby Charlton and Denis Law. Docherty admits that Charlton's decision to give up made things much easier. There was still, however, the question of what to do about Denis Law. Docherty clearly saw Law as part of the 'dead wood'. He persuaded the United board that Law should be given a free transfer, though Busby disagreed with the decision. And, much against his own wishes, Law left United to join his old club, Manchester City, but the move came only after an extremely unpleasant dispute with Docherty.

Law had confidently expected to stay at United. He says that Docherty had told him at least twice 'that when I had finished playing there would be a job for life for me at Old

Trafford'. According to Law, the manager then forgot these promises and offered him a free transfer instead. Law did not like the idea at all. So, to save the player any embarrassment, Law says the two men agreed that, rather than move to another club, it would be more dignified for him to announce his retirement from football altogether after his testimonial game, due early the next season.

Then, while watching television the following lunchtime in Aberdeen, where he had gone to collect his children, Law heard a report that he had in fact been given a free transfer. In the light of what had been discussed with Docherty twenty-four hours earlier, Law was astonished. He was also very embarrassed when his friends and family wanted to know why he had not told them. On returning to Manchester he complained to Sir Matt Busby, who said that Docherty had been forced into the announcement under pressure from the media.

Denis Law was only the first important United figure that Docherty seriously upset. In time he was to have bitter disputes with three others – Pat Crerand, Willie Morgan and Alex Stepney.

Another attempt was made, however, to restore George Best. While the Irishman was in hospital recovering from thrombosis of the leg, Sir Matt Busby walked in carrying some fruit. "Bout time you were back playing, isn't it?' Best recalls Busby saying as he left.

The Irishman worked hard to lose weight and get himself back to full fitness, doing extra training during afternoons and on Sundays. He played a dozen first-team games that autumn and scored twice, but often his performances were indifferent. A particularly ineffective contribution at Queen's Park Rangers on New Year's Day 1974 turned out to be Best's last appearance for Manchester United. The Irishman missed training for two days trying to recover from the New Year celebrations and so was dropped the following Saturday. The humiliation of not being able to hold his place, even in a struggling side, was just too much. In the years ahead he played for virtually any second-rate club that would have him in Britain, Ireland and America, but the old Best magic flickered only occasionally.

Docherty played George Best in midfield, but his presence did little to help what was now United's main problem – the team's failure to score regularly. In thirty-six competitive games, up to the end of March 1974, United had suffered the most barren run in club history. There had been twenty-six goals shared between thirteen different players and in half those matches United had failed to score. With Martin Buchan and Jim Holton in the centre of the defence, the forty-eight goals conceded was the best defensive record since the team won the championship in 1967. But because of the lack of scoring power United were now in bottom spot and relegation looked certain. Perhaps it was the apparent certainty of going down to the second division that produced the sudden change in United's style in the spring of 1974.

United began playing simple possession football with short passes. Instead of kicking the ball upfield, Alex Stepney would now throw it to the nearest defender and build up a new attack. Several of United's younger players were beginning to perform well together, including Gerry Daly, Sammy McIlroy and Brian Greenhoff. Two new recruits, Stewart Houston and Jim McCalliog, also improved the side.

United scored thirteen goals in a six-game spell and gained ten points out of a possible twelve. If not quite enough to save them from the second division, it was at least the necessary boost for the following season. United's defensive, aggressive style would be dropped in favour of more adventurous play, and eventually the adoption of two wingers. 'We tried to play tight, to play defensively,' said Docherty, 'and we were relegated. From now on we attack.'

'Busbyites' such as Pat Crerand claim that Sir Matt himself, not Docherty, deserves the credit for the sudden transformation in United's style. 'When do I get the sack?' Docherty is said to have asked Busby after another defeat at Old Trafford late in the season. Busby replied that

Docherty would not be sacked, that he would take the side down into the second division and rebuild it from there. It is claimed, by Busby's friends, that the former United manager then suggested that Docherty ought to return to playing 4–2–4, the formation Busby had helped pioneer in the 1950s, and indeed to which he himself had returned during the brief post-McGuinness era.

Whether such a conversation actually occurred is difficult to ascertain. Pat Crerand, Docherty's assistant, claims he was there when it took place. Sir Matt Busby himself told the *Sunday Times* in 1976 that he had said to Docherty towards the end of the relegation season: 'Let's go out with dignity, Tommy,' and suggested that now United's fate was known, the team ought to go back to its more attacking style. Whether it was actually that advice from Busby which caused the dramatic change may never be certain. The Busbyites' conviction that Sir Matt was totally responsible also illustrates the strength of feeling they now have against Docherty. Their contempt is so great that they could never accept that he himself was responsible for anything good at Old Trafford.

In spite of the new approach, a 1–0 defeat at Goodison Park made United's position desperate again. That Saturday, 27 April, United faced Manchester City at Old Trafford, the last home game of the season. In the City side was Denis Law, playing out the end of the season in preparation for the World Cup finals in Germany. Law's return to Maine Road had proved surprisingly successful, with twelve goals and a League Cup finalists' medal. United needed to beat City, and Stoke the following Monday, even to have a chance of survival.

By 4.35 p.m. there was still no score, and eight minutes left for United to do something. When the ball came across into the United penalty area, Denis Law, with his back to the goal, backheeled it instinctively towards the net. The result made him feel sick. That goal was Law's last touch in club football. In fact, other results were such that, even without conceding it, United were doomed.

Denis Law always felt bad about scoring that day, in spite of the way he had had to leave United a year before. Yet, if Tommy Docherty had kept the promise Law says he made, the Scottish forward might not have been playing for City at all. The Scot could have joined the United coaching staff or retired altogether. How typical of United that such a disastrous season should have ended with such a dramatic twist! 'Whether that is poetic justice, I don't know,' an Old Bailey judge would remark seven years later.

Throughout United's single season in division two there was never any great doubt that the reds would win promotion at the first attempt. The sixty points with which they took the second division championship was a comfortable total, but not outstanding. Docherty's youthful United team had an average age of twenty-three, like the 1956 Busby Babes, and an equally refreshing, confident pattern. Stuart Pearson, bought from Hull City, added new goal-power up front. The crude aspects of United's game had now disappeared. It was a highly enjoyable season for the fans, who were visiting many new grounds, and for most, but not all, of the players.

By the time the team emerged from the second division in 1975 there was some internal discontent within the camp which, remarkably, did not seem to affect team performances. The seeds of Docherty's eventual downfall were already being sown. One by one Tommy Docherty added to his enemies with players he tried to get rid of. In most cases it was not the axing itself that hurt – that was to be expected in football – but the way in which the United manager carried it out. Probably the player Docherty most angered was Willie Morgan, the other Scotland player who had originally recommended Docherty to Busby. Eventually Morgan and Docherty were to become embroiled in a libel action that would cost the former United manager more than £50,000 and which he would describe as the 'biggest mistake of my life'.

Publicly, the growing tensions between the two men did not show themselves until early on during the 1974–75 season, United's year in the second division. During a dour match at Portsmouth one October night, Docherty brought Morgan off and sent on a young substitute, David McCreery. Morgan was furious and made it clear as he left the pitch. Eleven days later the United captain was substituted again, at home against Southampton. This time Morgan was so angry that he left the ground before the final whistle. By the end of that season Morgan was in and out of the team, being challenged for his place by a young winger bought from Tranmere Rovers, Steve Coppell.

Morgan says that he was determined to stay and fight for his place. In the summer of 1975, however, the players were due to go on a six-week tour of Iran, the Far East and Australia, but Docherty suggested that after a hard season Morgan might like to rest at home. Morgan happily agreed, only to see it reported in the press that he had refused to go on tour. By now relations with Docherty had become impossible and Morgan agreed to go back to his former club, Burnley, for £35,000, widely regarded as less than his true value. Morgan was still playing first-division soccer – for Bolton Wanderers – five years later.

Docherty's version of events is simple. Morgan, he says, was never the same player after an eye injury suffered while playing tennis in the summer of 1974. This required an operation. Docherty actually cut short a holiday to visit him in hospital, an indication perhaps that the manager felt Morgan still had a place at Old Trafford.

Eighteen months after leaving, on a local Granada television programme, Morgan described Docherty as 'about the worst manager there has ever been'. That comment led to Docherty's unsuccessful libel action against Morgan and Granada, and his subsequent prosecution and acquittal on perjury charges. Morgan spent two years preparing his defence and drew up twenty-nine allegations against Docherty to support his claim, many of which were never mentioned in court. Morgan even went so far as to subpoena the minutes of United board meetings during the 1974–75 season, his last year at the club. These showed that Docherty had reported to the directors that Morgan wanted a transfer. Docherty recommended that the requests be rejected and the board quite naturally agreed.

Yet Morgan denies he ever asked to leave, and says the manager's reports to the board were completely false. He interprets Docherty's action as an attempt to present him, Morgan, in a bad light, so that it would be much easier to get rid of him when the time came.

Pat Crerand, who served as Docherty's assistant manager, was another who eventually left after, he claims, he had frequently been humiliated by the Doc and made to feel unwanted. On one occasion, for instance, before a game at Manchester City, Docherty even asked Crerand to leave the dressing room.

According to both Willie Morgan and Alex Stepney, Docherty also tried to get rid of his coach, Tommy Cavanagh. The two men say Docherty wanted them, as the club's senior professionals, to state that they were unhappy with Cavanagh because of his bad language and his treatment of younger players. Docherty also made efforts to transfer Morgan's successor as team captain, Martin Buchan, to Arsenal.

It was Docherty's quite extraordinary way of handling players that caused so much resentment. So long as you were in his favour he was all sweetness and light. But once he no longer saw a need for a man in his team, he could be totally untrustworthy and unpleasant. There were reports of how Docherty would rubbish some of his players to supporters he happened to meet casually around Manchester. On the training field he would criticise players with precise references to the amount of money they were earning. Invariably it was the more experienced players Docherty fell out with, while the younger members of the squad, men he had brought into the side, remained full of admiration for him. Some people argue that it was simply a matter of the older, more experienced players rumbling Docherty. Once they had got the full measure of the man,

they claim, he could not afford to have the older players
around any longer.

Not only did Docherty succeed in discarding all except
Stepney of Busby's senior players – McIlroy and Greenhoff
had been signed as youngsters by Busby but never played
in his first teams – but there is a belief among the Busbyites
that Docherty also tried to get rid of Busby himself. The
theory is that he deliberately struck up a close relationship
with Louis Edwards to do this. There is no doubt that
Docherty and Edwards did get on extremely well and often
socialised together at a time when, as we shall see later,
Edwards and Busby were themselves moving apart.

In contrast, many of the younger players benefited from
the other side of their manager. Steve Coppell was particularly impressed with the way in which Docherty insisted
that he should continue with his studies at university, and
then flew back from a holiday in Malta to attend his gradu-
ation ceremony in Liverpool. Coppell also remembers how
some months earlier he had been feeling depressed about
his form and his university work. Docherty came up to
him, took a piece of paper out of his pocket with the address
of a hotel in the Lake District written on it and told Coppell
and his girlfriend to go and spend the weekend there at his
expense. Brian Greenhoff tells of a similar experience. His
wife, expecting their first child, had not been feeling well,
and Greenhoff asked if he could take the next few days off
training so that they could both go off to Anglesey for a
short break. After a match at Coventry, Docherty handed
Greenhoff a bag with playing gear so that he could train on
his own while he was away. He told Greenhoff he did not
want to see him back until the following Thursday.

Coppell, now pursuing his own managerial career, still
admires 'the Doc' as a manager for understanding the real
spirit of Manchester United. 'He was smashing. He identified with everybody, especially the spectators. He would
go around the country visiting each supporters' club. He
was manager in the eyes of the spectators and helped create
a better club.' On one occasion Docherty even asked each

of the players after a match if they were going to a supporters' club dance that night. If they said no, Docherty wanted to know why not.

On the other hand Docherty would not miss a chance to make money, and sometimes upset others by doing so. Steve Coppell will not forget the time Gillette asked him to make a TV commercial:

> As it was the first commercial deal I had been involved with, I thought I had better obtain permission and advice from my manager. I took the letter with me to show him, and he told me to leave it with him and he would look into it. A week later he had sorted it all out, but it was no longer just me, but now Gordon Hill, Tommy Docherty and me. Doc, inevitably, was the star of the show and it was his car boot which was full of razors and blades rather than mine.

Relations between Docherty and some players were never the same again following the particularly acrimonious tour to Iran, the Far East and Australia in 1975. The players suddenly noticed in Australia that United were being advertised in the local papers as taking part in a head-tennis competition, yet most of them knew nothing about it. The United head-tennis team, it soon emerged, consisted of three relatively junior players, Brian Greenhoff, Sammy McIlroy and Steve Coppell, as well as Tommy Cavanagh and Tommy Docherty himself. It also became known that they were getting a large sum of money – around £1,000 between them – just for playing in the first round of the contest, and that further rewards would follow if they progressed beyond that. This arrangement ran completely against the spirit of the players' pool, whereby all such payments were shared equally amongst the first-team squad. The players quickly made their anger known.

The dispute came to a head in an extraordinary scene more appropriate to gangland than to Britain's most prestigious football club. Late one evening in Sydney, before a match the following day, Docherty gathered the players

together in the team's hotel. Realising that what was likely
to follow would be unpleasant, he even excluded Arthur
Albiston on the grounds that, at seventeen, he was too
young for such things. Docherty sat on his own at a table
at the front of the room, with the players sitting in chairs
around him in a horseshoe. Topping up his glass regularly
from a full bottle of spirits, the manager called on each
player to express his grievances. He next admitted to
arranging the head-tennis tournament with an agent in
Manchester long before the party set off. Then, addressing
each player one by one, progressing around the room, he
criticised them in detail in front of all the others, saying
just what he thought about them as players and, in particular, their shortcomings. The confrontation lasted about an
hour. By the end, says Alex Stepney, the bottle was empty.

This was clearly not the way a football manager should
act. In particular, it was not the kind of behaviour associated with Manchester United. And the directors came to
hear about such things. The experiences of Willie Morgan,
Pat Crerand and Alex Stepney quickly created an unflatter-
ing image of the United manager in the eyes of the Old
Trafford board.

None the less, the reds charged to the top of the first
division with delightful attacking football which attracted
the second highest average home crowds in the club's history. What made a particular difference was that a third of
the way into the season Docherty brought back the idea of
playing two wingers – Steve Coppell on the right and
Gordon Hill, just signed for £70,000 from Millwall, on
the left. The enthusiasm and confidence which had carried
United to the second division championship bubbled
through the first division too. It was a remarkably young
team, none of whom had great reputations in English football like the Best, Law and Charlton team of only three
years before.

United's exciting form carried over into the FA Cup,
where they reached the quarter-finals with a series of
comfortable wins. But Wolves looked to have upset the run

when they came to Old Trafford and went 1–0 up. Gerry Daly equalised, but then at Molineux the following Tuesday Wolves were 1–0 up in the nineteenth minute, scored a second only two minutes later and then, worse still, Lou Macari was taken off injured. The match might have seemed over, but only to those who did not know United. Brian Greenhoff moved to Macari's position while the young Jimmy Nicholl replaced Greenhoff in defence and had a super game. That night at Molineux was to exemplify the spirit of a United side for whom opposition goals were only an incitement to play even better.

'We weren't really bothered about being 2–0 down,' says Steve Coppell. 'We knew we were better than them.' Before half-time, Stuart Pearson had pulled one back. Sixteen minutes from the end Brian Greenhoff struck the equaliser after Parkes had saved a shot from Coppell. Sammy McIlroy's goal in extra time took United into the semi-final. For United fans it stirred memories of the glory days of the 1960s. Two goals from Gordon Hill against Derby County in the semi-final took United to a Wembley final to play second-division Southampton.

In the league, meanwhile, United were only a point behind the leaders, Queen's Park Rangers, at the start of April, and had a game in hand. Like so many teams in recent years who have had a chance of winning two or more trophies, United ended up with nothing. Injuries to Steve Coppell and Stuart Pearson were followed by the kind of pathetic result that United have so often suffered late in the season, losing 1–0 at home to Stoke City. The title went to Liverpool again, with Queen's Park Rangers second. United were third, four points behind Liverpool.

Wembley overwhelmed Docherty's young players in the final against Southampton. United started well but began playing badly after a header from Sammy McIlroy hit the woodwork. Bobby Stokes' goal for Southampton eight minutes from the end was perhaps offside, but it won the match. Again the drama was twisted further by the fact that Stokes had had the ball touched into his path by another of the Scottish players whom Tommy Docherty had discarded – Jim McCalliog.

When United returned to Manchester for a civic reception, Docherty made the usual FA Cup losers' promise about returning and winning next year. Few believed it.

In the 1977 FA Cup competition, Walsall, Queen's Park Rangers and Aston Villa were all eliminated at home at the first attempt, while revenge was taken on Southampton with a 2–1 win at Old Trafford in the fifth round, after a replay. For the third time in thirteen years United were drawn against Leeds United in the semi-final at Hillsborough. This time goals from Steve Coppell and Jimmy Greenhoff saw the red shirts triumph for the first time in the series.

At Wembley in 1977 United were the underdogs. Their opponents, Liverpool, had already won the league championship, and they hoped a European Cup final appearance four days after the Wembley final would mean the first treble in English football history. But Docherty told the squad that he would pay £5,000 in cash to share among themselves if they won.

Liverpool were superior over the first half, but the nearest they came to a goal was when Alan Kennedy hit the foot of the United post. Five minutes into the second half Jimmy Greenhoff headed the ball on for Stuart Pearson to open the scoring, only for Jimmy Case to equalise just three minutes later. But within two minutes United were ahead again with Lou Macari's shot accidentally glancing off Jimmy Greenhoff's chest, past Ray Clemence. It was the winning goal. Liverpool had to settle for the league championship, and the European Cup – becoming only the second English side, after United, to win the trophy.

Martin Buchan collected the players' £5,000 cash from Docherty a few days later. But with so many of the squad now away on holiday, Buchan had second thoughts about keeping that amount of money. He asked Docherty to hold on to it until the new season. Buchan never saw the money again.

A month after United's victory over Liverpool, reporters

were summoned to an unusual press conference at a house in Mottram, a village 10 miles east of Manchester on the edge of the Peak District. Crowded into a small room the reporters and photographers were faced by the United manager, Tommy Docherty, hand in hand with Mary Brown, the wife of the club's physiotherapist, Laurie Brown. Docherty announced that three weeks earlier he had left Agnes, his wife of twenty-seven years, to live with Mrs Brown, with whom he had been having a secret affair for three years.

At first it did not look as if the announcement would affect Docherty's job. He had after all just won the FA Cup, and produced the most exhilarating football at United for a decade. Initially Louis Edwards seemed unconcerned. When Docherty telephoned the Edwards' home to notify his chairman, it was Martin Edwards who answered. His father was not available, and when Docherty explained the situation, Martin said that he did not think it would matter. Louis Edwards later told Docherty not to worry and said that it would blow over within forty-eight hours. It was a personal affair and would not affect his job as manager. Edwards even opened a bottle of champagne and toasted Docherty's future at United. And the United chairman also stopped an approach from Derby County who had been trying to get Docherty as their manager. Edwards assured the Derby chairman that Docherty would be staying at United and publicly described reports that he would be sacked as 'nonsense'. That position prevailed until a full board meeting could be assembled.

Ten days after the initial revelation, while Docherty was staying in the Lake District, the club secretary, Les Olive, summoned him to Edwards' home in Alderley Edge. There the five directors told the manager to resign. When Docherty refused, he was suspended on full pay. To the press afterwards, however, both Docherty and the club secretary, Les Olive, denied that he had even been suspended.

On Monday, 4 July, the United board met twice at Louis Edwards' house. First, at 9 a.m., they spoke to Laurie

Brown. He explained how Docherty had used his position
as manager to pursue his affair. The two lovers had been
seeing each other at times when Docherty had told Brown
to come in and treat United players, and the manager had
arranged for other members of staff to keep Brown busy.
But Brown did not just give details of the affair. He told
of several other actions by Docherty, and in particular
explained how the United manager had used journalists to
publicise his request for a new contract.

The board was now resolute that Tommy Docherty had
to go. On top of everything else they feared that if Laurie
Brown left the club he would sell his story to a newspaper,
and knew he had already been offered a large sum to do
so.

At 4 p.m. the board held its second meeting. This time
Docherty was simply sacked. A statement said that it was
for a 'breach of the terms of his contract'.

Had Tommy Docherty simply been having an extra-
marital affair, he might have survived. But it was much
more complicated. Firstly, it was an affair with the wife of
a club employee who was actually under Docherty's control.
The board now knew how Docherty had been exploiting
his superior position as manager. Secondly, there was the
extraordinary way in which Docherty had handled the news
and the bad publicity it had brought the club. The manager
had sold the story to the *Sunday People* for an estimated
£5,000, then held a press conference to announce further
details, just as if he had signed a new player. Doing so was
just inviting the press to probe further. Moreover, Docherty
was reported to be charging £100 for interviews. He could
not have arranged for more coverage if he had employed a
PR company. It was on the front pages of all the tabloids.

Thirdly, there was also the question of what to do about
Laurie Brown. It would be totally unfair to compound the
misfortune of losing his wife and two daughters by forcing
him to resign. At first the physiotherapist had insisted to
Louis Edwards and Sir Matt Busby that there was no way
he could stay at Old Trafford, even if Docherty left the

RIGHT Matt Busby in his playing days with Manchester City. They were not always happy times though, and at one stage Busby talked about packing in and returning home to Scotland. (*Topical Times*)

BELOW Down Memory Lane. A happy re-union for Sir Matt and members of the 1948 FA Cup winning side, Johnny Carey, Jack Rowley and Stan Pearson. (*Manchester United Supporters Club*)

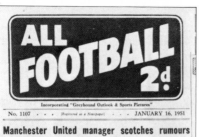

ALL FOOTBALL 2d

Incorporating "Greyhound Outlook & Sports Pictures"

No. 1107 · · · [Registered as a Newspaper] · · · JANUARY 16, 1951

Manchester United manager scotches rumours

'I'M NOT GETTING THE SACK'

by MATT BUSBY

LET me scotch first those rumours which, I am told, go the rounds—I am not resigning, I am not being sacked and there is neither trouble nor panic in our camp.

Those rumours seem to have started because we are not quite the glamour team we used to be. Maybe we are not. You cannot stay on top all the time and we had a longer run than usual.

A set of players hits such a wonderful peak only once in a lifetime. That goes for every sport. Now, I admit, we do not appear to be as good as we were—but we are not so bad, either. We are at the top half of the First Division and these are many worse teams in the land.

Do not forget we had a big shock when Charlie Mitten went off to Bogota. We were not prepared for that. Who was? We were left without an adequate deputy and Mitten's departure left a jolting effect on the club generally.

Some of my critics say I should have gone out and spent £ some of that £34,000 profit. Well, you can call me a real mump features, but I do not believe you can buy success.

I will not spend money for the sake of spending it. If we can buy a player we want at a sensible fee, all right. If not, no deal.

There is no panic

There is nothing to panic about. Before long, you will see Manchester United back on top, footing the field. Look at some of our young players. Den Gibson, just...

THE BARRATTS OF COVE

⚫ NEXT WEEK

LEFT Even the greatest United manager suffered rumours about getting the sack! This headline followed three successive defeats in the 1950–51 season. Fifteen months later Matt Busby won the first of his five league titles.

LEFT Even the greatest United manager suffered rumours about getting the sack! This headline followed three successive defeats in the 1950–51 season. Fifteen months later Matt Busby won the first of his five league titles.

BELOW First Division champions 1952. United went to America after winning the title, and so to did Louis Edwards. The trip was the first occasion that a number of players recall seeing the future chairman.

RIGHT Busby was one of the first tracksuit managers. Here he is seen with Duncan Edwards and Roger Byrne, two of his famous 'Babes'. (*Kemsley Newspapers*)

BELOW The 'Babes'. Six months after adding the Charity Shield to their second successive Championship trophy, Busby's hopes for the future were decimated in the Munich air disaster.

Daily Mirror
FORWARD WITH THE PEOPLE
No. 16,843
2ᵈ
FEB 7 1958

SOCCER AIR TRAGEDY

Manchester United plane crashes

21 dead

AN Elizabethan airliner—on charter to Manchester United football team, the famous "Busby Babes," crashed on take-off at Munich Airport, Germany, yesterday, and plunged the world of Soccer into mourning.

Among the twenty-one dead were United stars Roger Byrne (captain), Tommy Taylor (centre forward), Mark Jones (centre half), Eddie Colman (right half), Billy Whelan (inside right), David Pegg (outside left), Geoff Bent (left back).

Also dead was ex-England goalkeeper and sportswriter Frank Swift. While in hospital last night fighting for his life, was manager Matt Busby, who gave his name to the team and made it one of the most famous in football.

Twenty-three of the 44 passengers survived.

THE END The shattered Elizabethan airliner in which the Manchester United team was travelling lies in the snow. Planes scraped through the mud.

CRUNCHIE makes exciting biting! 4ᵈ

THE BEGINNING

ABOVE The *Daily Mirror*, 7 February 1958, the day after Munich. Eight players died, but it took Busby only five years to rebuild United.

RIGHT Many believed that Willie Satinoff would have eventually become a director. But the United supporter, who was a close friend of Matt Busby, was killed at Munich.

RIGHT Denis Law was Busby's most expensive signing when he moved from Torino to United in a £115,000 move in 1962. (*Daily Express*)

BELOW FA Cup winners 1963. United beat Leicester in the final at Wembley to end the season on a high note after fighting off relegation. The United chairman, Harold Hardman, is seated in the centre of the picture.

ABOVE Meat with Royal
approval! HRH Prince Philip is
shown around the Edwards'
meat factory by the two brothers,
Douglas (left) and Louis.
(*Manchester Evening News*)

RIGHT Alan Gibson, the vice-
president and former director,
whose decision to sell his
shareholding allowed first Louis
Edwards to buy the club, and
later Martin Edwards to gain a
majority. (*Manchester United
Supporters Club*)

ᴀʙᴏᴠᴇ Louis Edwards and Matt
Busby travel to Wembley for the
1968 European Cup final.
(*London Express News Service*)

ʀɪɢʜᴛ Tommy Appléby, the man
who introduced Louis Edwards
to Matt Busby nearly two
decades before, at one of his
Manchester Opera House parties.
(*Manchester Evening News*)

RIGHT Matt Busby with the European Cup at last, the trophy that had become his 'obsession'. It took United much longer to recover from the 1968 triumph than it had from the 1958 Munich disaster. (*London Express News Service*)

BELOW The Busby family – Lady Jean Busby, son Sandy, Sir Matt and daughter Sheena. Sandy Busby was meant to become a United director under an arrangement with Louis Edwards, but he had to be content with managing the souvenir shop, until the Busbys lost the lease in 1987. (*London Express News Service*)

club. He argued that United should compensate him for the loss of his wife and family and help him make a new start. Eventually Brown did agree to stay and was given a big pay rise.

Finally, once news of the affair broke, the directors came under tremendous pressure – from players, club staff and ordinary supporters. There were personal approaches, telephone calls and letters containing numerous other allegations about Docherty's activities, most of them totally unrelated to Mary Brown. The United manager had made many enemies in Manchester and it was inevitable that they would seek their revenge.

Tommy Docherty claims that it was the ladies who got rid of him – wives like Muriel Edwards and Jean Busby. Others say that Denzil Haroun was among those most vociferous in arguing that he had to go. Sir Matt Busby had created a club with high standards of public conduct. If only a few of the allegations were true, keeping Docherty would fly right in the face of United's traditions. There was even talk of a surveillance report floating around, supposedly written by a private investigator in Stockport called Steve Hayes. It was claimed that for two years Hayes had followed Docherty everywhere and built up a complete dossier of his movements.

The board had also seen at first hand how Docherty lost the support of leading players. A year earlier, at the club banquet, held at the Midland Hotel in Manchester after the 1976 FA Cup final defeat, Martin Buchan had been called on to say a few words in praise of the team's success but, much to everyone's embarrassment, he simply walked up to the top table, had a word with Les Olive and sat down again. It seems that he did not want his remarks to be construed in any way as praise of the United manager.

This explains why it had taken weeks that spring for Docherty to secure a new four-year contract with United worth £100,000. The board was only forced to agree when Derby County offered Docherty a job, though the contract remained unsigned at the time of his sacking. The United

manager might well have been sacked anyway had the team
lost to Leeds in the FA Cup semi-final. The relatively
disappointing league form during the 1976–77 season – the
reds finished sixth – would have been sufficient excuse.

Many of the accounts of Docherty's behaviour that
reached the directors' ears were to become public during
his unsuccessful libel action against Willie Morgan a year
later. Perhaps the most damning claim made in court was
that Docherty had demanded a personal payment of £1,000
to allow George Best to play for Dunstable Town in August
1974 and to arrange for United reserves to play a match
there. The Dunstable manager at the time, Barry Fry, a
former United player, stated that he was satisfied that the
money was for Docherty's personal use. Pat Crerand alleged
that he had actually seen Docherty being given the wadge
of £5 notes while he was sitting naked in his bath. Morgan
also intended to produce dramatic corroboration from Keith
Cheeseman, the Dunstable chairman, who had supplied the
cash. Cheeseman was by then in Albany prison on the Isle
of Wight, serving six years for fraud. Morgan had received
special permission from the Home Office for Cheeseman to
be brought to court to give evidence.

It was also alleged that Docherty had been selling Cup
final tickets on the black market. In 1974, it was said,
Docherty sold two £10 tickets for £100 each. In 1977 the
United manager had sold 200 tickets for £7,000 and, counsel alleged, he had even invited the ticket tout Stan Flashman into United's executive suite to carry out the deal.
Tommy Docherty himself said on radio in 1988 that Martin
Edwards told him that selling tickets was another reason
why he was sacked; this was contrary to his contract which
stated that he must uphold FA rules. Docherty says his
reply was that he had been selling Cup final tickets since
1959.

The profits from Docherty's ticket-dealing may have provided the £5,000 he had promised the players if they won
the FA Cup. After his dismissal, some United players were
furious with Docherty for never paying them the money.

So when Morgan was assembling evidence to defend his allegations against Docherty, there were members of the existing team only too happy to assist.

The two organisers of the United players' pool, Alex Stepney and Lou Macari, were lined up to appear in court for Morgan. Morgan's witnesses also included several of Docherty's other enemies – Laurie Brown, Ted MacDougall, Pat Crerand and Denis Law. The Busbyites in particular saw the libel case as another opportunity to put matters straight. Morgan even hoped to persuade Busby himself to take the witness stand. But Sir Matt, who was probably closer to Morgan than to any other former player, and played golf with him regularly, would not have involved himself to that extent.

In the end none of Morgan's star witnesses had to testify. The case collapsed before the prosecution had even finished its arguments. Docherty accepted under fierce questioning that not telling Denis Law about his free transfer 'was very wrong'. During cross-examination about discrepancies in his evidence, Morgan's barrister put it to Docherty that he had told 'a pack of lies'. The former United manager admitted that he had.

Docherty was ordered to pay Morgan's and Granada's costs, estimated at £30,000. His own lawyers and further action arising from the libel case cost him another £20,000–30,000. In 1981 a jury at the Old Bailey cleared the former United manager of two charges of perjury arising from the Morgan court hearing, having decided that his lies were not deliberate.

In the years since 1977 United fans have occasionally chanted Tommy Docherty's name at moments of crisis. To those on the Stretford End the street-fighter Docherty was one of the lads. Ticket-dealing and running off with a colleague's wife were something they might do themselves. It is his exciting young team they remember, a team which had attracted home crowds as great as those who followed the Busby Babes and the 1968 side.

6
The Edwards Family Business

'United have begun to think that "class" is something that comes with big office suites and fast motor cars.'

Harry Gregg, United goalkeeper 1958–67.

Louis Charles Edwards was born on 15 June 1914, two months before the outbreak of the First World War. His parents, Louis and Catherine, had married twelve years before, and although they already had two young daughters, Beatrice and Kathleen, this was their first son. The baby Louis, named after his father, came into the world at the family home in Liverpool Street, Pendleton, Salford. It was about 1½ miles from the impressive new football ground that had opened at Old Trafford four years earlier.

The Edwards family had a long history in the food and grocery trade. Louis' father, Louis Charles Panizza Edwards, is described on his son's birth certificate as a 'preserve manufacturer'. Their family had originally lived in Pimlico in London, then moved to Liverpool before settling in Salford. The 'Panizza' that Louis Edwards Senior carried in his name was that of his mother's Italian family, silversmiths who had emigrated to London from Florence.

In 1919, Louis Edwards Senior set up on his own in the meat trade in Salford, as a manufacturer and wholesaler of sausages. In 1921 he opened the first of several shops in the Manchester area, and in time both his sons, Louis and Douglas, born in 1916, helped out when they were not at school. Louis went to the local Roman Catholic grammar school, De La Salle College, but left at fourteen to work full-time in the family firm. Later, during the Second World War, he served in the Hussars in India, Africa and the Middle East.

Just before war broke out in 1939, the family business became a limited company, Louis C. Edwards & Sons (Manchester) Ltd. When the founding father died in February 1943, it passed to his two sons, Louis and Douglas, who ran the business together. But their father's will specified that Louis should inherit seventy-seven shares, and Douglas only seventy-five. Louis, of course, enjoyed the extra prestige of carrying the same name as the business. At that stage the company had a turnover of around £25,000 a year from a few butchers' shops in the Manchester area and a sausage and cooked meats factory. Within two decades the Edwards sons would turn this small operation into one of the largest meat suppliers in the kingdom.

During their early years of working together, Louis and Douglas Edwards found that the trade inevitably suffered from wartime and post-war meat rationing which did not end until July 1954. They were nevertheless determined to expand. As well as increasing the number of high-street shops, they made an important advance in the mid–1950s by winning the franchise for meat counters in dozens of Woolworths stores and in shops owned by Littlewoods. Another line was tendering for contracts with local authorities. Councils in Lancashire, Manchester and Salford were obliged by law to provide hundreds of thousands of school meals every day, and it proved a very lucrative business.

By 1962 the Edwards company had more than eighty retail outlets, including forty with Woolworths and Littlewoods, and it enjoyed an annual turnover of £5 million – 200 times the 1945 level. That year the company went public, and shares were floated on the stock exchange. The move made both brothers wealthy men and provided Louis

Edwards with the extra funds to buy his control of Manchester United.

Yet the business was not the ideal model of success. The Edwards meat firm thrived throughout the post-war years by providing low-quality meat, and by methods which were often corrupt. In 1978 and 1979 researchers for Granada Television's *World in Action* gathered considerable evidence about the company's dishonest business practices. Only a small portion was ever used in the programme finally broadcast in January 1980.

One of the firm's most important customers was the Education Committee of Lancashire County Council. Across the county, children were eating more than 300,000 school meals a day at one point, and by 1961 the authority's meat contracts were worth £393,000. That year Louis C. Edwards and Sons (Manchester) Ltd received £203,000 of the trade, and although the amount varied annually, the firm would nearly always get between a half and two thirds of Lancashire's meat supplies. By 1974 meat provided for Lancashire school meals was worth £1.5 million a year. Because of the size of the operation, and the extensive transport required, there were few firms in the North-west able to fulfil such contracts. The Edwards brothers' main rival, primarily in the north-eastern divisions of the county, was F. Lord & Son Ltd, the company owned by Bob Lord, the chairman of Burnley.

But the Lancashire contracts were acquired only at a price. Every few weeks a van would leave the Edwards' factory in New Street off the Oldham Road in Miles Platting. From there it would head north up the A6 to deliver a large consignment of meat to a house in a small village called Elswick, situated half-way between Preston and Blackpool. The address, 'White Gables', was the home of Sidney Hilton Whittaker, an assistant chief education officer of Lancashire Council and the man with overall responsibility for the county's school meals.

A former Edwards company sales manager, Thomas

O'Hora, told *World in Action* about one occasion on which he himself had delivered Sidney Whittaker's gift:

> It would be in weight roughly about 100 lb. I think it was about seven or eight parcels. It would appear as if Mr Whittaker was expecting me, and a lady, whom I've reason to believe was Mrs Whittaker, met me and showed me to an annexe where there was a very large deep freeze and I put the meat into it.

According to another former Edwards' employee, a typical order for Whittaker would include 'six sirloin steaks, six lamb chops, a leg of lamb, a leg of pork, a number of pounds of sausages and a number of pounds of best stewing steak'.

Similar gifts were regularly sent to officials and councillors concerned with school meals contracts for Manchester and Salford City Councils. Put bluntly, the Edwards company was bribing many of the people who recommended whether or not the firm should be given the councils' meat contracts. A list of the beneficiaries was kept in a slim, brown, hardback book at the New Street offices. Next to each name was written 'N.C.', which stood for 'no charge'. This was the kind of corruption that was common in local government in the Poulson days. Making gifts to chefs, catering managers and other people responsible for ordering meat is still a fairly common practice in the meat trade – 'danglers', such gifts in kind are called.

Between fifteen and twenty clients of the Edwards company would also get 'sweeteners', or cash bribes, delivered every month in plain brown envelopes. So common did these payments become that the extra expense of 'sweeteners' was automatically built into the figures whenever the cost of a contract was calculated. 'In some instances,' according to O'Hora, 'we renegotiated contracts within a couple of months of starting them. In this way, the cost of the backhander could be covered by the firm or council involved and the person who received the payment in the first place would invariably sanction the increase.' And

O'Hora insists that both Louis and Douglas Edwards were
fully aware of what was going on. Yet they were quick to
sack employees caught pilfering the tiniest amount of scrap
meat.

Executives and directors of Woolworths, including a
former chairman, Fred Chaplin, also received 'danglers', in
recognition of the Edwards' valuable franchise in many of
the company's stores. A van which left New Street on
Thursdays for the weekly tour of Woolworth employees'
homes in London and the home counties became known
inside the Edwards' company as 'the Oxfam run'.

At Christmas, Edwards' contacts would get an additional
large package delivered by the firm's drivers, usually a tea-
chest full of best-quality meat and bottles of spirits. Other
Edwards beneficiaries, according to Granada's extensive
research and affidavits, were ICI executives, managers of
several Butlin's and Pontin's holiday camps and even Sir
Billy Butlin himself.

Yet few of the firm's ordinary customers received such
good meat. Throughout the catering trade the Edwards
company became well known for the poor quality of its
product. A report by Manchester Council in 1966 complained of the bad supplies they were getting, and said that
the firm delivered the worst meat to the poorest parts of
the city. More than ten years later, in 1978, the company
was fined on several occasions under the Food and Drugs
Act for poor quality and excess fat in the meat supplied for
Cheshire County Council's schools. Shropshire and Staf-
fordshire Councils were also unhappy with the company's
supplies.

By the '70s, the public were also beginning to understand
what they were getting in Edwards' shops – 'second-class
meat at first-class prices', in the words of one former senior
executive.

Louis Edwards would often treat Manchester United
Football Club simply as an extension of his meat business.
United's affairs were sometimes transacted at the meat com-
pany offices in Miles Platting, most notably the sacking of

Frank O'Farrell as United manager in 1972. Similarly,
people from the meat business were often drawn into football matters. Thomas O'Hora regularly spent evenings
arranging the distribution of more than a hundred United
tickets for Edwards. Drivers would deliver them to a wide
range of contacts – councillors, local government officials,
health officers, senior policemen – though in the vast
majority of cases the tickets were paid for. In another
instance, in 1974, the meat company's property controller,
Norman Redfern, attended a United board meeting to
advise on plans for the club's proposed Executive Suite.
When the suite was opened, who should supply the meat
but a firm called Louis C. Edwards & Sons (Manchester)
Ltd. They had already been supplying the canteen at The
Cliff training ground for several years.

Officials at Old Trafford, and others in the football world,
were also sent regular free meat, though these parcels were
simply gifts not bribes. The home of Alan Hardaker, the
Football League secretary, next door to the League headquarters in Lytham St Annes, was one such delivery point.
To avoid embarrassment on these visits, the Edwards' drivers would be told to keep their vans parked away from
the house, preferably round a corner, and they were advised
not to wear their company overalls.

By the mid-1970s, however, Edwards' meat business,
like his football club, was in difficulty. In 1973 the company
made a profit of £360,000 on a £20 million turnover, but it
was the last year the company's shareholders were to receive
a dividend under Edwards' regime. The company planned
to expand by buying more retail outlets all over the country
and opening new stores selling a wide range of fresh food,
but things did not work out. In 1975 they had to announce
redundancies at Miles Platting, and though the accounts
returned to profit in 1976, by 1978 there was again a loss,
of £340,000.

Part of the problem may have been that both Louis and
Douglas had become distant from the company's affairs
and drawn into more glamorous activities. 'Mr Louis', as

employees called him, was more interested in running Manchester United, and in the Football League Management Committee, to which he was elected in 1968. His brother, 'Mr Douglas', was heavily involved in local Conservative politics. He had been a Manchester city councillor since 1951, and later became an alderman and city lord mayor. He also served as high sheriff of the new county of Greater Manchester. The men assigned to manage the company in their place lacked the Edwards brothers' determination and business style.

Alan Simmons, who was appointed chief executive in 1974, says that the business was being run in a 'fairly relaxed atmosphere with not much pressure being exerted to produce results'. Plans to expand by buying more retail outlets were abandoned. Other former Edwards employees argue that a major problem for the firm was Britain's entry into the Common Market in 1973. European meat regulations were much stricter than the rules that had applied until then in the UK. The Edwards company could no longer import carcasses from abroad which had been slaughtered inhumanely, for instance. And local government officials were also getting more fussy about the meat they were prepared to accept. In 1975 the firm lost the Lancashire Council contract.

The family's demoralisation would be compounded by the collapse in the late '70s of the building firm John Lee and Sons – Louis Edwards' daughter Catherine had married David Lee. Coincidentally the collapse came only a few months after the firm had built the United Executive Suite that Norman Redfern was consulted about.

In 1973, while his football club was recovering under the managership of Tommy Docherty, Edwards had called on Roland Smith, Professor of Marketing at the University of Manchester Institute of Science and Technology (UMIST). Smith is a fascinating character, a part-time businessman and part-time academic, who as chairman of British Aerospace was largely responsible for the dramatic takeover of the Rover Group in 1988. He also hit the headlines in the early 1980s with Lonrho's attempted takeover of Harrods. During his brief period as chairman of Harrods' parent company, House of Fraser, Professor Smith made a name for himself by telling Tiny Rowland to get his 'tanks off my lawn'.

In the early '70s Roland Smith was largely unknown outside the North-west of England. Yet already, when not teaching students at UMIST, the professor specialised in being a business consultant to companies in trouble, and was becoming known as 'the man of a thousand board-rooms'. The Edwards brothers made Smith a non-executive director and vice-chairman of their meat company. He gave them advice on how to reorganise their operations and suggested the appointment of Alan Simmons from outside as chief executive. While giving advice to Louis Edwards about his meat business, it was only natural that Professor Smith should turn his attention to Edwards' other concern, Manchester United Football Club. Roland Smith was himself a local boy and had been educated at Manchester Grammar School. Moreover, he claimed to be a life-long supporter of Manchester United.

Roland Smith saw great financial potential in United. He suggested to Edwards that it would be possible to devise a shares scheme which would not only raise a considerable amount of extra money for the football club, but which would also help Edwards realise some of his own investment in it. Louis Edwards found Smith's ideas attractive, not just because they might bring in cash to buy new United players, but also because he hoped they would make money for him at a time when the meat company was in deep financial difficulty. Moreover, Smith's plans would enable the family to retain control of the club.

In September 1976, a few months after United's defeat by Southampton in the FA Cup final, Louis Edwards and Roland Smith were accompanied by United directors Alan Gibson and Sir Matt Busby on a visit to the merchant bankers Kleinwort Benson in London. Among the possibilities the four men discussed with the bankers was a rights

issue – selling off new shares to the existing shareholders
in Manchester United Football Club Limited.

It was the start of a plan which would change radically
the whole nature of Manchester United, effectively transfor-
ming it from a football club into a business. The scheme
would eventually cement the Edwards family's control over
the club, and yet also cause a battle that would irreparably
rupture relations between Sir Matt Busby and his former
protégé, Louis Edwards.

The city bankers came up with several different schemes
that would raise money both for Edwards and the club. Yet
at one point Louis Edwards briefly considered a free issue
of shares, whereby each existing shareholder would be
entitled to a certain number of new shares in direct proportion to the number already held. Somebody with one
share might get ten new, free shares for instance, while
someone with a hundred would get a thousand more. The
idea was dropped when shown to be against FA rules. It is
highly significant, however, because the effect would simply
have been to increase the total number of Manchester
United shares, without raising any new capital. Why
Edwards should have wanted to do this may not seem clear
initially, but a clue may be provided by a comment Edwards
made to a colleague in the meat business shortly before the
1977 FA Cup final. 'How much,' Edwards reportedly
asked, 'would the fan in the street pay to have a Manchester
United share certificate on his wall?'

It seems that Louis Edwards partly planned to use his
greatly increased shareholding simply to sell off his spare
shares to supporters who would want them for sentimental
reasons and pay well above the commercial value.

Kleinwort Benson and Roland Smith eventually worked
out a proposal for Edwards that involved a rights issue
which would not only increase the total number of United
shares, but would also mean £1 million in new capital. That
money would then, it was argued, be used to buy new
players. Rather than issue shares to the general public and
anybody who wanted to buy them, they would be issued

only to existing shareholders. For every Manchester United share already held, shareholders were allowed to buy 208 new shares at £1 each.

While details of the scheme was still being negotiated in private between United directors, Roland Smith and the merchant bankers – and before the plans had been made public in any way – the Edwards family had already embarked on a second round of frantic share buying to rival that of 1962 and 1963.

Since Louis Edwards had succeeded Harold Hardman as chairman in 1965, neither the United board nor the share register had changed significantly. Apart from Sir Matt Busby's election as a director in 1971, the only other change was the election of Louis Edwards' elder son, Martin, in 1970.

Alan Gibson, who had sold most of his existing shares to Louis Edwards in 1963, had his portfolio greatly replenished when he inherited 894 shares from his mother in 1971. Apart from that, the only other major share change had been the promised allocation of 500 new shares to Sir Matt Busby in 1971, but these were being held in trust for Busby by his solicitor. Because this increased the overall number of shares to 4,644, Louis Edwards' own holding had in fact been diluted below the 50 per cent mark, to around 47 per cent. But the United chairman had little need to fear a takeover bid since a rule change in 1973 had restricted the price at which shares could be bought. In addition Edwards had placed 1,500 of his own shares into a trust for tax reasons so that they could be passed on to his sons in due course.

Another rule change, at the 1977 Annual General Meeting, was the prelude to the second round of Edwards' share buying. The shareholders agreed to the board's recommendation to remove the 1973 limit on the price of shares. Now the Edwards family were again free to start offering people prices they could not refuse, in an operation which over six months radically increased their holding from 47 to 74 per cent of the club. Their targets were the three largest remaining shareholders apart from Sir Matt Busby, all of whom were the descendants of important figures in the club's history.

The first to sell, in November 1977, only a few weeks after the AGM, was Beryl Norman. She had fifty-one shares which she had inherited from her father, the former club secretary, Walter Crickmer, who had died at Munich. One evening she received a telephone call from Jim Smart, the sales manager at the meat company. Smart was acting as Edwards' fixer, in much the same way Frank Farrington and Thomas McKeown had in 1962 and 1963. Smart asked if she would be willing to sell for £200 a share. Smart told Beryl Norman that Louis Edwards needed the shares to retain control, having handed over some of his holding to his sons. 'To tell you the truth,' she remembered later, 'the offer he made us was absolutely gorgeous. I'd always wondered what the shares were worth but as I'd have to offer them to the United board I didn't think they were worth anything.'

Smart went to Beryl Norman's house in Timperley with a cheque for £7,650. A further £2,550 was paid in cash – in used £5 notes taken from Smart's briefcase – to avoid capital gains tax. But the United minute-book and the share register simply recorded the transaction as having cost only £7,650 – £150 a share, £50 less than the actual price.

Then, in December 1977, Jim Smart went to see Elizabeth Hardman, the daughter of the former chairman, Harold Hardman, and arranged for her seventy-one shares to be sold to Louis Edwards' wife, Muriel. These shares also cost £200 each – £14,200 altogether.

Just as in 1963, the last and most important decision to sell to the Edwards family was taken by the long-serving club director, Alan Gibson. In February 1978 he agreed to sell 1,138 shares to Martin Edwards at £172.70 each. The deal cost the United director £196,545 in all, for which he had to take out a £200,000 overdraft. Martin Edwards' bank manager was told that the money would easily be recouped later by selling off a small part of his stock.

Edwards intended to sell up to 10 per cent of the total holding in two separate batches of 5 per cent and make around £125,000 for each batch. In other words Martin Edwards was hoping to make more than £1,420 each from shares that Alan Gibson had sold to him for only £172.70.

Between them Louis Edwards, his wife, his two sons, Martin and Roger, now owned nearly 74 per cent of United's ordinary share capital. The first two transactions – with Beryl Norman and Elizabeth Hardman – were carried out before the women could possibly have known about the intended rights issue – an issue which would have considerably increased the value of their holding. Alan Gibson, of course, had been on the trip to Kleinworts. He only agreed to sell his holding, he says, because Louis Edwards assured him the rights issue had been dropped. He later felt deceived on discovering it was still going ahead.

What the Edwards had done was insider trading, since the family was taking advantage of their own private knowledge that the shares were likely to increase in value. At that time, such transactions were regarded as unethical, but not illegal. Nowadays they are against the law. The Edwards knew that the more shares the family accumulated, the easier it would be to retain 50 per cent control and sell off the surplus at a large profit.

The deals also breached United's articles of association, which stipulated that shares had to be offered to the board of directors first – a rule passed in 1973 to prevent a threatened takeover bid. Yet even had the board been offered the Norman, Hardman and Gibson shares, it seems unlikely that any director apart from Louis or Martin Edwards could have afforded them at the prices they sold for.

When the rights issue formally came before the board in September 1978, Louis Edwards easily won approval for it, though not all the directors were keen on the idea. Alan Gibson said that he had reservations about whether it was necessary to raise money in this way, but that he would vote in favour if the meeting felt it was in the best interests of the club. Bill Young said that he agreed with Alan Gibson and asked whether the club needed the money. Yet he would vote for the plans if the money was free of tax. Louis Edwards' brother-in-law Denzil Haroun and his son Martin, spoke and voted in favour. Martin Edwards argued that the club might need £350,000 to buy a new goalkeeper since Alex Stepney was nearing the end of his career.

Only Sir Matt Busby spoke out strongly against the scheme. He argued that the club did not need to raise money in this way, since there were more than 50,000 regular spectators, £425,000 in the Development Association accounts, and the club had no financial troubles. He was, he said, completely against the principle of a rights issue and, moreover, insisted that his opposition be registered in the minutes. By five votes to one, however, the board gave its approval. Yet of the six directors, only the three members of the Edwards family, Louis and Martin Edwards and Denzil Haroun, were enthusiastic. Strangely, both Alan Gibson and Bill Young voted with them in spite of voicing strong reservations.

When the rights issue was made public, many people, including highly experienced local businessmen, argued that it was not the best way to raise capital for United. Instead they suggested that it would be better to raise a bank loan or to make a public share issue. Even the Stock Exchange described the scheme as unusual. Louis Edwards replied that bank loans would involve heavy interest payments and debts, while a public issue might mean his family lost control of the club. The Edwards family said that, simply to keep that control, they were willing to spend £740,000 on the new shares they would be entitled to under the rights issue. Moreover, they also promised to buy any entitlement to shares which other shareholders did not want to take up.

There were few observers who did not see the scheme as a money-making exercise for the Edwards family. They would expect to sell their new shares for much more than the £1 they would have to pay for each of them, possibly

or as much as £8 apiece or even more. In addition the
greatly increased capital within the company would mean
much greater scope for annual dividend payments – up to
a total of £150,000 under the then Football Association
limits. Previously the maximum amount the company could
pay out in dividends had been about £600 a year.

Ted Croker, the secretary of the Football Association,
was also extremely concerned about the plans. Sir Matt
Busby was so worried that he went to visit Croker in
London to see if the scheme could be stopped. Busby even
considered resigning from the board, but friends persuaded
him not to. The former United manager felt almost as hurt
by Edwards' plans, according to one friend, as he had been
after Munich, although obviously in a different way. It was
particularly upsetting since Sir Matt had himself brought
Louis Edwards to United in the first place. This dispute
came on top of the Docherty scandal, in which Busby must
have felt Edwards had let Tommy Docherty get away with
far too much for far too long.

Even though Edwards had given up his place on the
League Management Committee to Busby in 1972, other
tensions had developed between the two United men. At
one time Sir Matt had an understanding with Edwards that
he would be the next chairman of Manchester United.
Indeed, Jack Crompton remembers Edwards saying so publicly, and at one point Edwards had even agreed to hand
over straight away, but Busby had insisted that he remain
in place. This gentlemen's agreement was less important,
however, than the understanding between the two men that
both their eldest sons, Martin Edwards and Sandy Busby,
would eventually be placed on the board. The young
Edwards had been duly elected as long ago as 1970, before
Sir Matt himself. But Busby's son was still waiting.

Sandy Busby had never managed to emulate his father's
success in football. After having his son-in-law Don Gibson
– Sheena's husband – at Old Trafford in the early '50s,
Matt Busby decided it would be best for his own boy to
play elsewhere. Sandy went to Bury and Oldham, and then

played under Johnny Carey at Blackburn, without ever
getting into first-team competitive football. He also played
for the Surrey side, Kingstonian, in the FA Amateur Cup.
Later Sandy Busby set up a bookmaking business, but this
in itself delayed any possible election to the United board
since Football League rules prohibited football directors
from owning betting shops. But by 1978 Sandy Busby's
betting business had long been sold.

Busby first became worried during an informal directors
meeting on a summer tour to Majorca. When Louis
Edwards suggested the election to the board of his youngest
son, Roger, Busby had expressed his opinion that his own
boy should have priority. When Sir Matt formally proposed
the election of his son in August 1977, the matter was
deferred to the next meeting, whereupon it was put off
again. Sir Matt Busby gave up. It was becoming clear to
the former United manager that the Edwards boy was now
being groomed as the future chairman, and his own son
was not even going to be elected a director.

Once it was obvious that the Edwards rights issue could
not be stopped either, Sir Matt gave up his public opposition in the long-term benefit of United. 'I decided that it
is in the best interests of Manchester United Football Club
that I should drop this matter,' he declared. 'I do not think
that to carry on with it would be good for the club's image,
and that matters to me more than anything.'

Privately Busby felt betrayed. Friends say that directors
of other first-division teams came to offer him well-paid
positions with their clubs. One chairman even turned up
at Sir Matt's home in his Rolls-Royce. Again, though, the
overwhelming loyalty to the club he had built forced Busby
to turn such offers down.

But Sir Matt was not the only long-serving United insider
to have great reservations about the rights issue. The club
secretary, Les Olive, wrote to Edwards on 9 October 1978
advising him to prepare for the probable criticism when the
issue was announced. Olive warned of 'personal attacks on
the directors who might be thought to benefit most from

the issue', and pointed out that legally it would be necessary to disclose details of the Edwards' meat supplies to the club, and of Sir Matt Busby's ownership of the souvenir shop.

Ten days later Olive sent Louis Edwards an even stronger letter, asking him to 'reconsider' the rights issue. 'I am convinced that in the long term it will cause many problems,' the United secretary cautioned, 'if not for yourself then certainly for some future chairman.' In his carefully reasoned appeal Olive set out in detail several strong reservations he had about the scheme. First, he argued, it could not be 'justified for financial reasons' – not only did United have good reserves, but there was also a healthy income from the Development Association. Then, in his role as company secretary, Olive warned again that the scheme might mean dividends of nearly £75,000 a year, or possibly double that amount if FA rules were interpreted in a certain way. 'This can be paid EVERY year,' Olive added prophetically. 'You may argue that a dividend is only paid at the discretion of the club but it is quite possible at some future date that the private financial position of your family (or of anyone else holding control) could be such as to influence the payment of a dividend even when it was against the interests of the club.' And Olive expressed particular concern about what might happen if control passed out of the hands of the Edwards family 'in 40, 50, or even a hundred years' time'. Mentioning the Football Association's disquiet, and the likely press criticism and comment – particularly if there was a split among the directors, Olive appealed to Louis and Martin Edwards to explore other possibilities. 'Is there any reason why you cannot sell some of your existing shares for a substantial price without losing the balance of power? I am sure this would avoid a major upset for the club and would still be beneficial to yourselves, and in the long-term interests of the Club I beg you to take this alternative.'

It was a courageous letter for Les Olive to write to the man who was effectively his employer. And his carefully thought-out arguments were remarkably prophetic, especially on the question of dividend payments. But Olive's warnings had absolutely no effect.

Publicly, the strongest opposition to the scheme came from John Fletcher, a United supporter for more than forty years and the millionaire owner of Trumann's Steel in Walkden, a firm which often advertised in the United programme. He argued that under Louis Edwards' plan the shares were being sold too cheaply, and that the sale was benefiting the Edwards family. There was enormous goodwill among United supporters, he claimed, which would enable a much larger public rights issue instead. Fletcher formed the Manchester United Action Group '78 and put advertisements in the press. He organised a petition against the Edwards' plan and attracted 6,000 signatures.

John Fletcher offered to underwrite his own proposed alternative share issue which would raise twice as much capital for the club – £2 million. A million shares would simply be offered to the general public at a price of £2 each. Fletcher even went so far as to deposit £2 million of his own money with his solicitor as surety, and as a sign of his sincerity.

The United board refused to see Fletcher, and came out with the rather odd argument that the club did not need as much as £2 million. So Fletcher went to the High Court to try to stop the Edwards' scheme going ahead. The judge ruled against him on the grounds that it was unreasonable to expect the Edwards family to support a plan which would dilute their control of the club and make them vulnerable to a takeover.

Meanwhile, Martin Edwards was preparing to finance the purchase of his share of the issue. He was the largest individual shareholder with nearly 400,000 shares, and so would have to pay almost £400,000. According to Granada TV's research, various local businessmen were approached, including Archie Thornhill, a Manchester bookmaker, John Lawlor, a building contractor, and John Tabner, the owner of a taxi firm named Mantax. Martin Edwards suggested that if they were prepared to help finance his share buying, they would get a cut of any profits when some of the shares were sold later. It seems that none of those he approached was able to go along with the idea, and in the end he had to go to the bank.

Martin Edwards could have calculated that after the £200,000 he paid Alan Gibson, and the £400,000 spent on the new rights issue, each of the 400,000 shares he now owned had cost him about £1.50. How many shares he would need to sell to recoup his outlay would obviously depend on the amount at which they were valued after the issue. He approached friends to ask if they would promise to buy some of his shares later.

With Fletcher defeated, Busby silent and Olive ignored, the rights issue sailed through United's Extraordinary General Meeting on 18 December 1978 in less than half an hour. By thirty-seven votes to three the allotment process went into operation.

Martin Edwards' new bankers, National Westminster, had made it a condition of granting him the necessary overdraft that afterwards shares should be traded freely on the open market. Indeed, he would need this to have any hope of selling shares at a profit later. Board approval must no longer be necessary to make share transfers, they insisted, and there should be no restriction on the share price. Ever since then, whenever United shares have been sold, the price has been given in the following Saturday's *Financial Times*. The change also meant that the total number of shareholders eventually shot up from ninety to almost 2,000. United's Annual General Meetings became large gatherings of several hundred people, who were often prepared to voice strong criticisms of the board and management.

In the early days of trading, however, in February 1979, Manchester United shares did not reach anything like the £8 apiece that Martin Edwards had hoped for. A few changed hands at around £4.50 or £5, but then the price fell to between £1.50 and £2.75.

At first, Martin Edwards sold around 60,000 of his allocation to relatives and friends. Many of them went to people who bought only small blocks of a few hundred. One block of 15,400 shares, however, was sold to a Manchester fur trader, Mike Edelson, for £125,000 – just over £8 a share. The agreement, referred to in the accounts of one of his fur companies, gave Edelson the option of selling the shares back to Edwards at the same price at a later date. This condition was probably incorporated to ensure that Edwards carried out a promise to get Edelson elected as a United director in due course. It would also explain why Edelson paid twice as much as other people, and never insisted on selling the shares back. It would take him nearly four years, though, to get into the boardroom.

Although Martin Edwards made £320,000 on immediate sales of United shares, he retained most of his £600,000 overdraft. Ten years later, he still claimed to be burdened with much of that debt. The reality was, however, that he could have paid it off years ago by selling off his substantial shareholdings in other companies. Edwards obviously calculated that the rate of interest payable on the overdraft was less than he could earn on investments elsewhere. Meanwhile, his bank demanded that so long as his overdraft persisted his United shares should remain in the hands of a company run by the bank, Control Nominees Ltd. This gave Edwards the voting power to which his shares entitled him, but also gave the bank security.

Just four days before the United shareholders approved the rights issue, Louis and Douglas Edwards agreed to hand over the family's control of the meat business to the second dynamic businessman to become embroiled in the affairs of Manchester United. Like Professor Roland Smith, James Gulliver has achieved considerable national fame in the years since then.

Gulliver, a Scot, had been negotiating with the Edwards to purchase their business for nearly two years. It was a natural target after his career in the food industry with Fine Fare supermarkets and Oriel Foods. Gulliver believed that the Edwards company would provide him with something he had long wanted, a stock-exchange-listed company which would be a vehicle for rapid expansion into the food-processing industry.

The deal struck with Louis and Douglas Edwards in December 1979 involved Gulliver buying 500,000 of the family's shares at 5p each, and then the company issuing Gulliver with a further 1.5 million shares, also at 5p each. The whole deal cost the Scotsman just £100,000. In addition, Gulliver was granted an option to buy a further million shares from the family over the next forty months at a much higher price. The family also agreed to wield 2.4 million of its votes in favour of whatever Gulliver proposed at any company meeting. Together with his own shares, this provision gave him 44 per cent of the company's votes.

James Gulliver was also given an important management role in the firm. Both Louis and Douglas Edwards retired from the board, and from their positions as joint chairmen and managing directors. In return they both received golden handshakes, pensions, consultancy contracts and company cars. Martin Edwards, though, carried on working for the new owner as a director.

It was a sign of how close the Edwards' firm was to bankruptcy that James Gulliver's effective takeover of the business in 1978 cost him so little. 'I'll make it one of the largest food and drinks groups in Britain,' he is reported to have promised at the time. 'Just wait and see.'

And he did. Louis C. Edwards and Sons (Manchester) Ltd was valued at around £½ million by the terms of Gulliver's takeover, though at £2.3 million by the quoted share price at the time. Twenty months later the firm's name was changed to Argyll Foods, after the part of Scotland where Gulliver grew up. Within less than ten years Argyll had become one of Europe's largest food firms. What happened to the Edwards company in James Gulliver's hands is one of the most extraordinary recent growth stories in British business.

Once in charge, the new owner launched a rapid series

of successful takeover bids for bigger and bigger targets, including Yorkshire Biscuits, Cordon Bleu, Dalgety Frozen Foods, Oriel Foods, Allied Suppliers, and later Safeway supermarkets. Argyll's swift expansion was interrupted in 1986 only by the unsuccessful and notorious battle with Guinness to acquire the drinks company, Distillers. Even so, by 1988, thanks largely to Gulliver's hard work and clever dealing, the Argyll Group was worth an astonishing £1.7 billion, in other words 34,000 times what the Edwards company had initially cost him ten years before.

Gulliver took up his options to buy a million more shares early in 1981. One by one the Edwards family sold most of the rest of their remaining 43 per cent stake in the firm. Between them they received an estimated £8 million, eighty times more than the price Gulliver paid for his initial purchase. Sir Matt Busby was less fortunate with the Edwards shares he owned, and failed to realise several thousand pounds, having already sold near the bottom. Had Gulliver not come along, the meat company would probably have gone into liquidation. On the other hand, if the Edwards family had held on to their remaining stake in the firm, between them they might be worth hundreds of millions today.

Just six months after James Gulliver rescued the Edwards' ailing meat firm, the Scot was to strengthen his business links with the family still further. At the dramatic FA Cup final in 1979 when United lost 3–2 to Arsenal, James Gulliver was Manchester United's guest in the Wembley royal box. Soon afterwards Gulliver bought 100,682 of Louis Edwards' United shares for around £¼ million. He had spent almost three times as much investing in the football club as he had initially in the firm that was to become the Argyll Group.

Gulliver promised that he would get involved in making the club more profitable and help to develop United's marketing potential, and that he would also try to organise a better market for United shares. He arranged for the accountants Arthur Andersen to carry out an inspection of the club's finances, partly to ensure that he was making a worthwhile investment. And there was one further condition that Gulliver insisted the Edwards agree to before buying his United shares. Accordingly, on 26 July 1979, the board co-opted James Gerald Gulliver as a director of Manchester United. Sir Matt Busby, however, abstained from the vote, saying that he did not know who Gulliver was.

Meanwhile, what had happened to the £1 million that the rights issue had supposedly raised for new players? Contrary to Martin Edwards' suggestion, it was not spent on a new goalkeeper. Agreement was originally reached to buy Jim Blyth from Coventry, but he failed a medical test. Then, a month before the rights issue was approved, United gave a debut to young Gary Bailey, who wore United's number 1 shirt for eight years before injury forced him to retire in 1987. Bailey cost no more than a £5,000 donation to the football club at De Witts University in South Africa where he had come from.

Most of the rights issue money was spent when United signed the England midfield player Ray Wilkins for £700,000 in August 1979. But the United board seemed to take the attitude that it was a deal they could barely afford and forced the price down to well below the £825,000 figure that was publicly stated. It was as if the rights issue had never happened. They also insisted that Dave Sexton, the team manager at the time, should balance the books by selling other players. So Stuart Pearson went to West Ham for £200,000, David McCreery to QPR for £170,000 and Brian Greenhoff was transferred to Leeds for £350,000. The directors' instructions to Sexton looked even stranger after their arguments against John Fletcher less than a year before – that the club did not need £2 million and that £1 million would be sufficient.

After his retirement from the meat firm, Louis Edwards was able to devote himself almost entirely to Manchester United – apart from his four-days-a-month consultancy for Gulliver, of course! He would now come into Old Trafford

most mornings. Here was the opportunity to concentrate
on achieving his ambition of building up an income from
United's commercial activities that would at least match the
club's turnstile receipts. Louis Edwards wanted to step up
the process of turning the Manchester United magic into
money, profit and dividends.

But during the course of 1979, Louis Charles Edwards'
past quickly caught up with him. On 28 January 1980,
Granada Television's *World in Action* broadcast a programme called *The Man Who Bought United*. It was the
result of sixteen months' meticulous investigation by a
research team which included Paul Greengrass, the journalist who was recently the ghost-writer of Peter Wright's
controversial book, *Spycatcher*.

Granada's half-hour report explained how Louis Edwards
had quietly acquired his majority shareholding in United
in the early '60s, and then bolstered his family's holding in
the late '70s in preparation for the rights issue. The broadcast included a secret recording of a telephone conversation
in which Louis Edwards told Beryl Norman's son that she
committed only a 'technical offence' by not paying capital
gains tax on the profit on her shares.

The programme also provided details of how, over many
years, Edwards had used bribes to secure and maintain his
company's meat contracts. Thomas O'Hora gave details on
camera of the corruption that had been carried out, while
Granada had evidence from numerous other Edwards
employees to back the claims. *World in Action* also showed
how, over many years, Manchester United had used similar
inducements to parents to get their teenage sons to sign for
the club. A cash reserve had been built up for such payments in a secret 'No. 2 account'. Brian Greenhoff was one
of the players the account had been used to acquire.

For well over a year both Louis Edwards and Manchester
United had been fully aware of what Granada were investi-
gating. The club consulted a solicitor, John Gorna, who
contacted Granada about the planned broadcast. Later
United went to see George Carman, the clever Manchester

QC who had helped to get Jeremy Thorpe acquitted of attempted murder only a few months earlier.

Once the programme was broadcast, Louis Edwards' solicitors advised against suing Granada. The United chairman should let the wind blow over it, they argued. And no legal action was ever taken. Granada's evidence was rock solid and had been examined by one of the most formidable firms of solicitors in the land, Goodman, Derrick and Co. – Lord Goodman's practice.

The Inland Revenue began asking questions about United's hidden 'No. 2 account'. The Manchester police started investigations too. Both inquiries lasted no more than a few weeks.

While having a bath at his home in Alderley Edge, Louis Edwards had a fatal heart attack. It was almost exactly four weeks to the hour since the *World in Action* broadcast.

'Let's not kid ourselves,' said Martin Edwards at the news. 'This is what brought about his premature death. What Granada did was a complete character assassination. I have never seen anyone deteriorate so quickly.'

Louis' brother, Douglas Edwards, said he was less certain that the programme was the reason. Louis Edwards had a history of cardiac disease and had been badly overweight. Indeed, members of the United staff could tell of embarrassing situations in which he had collapsed before.

We'll Support You Evermore

' "Manchester United" stands for something more than any person, any player, any supporter. It is the "soul" of a sporting organisation which goes on season after season, making history all the time.'

United Review, August 1937.

The concourse of Euston station is remarkably busy around ten o'clock on winter Saturday mornings. The crowds are swelled by hundreds of London football supporters following their teams around the country. Often the biggest contingent, meeting friends, selling lottery tickets to each other, stocking up with sandwiches, waiting for the 11.00 departure, are the Cockney reds embarking on their fortnightly pilgrimage to Manchester. The journey has become routine by now. The same transport police travel with them to avoid clashes with any rival supporters, and if the trains run on time, the Cockney reds should be back in town by 8.40 that evening. Indeed, until the early '80s so many London United supporters used to go to Old Trafford by train that British Rail arranged special services. Not many London clubs need special trains when they play in Manchester.

By the time the train is whistling through Bletchley, a coach has already set off from Holyhead with a party of fifty or so Irish supporters who sailed across the previous

vening by ferry from Dun Laoghaire. These are just some
f the dozens, sometimes hundreds, of Irish United fans
vho go to matches at Old Trafford. Some begin as far away
s Cork or Limerick.

A party from Belfast often takes the early morning British
Airways flight to Manchester, stays in a hotel in West
Didsbury and does not return home until Sunday or
Monday. Other Irish fans travel north to Larne for the
hort crossing to Stranraer and stop off for breakfast in the
Lake District on the way. Yet more come on trips organised
y agencies such as Tara Travel, run by the former Man-
hester City player Dave Bacuzzi in Dublin, or by International Sports Travel in Manchester, a firm jointly owned
y Norman Whiteside and Pat Crerand.

Meanwhile, on the motorways leading to Manchester –
he M1, M5, M6, M56, M61, M62 and M63 – coaches are
ringing yet more fanatical supporters from all points of
he compass. Parties set off at 7.00 a.m. from Torbay in
Devon and from Colchester in Essex, others at 8.00 a.m.
rom Glyncorrwg in South Wales and from Epsom in
Surrey. More supporters leave at 8.15 a.m. from Witney
n Oxfordshire, at 9.00 a.m. from Carlisle and at 10.00 a.m.
rom Leamington Spa and Birmingham. Some will not get
ack until after midnight. And throughout the morning
lanes landing at Manchester Airport bring small groups
f fans from all over Europe – Scandinavia, Holland, Malta
nd Austria.

No other club in Britain can boast such consistent and
vorld-wide support as Manchester United. When Celtic
nd Rangers play in England they bring tens of thousands
f supporters south of the border, yet often in the past
hese same supporters have not bothered to attend the next
ome game in Glasgow against, say, St Mirren. When Sunderland or Newcastle get to the Cup final, tens of thousands
f Wearsiders and Geordies may rediscover their red and
vhite or black and white scarves, and the words of 'Ha'way
he Lads' or 'Blaydon Races'. Anfield and Goodison may
verflow when Liverpool and Everton battle with each

other, or against United or a top European side, but no
club in Britain can boast a following that has been as con
sistent, as faithful and as widely based, through good time
and through bad, home and away, week in and week out
year after year.

During the season of 1967–68, in which Mancheste
United won the European Cup, more than three millio
people watched the reds at home and away. The averag
home attendance figure was a remarkable 57,759 – a recor
in English football history. At thirteen home games tha
season – nine in the league – more than 60,000 were packe
inside the ground. Only once did a home game attract fewe
than 50,000. It is a record that Manchester United are likel
to retain for many years, if not forever: no club ground i
England now has the capacity to house 57,000. Even Ol
Trafford is restricted to 50,837 these days following th
recommendations of the 1989 Taylor report on the Hillsbor
ough disaster.

It seems strange, therefore, that the present Mancheste
United Supporters' Club was not formed until after Unite
won the European Cup in 1968. The explanation lies in th
troubled history of relations between the club and fans wh
have tried to organise into a representative body over man
years. The first recorded supporters' club was forme
around the mid–1920s, with a local taxi owner called Green
hough as the main driving force. It was an era when eve
top football clubs depended on supporters to help wit
refreshment huts, ground maintenance and, in some cases
money, raised from supporters' social events and raffles.

Greenhough's attempted boycott of Old Trafford afte
the atrocious string of results in 1930 contributed to th
suspicion which has often existed between football club
and their supporters' organisations. The delicate state o
the relationship at clubs in general eventually led to the F
rule: 'It must be realised that there is no official lin
between a Supporters' Club and a Football Club – they ar
two distinct clubs.'

By the time of Matt Busby's arrival at Manchester Unite

in 1945, the club founded by Greenhough had collapsed through inactivity and there seemed little interest in forming a new one. And until the Busby Babes era in the mid–1950s, Manchester United were no better supported than many other big city clubs. Indeed, in the decade after the war when football as a whole was booming, United's average home crowds were often lower than today. The season 1947–48, the year United won the FA Cup, was exceptional, with an average home gate of 54,890, but in subsequent seasons attendances dropped rapidly.

In the early 1950s crowds of 40,000 or more were not unusual at most first-division grounds. Several clubs could regularly boast more support than United – Sunderland and Newcastle in the North-east; the two Merseyside clubs; Wolverhampton Wanderers in the Midlands; Arsenal, Chelsea and Spurs in London. Even Cardiff City, West Bromwich Albion and Sheffield Wednesday attracted better crowds than United in one or two years during that period. In the 1953–54 season United's average home gate of 33,637 was actually below the first-division average, and in 1954–55 even Manchester City were better supported at home than United. Throughout most of Busby's first decade, from 1946 to 1956, the crowds United attracted to away grounds were barely better than clubs welcomed for most visiting teams.

The transformation came after the Busby Babes' first league championship in 1956. Everywhere fans flocked to see United in unusual numbers. At Old Trafford gates were roughly 50 per cent higher than the rest of the first division, while at away venues United increased normal attendances by 30 or 40 per cent – an extra 10,000–15,000 spectators at each game.

The greater enthusiasm led naturally to the formation of a new supporters' club. Its headquarters were in Collyhurst, not far from United's roots in Newton Heath. But the club did not receive much encouragement from Old Trafford in the two years before Munich. The Manchester United secretary, Walter Crickmer, had witnessed the rebellion in the 1930s of the Greenhough organisation and kept the new group at arm's length. It was only after Crickmer's death at Munich that more encouragement was shown. At Christmas in 1958 Bobby Charlton, Dennis Viollet, Wilf McGuinness and Gordon Clayton acted as judges when the supporters' club held a *Miss Manchester United* contest at Chorlton Palais.

By 1963, the supporters' club needed new premises because of redevelopment in Collyhurst. There were also rumblings within some local branches that United should recognise the club as an official body. The dissidents were actually expelled for making these protests, to the long-term detriment of the supporters' club. New headquarters were found in the basement of Ralli Buildings, off Deansgate in the city centre, and a social venue was established with a loan from a local brewery. But it was too far from Old Trafford and not enough fans used it. In 1966 the organisation folded, with outstanding debts of about £5,000.

It seems odd that the club should collapse in the mid-1960s, the halcyon days of Manchester United, when support for the team had never been greater. Never had one English football club boasted three such entertaining world-class players as George Best, Denis Law and Bobby Charlton. This exciting line-up, and the new silverware that the side were collecting, brought crowds back after attendances had fallen in the immediate post-Munich era to around 33,000 again. People would go out of their way to see any one of the trio of Best, Law and Charlton. In 287 competitive games between 1963 and 1973 United presented all three for the price of one. Analysis of attendance figures for away matches during the decade the three world stars played together shows United's remarkable drawing power (see Appendix A, page 306). The team would add between a third and a half to normal gates, and the official figures would have been higher still if many thousands had not regularly been locked out.

It was often said that George Best alone put several thousand on the gate, and figures up to 12,000 were cited. In fact, the Best factor was probably overemphasised. When the Irishman was suspended in 1970, 41,000 still flocked to watch United at West Ham and 60,000 saw the reds at home to both Derby and Leeds. Again, when Best was dropped in 1971, Chelsea still attracted 53,000 for United's visit.

During this period Manchester United could also guarantee to score eighty or ninety league goals a season at a time when scoring seemed a dying art. Denis Law, David Herd, George Best and Bobby Charlton enjoyed regular hat-tricks, and spectacular goals. Yet United were also extremely unpredictable. While locals might expect a magnificent display from the visiting reds, they might also see the local home team humble the mighty Manchester United. Such uncertainty only added to the aura that surrounded the club. United's pulling-power at away grounds has rarely been the same since 1973, when Best, Law and Charlton all left within eight months of each other.

Outside Manchester, it was in London that the public's love affair with United was most passionate. In the late '50s, '60s and '70s there seemed almost as much support for United in the capital as for the top London sides. From the days of the Busby Babes, Manchester United have given many of their best performances on London grounds. In 1954, 56,000 at Stamford Bridge watched the emerging Babes side, with Roger Byrne, Tommy Taylor and Duncan Edwards, beat that season's champions, Chelsea, by the extraordinary score of 6–5. A crowd of 63,000 at Highbury on 1 February 1958 saw Arsenal beaten 5–4 by the Babes in their historic last appearance in Britain, five days before Munich. The post-Munich reds won 6–3 at Chelsea in 1959. Other big London victories were 5–1 at Charlton in 1957, 5–3 over Fulham in the 1958 Cup semi-final replay at Highbury, 5–0 at Fulham in 1960, and 5–3 at Crystal Palace in 1971.

In 1967 London was the stage when United clinched the league title with the famous 6–1 victory at Upton Park;

and the 1968 European Cup triumph, of course, was at
Wembley. On other occasions United might produce more
normal scorelines, but fabulous matches. No wonder that
Arsenal, Spurs, Chelsea and West Ham would often secure
their biggest crowds of the season for visits by 'Man U', as
Londoners called the team, rather than for London derby
matches. Geoffrey Green points out that in 1959–60, for
instance, the league's biggest crowd, 66,579, was recorded
for United's 6–3 win at Chelsea. The second biggest league
crowd anywhere that season, 62,602, saw United at Spurs.
Even in the dismal 1972–73 season, when United were
almost relegated, seats for the final game of the season, at
Chelsea, were sold out four months earlier, just before
Christmas.

In the mid-1960s London boasted one of the biggest
United supporters' club branches, with more than 3,000
members. When the Manchester headquarters folded in
1966, the London and district affiliate quite understandably
dissociated themselves from what had happened. Old Trafford officials encouraged the London club to continue on
their own, and for a year or two London became the unofficial headquarters of the Manchester United supporters'
movement. There arose the extraordinary state of affairs
whereby applications to Old Trafford for details of how to
join the supporters' club were referred to an address 180
miles away.

After the fall of the main Manchester body in 1966,
two small groups – the Association of Manchester United
Supporters that met at the Manchester Arms Hotel in Mill-
gate by the side of Victoria station, and the Manchester
United Social Club based at the Bay Horse, a pub on
Thomas Street a few hundred yards away – continued to
organise sports, social events and travel to matches. The
minutes of a meeting of the Association in September 1968
report, for example, details of a trip to Sunderland costing
£1 per person and with a return time of midnight so that
members could be entertained by Sunderland supporters in
the Black Cat social club at Roker Park. It was obvious

that by combining forces the two pub groups could form the nucleus of a new supporters' club in Manchester. Agreement to merge came in October 1968.

On 18 November 1968, six months after the European Cup win, the inaugural meeting of the new club took place at the Seven Oaks Hotel in Nicholas Street, Manchester. The new organisation had to call itself the Manchester United Supporters Association (MUSA) – the word 'club' was avoided so as not to become liable for the debts of the defunct organisation. The force behind the amalgamation, and the club's first chairman, was Roy Priestley, a fan who had moved to Manchester from Suffolk. The new committee, comprising members of both bodies, included Anne Gilliland, Michael Goldstone and David Smith – each of whom remained involved until Martin Edwards announced twenty years later that the organisation was 'surplus to requirements'.

It was another three years before MUSA made much progress, however. Developing good relations with United officials proved difficult, largely because of previous misfortunes, and in particular the financial embarrassment from the winding up of the recent Ralli Buildings group. It did not help that one of MUSA's aims was 'to provide supporters of Manchester United with the one facility they are lacking – a social club', for this was the very problem that had caused the previous organisation to fold. Negotiations were already under way with Vaux Breweries about sponsoring the facilities.

Manchester United were quite happy to continue dealing with the London and District club and the half-dozen or so other local bodies then in existence. The London organisation was keen to remain the 'recognised' headquarters and their secretary even wrote to United objecting to the formation of the new Manchester club. During the 1970–71 season, however, the new supporters' association established itself as a serious organisation, and relations with the football club slowly improved. In September 1971 Les Olive wrote to Anne Smith (*née* Gilliland) to say that he needed more marshals at the ground on match days and asked her to 'recommend a dozen of your members who may be interested in coming along and assisting in this way'. It was a small but significant request – a sign that Old Trafford was impresséd at the way the new club was run.

Six months before, the supporters' club had sent a petition to the FA about the annual problem of Cup final tickets. The protest was strengthened by the fact that United had already been knocked out of the FA Cup that year: the request for more tickets for supporters of the finalists could not be seen as self-interest. MUSA also had new premises for match days – the 'Red Room' at the Dog and Partridge Hotel on Chester Road, a few minutes' walk from Old Trafford. This became the focal point of the club's growing activities. As well as weekly social events in their new headquarters, two dances were arranged every year at Belle Vue. The *Miss Manchester United* contest was resurrected and a Player of the Year award began. Denis Law agreed to be club president.

Club newsletters, published almost from the start of the new organisation, developed from duplicated sheets to a more professional quality. August 1972 saw the first *Manchester United Supporters' Yearbook*. By now the organisation felt legally able to call itself the Manchester United Supporters' Club.

The new club had emerged while United fans were gaining a reputation for being among the most violent in Britain. Against AC Milan in the 1969 European Cup semi-final, a piece of brick was thrown from the Stretford End. It knocked out the Italian goalkeeper, held play up for five minutes and possibly put United out of their stride when they seemed to be getting on top. In 1971 a knife was thrown on to the pitch in a home game against Newcastle. As punishment United had to play their first two home games the following season at neutral grounds, and part of the Stretford End was closed.

In the mid-1960s gangs of United fans often attacked

programme sellers at away grounds – the programme covers were valuable for applications for cup tickets. Soon the violence and vandalism became widespread. Train seats were carved up and windows of shops and houses smashed as United followers went on the rampage at away matches. Cars would be overturned, shops looted and battles fought in the streets with opposing fans. The police could not cope, and the violence was so extensive that serious incidents outside grounds, away from the press, sometimes went unreported.

The supporters' club, therefore, might have appeared rather unwise in starting its own excursions to away matches. But the move helped the club show its organisational skills and greatly increased membership. The trips began on a small scale when, for United's final match of the 1972–73 season at Chelsea, Anne Smith hired a carriage from British Rail on an ordinary train to London and thirty-one members bought tickets. That summer, BR asked if the club would be interested in organising the notorious 'football specials' they already ran for United fans. It was a daunting prospect: in two seasons £50,000 of damage had been done to railway property by United followers. The challenge was accepted. The club hired its own trains and insisted on complete control over tickets, stewarding and refreshments.

The first supporters' club 'special' left Piccadilly station at 8.30 a.m. on Saturday, 8 September 1973, bound for Ipswich. David Smith recalls it as a 'hairy occasion, a journey into the unknown'. Longstanding club members were appointed stewards, and Smith spent £150 on two bouncers who normally worked at a Manchester nightclub.

The 'special' completed its 500-mile round trip without trouble. Smith insisted that only members could use the trains, and as a result the club gained thousands of recruits and large profits. And there was little hooliganism on the trips. British Rail agreed to overlook minor incidents, such as stolen light bulbs, and the damage bill over two years was just £70. Meanwhile, the travel arrangements got so hectic that David Smith, who was by now club chairman, gave up his job as a milkman to work full-time. He received no regular salary, just the profits from the travel, which in 1974–75 were £4,509.

The supporters' organisation was now on excellent terms with Old Trafford. In 1974, after Smith had lobbied both Sir Matt Busby and Louis Edwards, he was given an office at Old Trafford free of charge at the back of K stand in order to sell rail and coach tickets. The club also got a free half-page in every match programme. United players and directors became regular visitors at supporters' gatherings.

Tommy Docherty's period at Old Trafford saw the second great surge in United support, even though the club no longer boasted stars of the Best-Law-Charlton calibre. Regular crowds of more than 50,000 at Old Trafford appeared at a most unexpected time – after United's drop to division two. The average home gate of 48,388 was more than any first-division side enjoyed, while a United visit doubled most clubs' normal crowds.

If anything, though, the fans' violence grew worse in division two. Many towns were not ready for the great United invasions. In the first match at Orient, Sir Matt Busby had to appeal to the fighting fans over the loudspeakers, while glass was thrown into the Orient goalmouth. Tommy Docherty even banned his eighteen-year-old son from away games because of the danger.

In 1975 the supporters' club abandoned its highly successful rail travel. The problem was that railway stations became the focus for opposing fans preparing an ambush, and the streets between the station and the ground were often a chance for further trouble. The 3-mile walk to the grounds at Liverpool, Everton and Leeds always caused problems, while the route along the river at Norwich saw cars pushed into the water. Instead the club organised coaches for away matches. They could drop United fans much closer to each ground and so avoid most opposition supporters.

Club membership rose to a peak of 22,500 during

Tommy Docherty's time, and there was a profit of £9,912 in 1976, but it was difficult to know how to spend it. An offer to donate the surplus to United was turned down. So too were plans to pay for a clock inside the ground, and a platform for wheelchair fans. The fear seemed to be that it might place United under an obligation to the supporters' club, although that was not the intention. Instead the money went towards better club publications, and membership fees remained unaltered despite high inflation.

Even with supervised travel, however, the violence at grounds and in surrounding streets continued, and a match at Norwich in April 1977 led to action by the Government. United fans attacked the home crowd and destroyed part of the stand, and it was recorded by television cameras. The sports minister Denis Howell decided that the only option was to prohibit United fans from attending away games.

Court reports showed that much of the trouble was caused by United followers from outside Manchester. To tackle this David Smith had been developing supporters' branches nationwide. Well-organised cheap coach travel from around the country, he thought, would reduce the numbers who travelled independently. These followers often arrived at venues early and spent the time before matches in local pubs. In the mid-1970s drink was a major cause of football hooliganism, though nowadays football violence is more organised and it seems that many hooligans regard drink as an impairment to fighting.

David Smith would often denounce the trouble-makers in the press and on radio and television. He was regularly consulted by the sports minister and when Denis Howell imposed his all-ticket restriction, Smith refused to organise coach trips to away matches even though it drastically affected his personal income. He also insisted that club branches should not organise travel either. Individual supporters still travelled to away matches in the hope of gaining admission, but the numbers were greatly reduced, making it far easier for police to control them.

Further violence during a European Cup-Winners Cup tie at St Etienne in France in 1977 initially saw United expelled from the contest. David Smith helped them appeal against the decision by collating a detailed report of the travel arrangements and first-hand accounts from United fans. UEFA's reprieve involved United playing the home leg well away from Manchester, in Plymouth.

After fierce fighting at Valencia in Spain during a UEFA Cup game in 1982, the supporters' club imposed its own ban on overseas travel. David Smith took the decision on the way back from Valencia's stadium to the airport. The previously promised police escort was refused and the United coaches were attacked by Spanish fans. Windows were smashed on every coach, supporters were cut by flying glass and two ended up in hospital. It was a difficult decision for Smith since it meant a further drop in income. He felt the possibility of having to tell parents that their sons or daughters had been seriously injured far outweighed any personal financial loss.

By the early 1980s, Smith was increasingly involved in other activities at Old Trafford. He supplied nearly all the photos for the *United Review*; he collated the programme's statistical records and proof-read all copy. This work, along with producing the supporters' club's own publications, demanded long hours. He often worked until midnight seven days a week.

The supporters' club finally found a way of contributing towards the football club by buying the photographic equipment and materials Smith needed for his work for the United programme, and paid for a darkroom extension to the club office. At one stage United even considered bringing the club in house. The plan, which might have meant Smith's becoming a United employee, was even discussed by the board. However, Denzil Haroun, a director who took a friendly interest in supporters' club affairs, advised against this idea. He argued that such a move would deprive United of invaluable political support from an independent body. Moreover, Haroun told Smith privately that the sup-

orters' club was not seen as a viable commercial enterprise
y the board, which had been one of the main reasons the
lea was considered at all.

Through his involvement with the National Federation
f Football Supporters' Clubs, Smith found many fans com-
laining that their organisations were being eroded by a
ew breed of football club employee – the commercial man-
ger. Not having experienced this problem himself, and
aving had only cooperation from Bill Burke at Old Traf-
ord, Smith argued vehemently that supporters' clubs
hould work closely with the commercial departments of
ne football teams they supported. In the years ahead, how-
ver, he was to discover at United that the fears of feder-
tion members had been fully justified. The first sign came
n the day United played Liverpool in the 1983 Milk Cup
nal. The Wembley programme contained a full-page
dvertisement encouraging people to join an 'Official Man-
hester United Fan Club'. This new body had been set up
y a company named Scanlite. Scanlite had already started
similar fan club for Liverpool and had reached an agree-
nent with United officials to do the same at Old Trafford.
Jnited were promised large royalty payments.

Remarkably, the Milk Cup programme was the first
mith knew of the fan club. He challenged the new United
ommercial manager, John Lillie, about it the following
eek. Although sympathetic, Lillie explained that Scanlite
ad made an offer United could not refuse and suggested
nat Smith contact the firm to see if the supporters' club
ould be linked with it in some way. Smith was furious at
ow the deal had been agreed by United behind his back
especially in view of the board's previous refusal to accept
noney from his own organisation. It was a sign of the new
ommercial spirit that was prevailing at the club. And there
as little doubt that his own club's membership would be
it by the new group. Meeting the Scanlite organisers only
ncreased Smith's fears. It was also obvious that the fan
lub's membership fee of £2.99 could not cover its costs.

The supporters' club had to decide whether to boycott the venture or become involved.

A boycott would have put Smith in conflict with the football club. He decided that the only option was a degree of cooperation between the supporters' club and Scanlite' fan club, partly to ensure some control, and in the hope that fans would not be cheated. It was agreed the supporters' club would contribute articles and photos for fan club magazines, and process membership applications. Smith wrote to United explaining that the subscription fee for his own organisation would be cut, and in future his members would receive only an annual yearbook. But supporters' club members could join the new fan club at a special reduced rate of £2. Smith also told United that because of the financial effect of the new body, the supporters' club could no longer afford to pay the costs of providing photos for the *United Review*. United therefore agreed to pay all film and processing charges in future.

The supporters' club restructured its work to fit in with the commercial fan club operation. But it was not long before problems arose. The printers of the first fan club magazine had not been paid and the work was swiftly switched to another company. Fan club membership cards were proving difficult. A computer system embossed names on to cards that were similar to credit cards. In theory the idea was good; in practice it was disastrous. A backlog of applications built up and the computer regularly broke down. Many applications were made by parents for their children, but the names embossed on the fan club cards were taken from the cheques with the result that hundreds of cards were incorrectly labelled and had to be altered.

By the time the fourth fan club magazine came out in January 1984, the creditors were already at Scanlite's door. The Post Office, the printers, the computer company and other suppliers were all owed large sums of money. United too claimed that they had not received royalty payments. The only people not to have lost money were the supporters' club. Because of his suspicions David Smith had deducted the sums his club was owed for contributions to the fan club magazine from money received with membership applications at the office.

Meanwhile, problems were arising over David Smith's photography for United, and John Lillie was questioning the costs. At one point United's lawyers even drew up a draft agreement which would have resolved the matter by making Smith the official club photographer. It was never offered to him. The problems were soon reconciled, but because of the uncertain future of the supporters' club, Smith would undoubtedly have signed the contract.

In January 1984 the fan club finally folded when Scanlite went into liquidation with estimated debts of £1 million. In spite of its poor administration, the fan club's basic strategy had been reasonably sound. Thousands of United fans had applied to join and the publications were good. Smith decided that thereafter the supporters' club would provide equally attractive colour magazines and subscriptions were increased to cover costs. Although his membership was now down to roughly 11,000, the new plan proved reasonably successful.

But relations between David Smith, his supporters' club and United never really recovered from the Scanlite affair. They grew worse in 1986 when Smith tried to defend a friend, Tony Woodward, who was wrongly accused of fraud in the United Development Association. There are those still employed at Old Trafford who are convinced that Smith's involvement in the Woodward affair, and his knowledge of irregular practices within the Development Association, had a bearing on Martin Edwards' eventual decision to tell him in March 1987 that, with the introduction of United's in-house membership scheme, he and his club were no longer wanted.

David Smith felt that his supporters' club was being sacrificed purely so that United could make money from their fans. He had expected that United followers would be charged only a small administrative fee for their ID cards, or perhaps nothing at all. The supporters' chairman was not in principle opposed to an identity card scheme, but the £5 charge, and the fact that internal club documents showed that United expected to make a profit on each member, persuaded him against it. He felt it would be wrong, and indeed a betrayal of United supporters, to provide United with either the goodwill or the membership lists that Martin Edwards was asking for.

Edwards denied at a press conference that the new membership scheme was a money-making exercise. The United chairman referred to the fact that, in the fight against hooliganism, the Government and the football authorities were asking all clubs to introduce membership schemes for specific areas of their grounds by the beginning of the 1987–88 season. Edwards admitted that up to eighty of the ninety-two league clubs might not comply with the recommendations, but he felt it was in football's interests that Manchester United be seen to support the plans. This was despite the fact that Old Trafford had long been one of the safest grounds in the country. Only two months earlier, United had been distributing a pre-printed condemnation of identity-card systems to supporters who asked about the club's position on the matter.

Rejecting Martin Edwards' offer of £15,000 compensation, David Smith decided that he would continue running his Manchester United Supporters' Club even if it meant that the club no longer enjoyed any assistance from Old Trafford. Enrolment, of course, was bound to suffer from the existence of United's own membership operations. But he was determined to continue publishing club newsletters and a yearbook, and to carry on running coaches to away matches, the activities that had built such a successful supporters' organisation in the 1970s.

Thanks in some part to the supporters' club's work over the previous twenty years, the burden United once carried of the most violent supporters in football had by the mid-1980s passed to other clubs. Leeds United, Millwall, Chelsea and West Ham are much more likely to be involved in violence, though there are still occasional outbreaks of trouble when United play away. There have been few problems at Old Trafford for more than a decade, mainly because of the segregation of opposing fans and advanced policing methods. Old Trafford saw the Manchester police using high powered binoculars to watch the crowd nearly twenty years ago. If there is any ground where a membership scheme is least needed, it must be Old Trafford. During the early months of the 1987–88 season it was publicly acknowledged by United that the new scheme had lost them around £80,000 in reduced attendances. And David Smith is not alone in believing that the £5 United scheme is only the most blatant example of the way in which the present administration at Old Trafford is gradually trying to turn United's keen following into hard cash – to convert the red magic into money.

In generating United's fanatical support, and casting the club's magic spell, the winning of trophies seems to have been less important over the decades than the nature of the teams that have worn the red and white shirts. Three FA Cup triumphs since 1968, coupled with relegation in 1974, cannot account for the sustained levels of fanaticism enjoyed over the last twenty years. Relative to football as a whole, United's support in the mid-1980s was higher than ever (see Appendix A on page 311). In the 1986–87 season there were twenty-two first-division grounds, but one in nine spectators who went to a first-division match that year went to Old Trafford.

The great surges in United support have occurred when the club has boasted attacking skilful teams – the Busby Babes; the 1960s team of Best, Law and Charlton; Docherty's two-winger side of the mid-1970s; and Ron Atkinson's cup-winners of the mid-1980s. While the last two teams never won the league title, they often led the first division or were in a challenging position for much of each season.

Not even United's reputation for entertaining football over the years can provide the whole answer. Tommy Docherty's 1972–74 relegation side played very unattractive,

physically aggressive football in which goals and victories
were rare. Sexton's team in the year before he left was
extremely dull, yet during both periods United boasted the
strongest following in the league. To some extent fans may
still have been going out of habit, in expectation of seeing
the United that had once been. In Docherty's case the fight
against relegation itself seemed to generate interest, and it
is interesting that the most popular player of that era was
a tough defender, Jim Holton. Yet part of the explanation
has to be less tangible – the aura, the charisma, the magic
and the tradition of the club.

The magic casts its spell too over those who have worn
United's red shirts. For many players United was just one
team in a long football career, and after leaving Old Trafford they went to clubs in other parts of the country.
But in retirement many ex-players find themselves attracted
back to the North-west and make the area their home.
Glasgow-born Pat Crerand became landlord of a pub, The
Park, in Altrincham. Tony Dunne, who came to Manchester from Ireland, began a golf driving range in the same
town. David Sadler still lives in Hale and until December
1988 was managing a building society branch in Liverpool.
Another Scot, Denis Law, lives in Bowdon and combines
his job as a sales representative at a local printing company
with regular football commentary work for the BBC. Martin
Buchan joined Puma sportswear in Manchester and lives in
Wilmslow. Even Tommy Docherty, the manager sacked in
disgrace in 1977, cannot get away from Manchester and
acknowledges his time at United as the peak of his stormy
career. He finally married Mary Brown in May 1988 and
they live with their children in Charlesworth on the edge
of Derbyshire.

In 1985 several ex-United players got together to form
the Association of Former Manchester United Players, the
only known organisation of its kind with the exception of
the Ex-Clarets at Burnley. They meet together regularly for
social occasions and to raise money for charity. Though few

former players go regularly to matches, they still consider themselves United fans. It is hard for anyone to escape the Manchester United magic.

8
The Butcher's Boy

'All the money is ploughed back into the football
club.'

Martin Edwards, 1988.

The question of who would succeed Louis Edwards as
chairman after his death in 1980 looked simple to outsiders
– it was a choice between Sir Matt Busby, the man who had
effectively built Manchester United, and Martin Edwards,
whose family had bought it.

In fact, there was no contest. Those close to Sir Matt,
like Pat Crerand and the former nightclub owner Paddy
McGrath, urged him to go for it. But Busby was now highly
disillusioned. His rebuffed attempts to get Sandy Busby on
to the board, the rights issue and the election of James
Gulliver had shown that the Edwards family now intended
to run Manchester United as their new family business.
The former United manager had spoken at Louis Edwards'
funeral service, but relations between the two families were
now extremely strained. Even if Busby still harboured any
ambitions to be the United chairman, he knew it was
beyond his reach anyway. He might have had the fans and
the sentiment on his side, but if it came to the crunch
Martin Edwards had the shares behind him.

The directors met to make their choice on the morning
of Saturday, 22 March 1980, before United's home league

ABOVE Sir Matt Busby announces his retirement in January 1969. It was three months before his successor, Wilf McGuinness, was named. (*Manchester Evening News*)

BELOW Wilf McGuinness (third from right) meets the players for their first training session under his command, but Busby remained in the background as general manager. (*Syndication International Ltd.*)

ABOVE Wilf McGuinness, Ian Ure, Jimmy Murphy and Sir Matt Busby, after Ure had been signed from Arsenal for £80,000 in 1969. It was Busby's initiative to sign the Arsenal centre-half, one of only two players bought by United between 1967 and 1972. (*London Express News Service*)

BELOW Sir Matt Busby introduces Frank O'Farrell and his wife, Ann, to Old Trafford. It was on this occasion that the men first clashed – over who should occupy which office. (*Syndication International Ltd.*)

RIGHT This photograph from the official club Christmas card of 1969 showed George Best, European Footballer of the Year, receiving his award from Sir Matt Busby C.B.E. and former holders of the award, Bobby Charlton and Denis Law. (*Manchester Evening News*)

ABOVE George Best scores at Newcastle United in October 1971. Before the game the IRA had threatened to kill him, and his brilliant form for United that season was rarely the same thereafter. (*Syndication International Ltd.*)

RIGHT No, he hadn't. Best made two comebacks for United, and several more with a stream of other clubs. (*Syndication International Ltd.*)

ABOVE Steve Coppell and Gordon Hill have Tommy Docherty firmly in their sights. A number of other United players would have jumped at the opportunity. (*County Press*)

BELOW Denis Law (second from right) scores the goal for Manchester City in April 1974 that confirmed United's relegation to division two (*Manchester Evening News*)

RIGHT Exactly a year later United
paraded with the second division
championship trophy, though
judging by their expressions it
looked as if they had been
relegated again! Lou Macari
(fourth from left) felt the celebration, for a club of United's
standing, was a big embarrassment. (*Manchester Evening News*)

LEFT Lou Macari celebrates after
his shot hit Jimmy Greenhoff
and led to the winning goal
against Liverpool in the 1977 FA
Cup final. (*Manchester Evening
News*)

RIGHT Tommy Docherty and his
team run round Wembley after
beating Liverpool 2–1 in the
1977 FA Cup final. The players
never got the £5,000 Docherty
had promised them for winning
the trophy. (*Syndication International Ltd.*)

LEFT Three weeks later Docherty announced he was setting up home with Mary Brown, wife of the United physiotherapist, Laurie Brown. This gave the United board a good reason to sack Docherty. (*Syndication International Ltd.*)

BELOW Barry Fry, Willie Morgan and Pat Crerand celebrate outside the Law Courts after the collapse of Tommy Docherty's libel action against Morgan in November 1978. Fry and Crerand would have testified in support of Morgan's allegation that Docherty received £1,000 after allowing George Best to play for Dunstable. (*Mail Newspapers p.l.c.*)

ᴀʙᴏᴠᴇ Some of the estimated
ᴀ,000 who welcomed United
ᴋ to Manchester *without* the
Cup, after the dramatic 1979
Cup final. (*Manchester Evening*
ᴡs)

ᴀɪɢʜᴛ Ray Wilkins joined Dave
ᴛᴛᴏɴ at United in August 1979
ɪs £700,000 fee accounted for
sᴛ of the £1 million raised by
1978 rights issue. (*Syndication*
ɪʀnational Ltd.)

LEFT Dave Sexton signs Garry Birtles for £1,250,000 in October 1980. It took Birtles thirty games and eleven months to score his first league goal. After two years he returned to Nottingham Forest for £275,000, just one of several strikers who have failed after moving to Old Trafford. (*Syndication International Ltd.*)

BELOW Bryan Robson became Britain's costliest player when Ron Atkinson bought him for £1,500,000 in 1981. Despite regular absences through injury he has probably been the most successful of all Atkinson's signings. (*Manchester Evening News*)

match against Manchester City. It was an unusual time for a board meeting, but the best way of ensuring that James Gulliver could pull himself away from his other hectic business affairs. When they reached the election of a new chairman, Sir Matt informed his fellow directors that he did not wish to be considered. The vice-chairman, Alan Gibson, said the same thing. Gibson then proposed that Martin Edwards be elected chairman. There were no other nominations. Bill Young suggested that Sir Matt Busby be elected to the position of club president and remain a member of the board. The directors readily agreed, though the position had been vacant since the death of James Gibson in 1951.

At thirty-four, Charles Martin Edwards was, after Elton John at Watford, the second youngest chairman in the Football League. So young, in fact, that on 24 July 1945, the day he was born, at Adlington near Macclesfield in Cheshire, five months had already passed since Matt Busby had accepted the manager's job at Old Trafford. Martin Edwards used proudly to take out of the bookcase in his office the programme for a match against Wolves in March 1952, six weeks before Busby won his first league championship. Edwards was just six years old at the time and it was the first occasion on which his father and mother had taken him to Old Trafford. In those days Louis and Muriel Edwards would sometimes watch from the directors' box as guests of their friend, Matt Busby.

Such visits were largely confined to the holidays when the following year Martin was sent to Terra Nova, a preparatory school near the Jodrell Bank telescope at Holmes Chapel in Cheshire. The Edwards' eldest child was not an outstanding pupil according to some of his teachers. The general view was that he was a diligent lad who showed plenty of effort, but he needed time to take in his work. At thirteen Edwards failed to achieve a good enough mark in the Common Entrance – the qualifying exam for public schools – to get into his parents' first choice, Stowe in Buckinghamshire, one of Britain's most prestigious independent schools.

Instead he had to settle for Cokethorpe, a far-from-distinguished private school of about 200 boys which had just opened in 46 acres of parkland near Witney in Oxfordshire. His former English teacher, Ron Lyle, remembers Edwards as 'an ordinary boy who was very keen on sport'. He enjoyed playing rugby in the first XV, was captain of his house cricket team and played basketball. But for a man who would one day have to juggle with millions of pounds as chairman of Manchester United, he was slow at maths.

By the time he was eighteen and a half, Edwards had collected six 'O' levels – in British History, English Literature, Bible Knowledge, Economic and Public Affairs, Economics and English Language – though only after several unsuccessful sittings. He was not good enough to take 'A' levels or to go on to further or higher education. The nearest Martin Edwards got to university was a summer marketing course held at Emmanuel College, Cambridge, many years later.

He had no need to worry, however. A job awaited him back home in the family meat firm. Both Louis and Douglas Edwards had followed their father into the business he had founded, and in due course all their four sons were to follow them into the firm. The company house journal later reported how Martin Edwards began as a trainee in the summer of 1964, working initially as an assistant in Edwards shops and on meat counters around the Northwest. Then he moved to head office in Miles Platting to work for the quality control and sales departments of the manufacturing division. After that he was in the sales office of the catering division.

Martin Edwards was then promoted to the post of assistant to the managing director, Arthur Peacock. In the summer of 1967, Peacock arranged for the twenty-one-year-old Edwards to act as a relief manager in various Edwards shops, including the store in King Street, Stretford, near Old Trafford, in order to understand meat finances on a small scale. This job was followed by appointments overseeing retail stores and working in the property division. In

1973, as part of the firm's reorganisation, Edwards achieved
the position of retail/wholesale controller.

After his return to Manchester, Martin Edwards had
also begun playing rugby for Wilmslow, as a centre three-
quarter. This regular commitment every Saturday meant
that Manchester United had to come second. Trips with his
mother and father to matches were now generally limited to
midweek fixtures. Many United fans would give the world
to sit regularly in the Old Trafford directors' box. Yet even
after Louis Edwards had his son elected to the United board
in March 1970, at the age of only twenty-four, Saturdays
for Martin Edwards were still devoted to Wilmslow and his
'first love', rugby. According to Martin Edwards, his father
had in fact suggested his election to the board in the hope
that it would make him give up rugby. He had just suffered
a serious concussion which required a lumbar puncture.
When he was concussed a second time, in 1971, Wilmslow
did indeed make way for Manchester United, though he
still maintained a great affection for rugby.

Martin Edwards was not a very frequent attender of
board meetings in his ten years as an ordinary United director. Business commitments and regular holidays caused him
to miss more meetings than any other board member. He
had no special responsibilities, nor, it seems, did he say
much. He was less than half the age of any other director
and it appears that he was mostly prepared to listen and
watch. Martin Edwards' only notable contribution recorded
in the minutes throughout most of the seventies came after
United had just met Norwich City over two legs in the 1975
League Cup semi-final. He thought it was unfair that the
gate receipts should have been divided equally between the
two clubs when the attendance for the game at Old Trafford
was almost twice as high as for the second leg at Carrow
Road. The other directors said that the League would be
unlikely to change their minds on the matter, but it was a
sign of Edwards' thinking in years to come.

The junior United director clearly found that his position
in the Old Trafford boardroom provided useful business

contacts. In 1974 he explained to the Edwards company's
house magazine how football had helped the firm win meat
counter franchises in five Cee-N-Cee supermarkets in Manchester. 'As a director of Manchester United I have many
friends in the world of football, including Mr Alex Humphreys, the managing director of Cee-N-Cee and a director
of Stoke City,' he stated. Humphreys confirms the story.
Again, it was indicative of the way Martin Edwards would
operate in future.

In his new job of retail/wholesale controller in the family
firm, Edwards helped close many of the firm's high-street
stores in the mid-1970s as the business tried to turn itself
round. On the other hand he developed what the company
regarded as 'an entirely new concept in shopping' – fresh
food markets, where people could buy not only meat but
also dairy products, ground coffee, fruit and vegetables.
But there is evidence that Martin Edwards did not entirely
have his heart in the job as the company battled for survival.
One colleague recalls him saying, round about 1976, how
he would be quite happy to sell up, move to the south of
France and do nothing. Another remembers that Louis
Edwards was fairly contemptuous of both his sons' abilities.

Edwards still found an outlet in sport, though, and not
just in watching it. Readers of his local newspaper,
Wilmslow World, learnt how in 1976 and 1977 the United
director triumphed in the Alderley Edge Cricket Club fun-
day. Edwards achieved the highest combined score in nine
events – the shot-putt, standing jumps, press-ups, squat
thrusts, interval running, the 100 metres, shooting, throw-
ing a medicine ball and welly chucking! On the first
occasion, when he was only joint winner, Edwards had the
honour of receiving his trophy from the former Manchester
City winger Mike Summerbee. Edwards swam regularly
too and played cricket, tennis and squash.

After the takeover of the family meat company by James
Gulliver in 1978, Martin Edwards was kept on by the new
owner and, unlike his father and uncle, retained his position
on the board. But he resigned from his full-time job in

April 1980 within a few weeks of his election as United chairman and received a golden handshake of £12,500. Gulliver also kept Edwards as a non-executive director, and paid him a consultancy fee of £5,000 a year. Edwards remained on the board of what shortly afterwards became Argyll Foods for three and a half years, though now nearly all his time was spent on United.

So the new United chairman had no full-time income, though his consultancy money from Argyll was nevertheless far more than some clerical staff at Old Trafford earned. He was preparing for a proposed change in FA rules which would allow each soccer club to have one paid director – a reform designed to bring football into the modern business world. Edwards cast United's vote in favour of the reform at a special FA meeting in November 1981. Within two months, in January 1982, the United board had appointed him as one of the first full-time chief executives of a British football club. His appointment took effect from December 1981.

The United accounts for the 1981–82 financial year show that Edwards was paid £15,000 in that year and contemporary press reports gave the impression that this was his *annual* salary. Edwards himself remarked at the time that he would be 'very surprised if my salary was among the top ten at Old Trafford'. In fact his annual rate of pay was £30,000, and it was only because he had held office for six months that half the figure was paid. As for not being among the top ten earners at Old Trafford, his full annual salary was exceeded only by that of eight other employees. Within a matter of months he had progressed even higher up the wages table, and there were also many perks associated with the job. In 1982 the directors authorised several thousand pounds to be spent on a new bathroom and toilet facilities next to Edwards' office, which at that time was situated in the new executive suite complex.

In August 1982, Edwards' salary was increased to £40,000 a year – only four United players, according to the 1982 accounts, had earned more than that amount over the previous year. Denzil Haroun explained that it was in recognition of more than £500,000 the new chief executive had brought into the club since he had begun his full-time job. It is true that several commercial deals had been secured during Edwards' first few months of full-time employment by United. But these were arranged in conjunction with Bill Burke's successor as commercial manager, John Lillie, who had previously worked for Makro, the Dutch wholesalers, and also at the Edwards meat company, before opening his own business in Birmingham. A contract worth £500,000 had been signed with the Japanese firm Sharp Electronics, under which United players would carry the Sharp name on their shirts. Sharp were introduced to United by Harrington Kilbride & Partners Ltd, an agency who then negotiated the contract. (For further information see Chapter 13.) Yet football clubs everywhere were arranging such deals at that time. Indeed, Everton and Liverpool had carried shirt advertising since 1979. The Sharp contract was hailed as the biggest football sponsorship arrangement ever, yet anybody could have secured a lucrative sponsor for United, Britain's most watched club both on television and in the flesh.

There were two other projects by which Martin Edwards justified his large salary increase – a joint prize competition planned with Glasgow Rangers and a scheme to hold Sunday markets in the club car-park. Both schemes failed. Another idea Edwards came up with – pop concerts at the ground – also fell through. Plans for a performance by the group Queen were delayed after protests to Trafford Council from local residents, and the group went to Leeds United instead.

Martin Edwards was determined to run Manchester United in a more businesslike manner. When he took over at Old Trafford there was, he says, 'no such thing as a club budget. . . . We worked out cash-flow on the back of an envelope.' Edwards' comments may not be entirely fair: there had long been a directors' finance committee, which

ept an eye on weekly expenditure. He might also have
called that his father was once its chairman.

Gradually matters that would previously have been dealt
ith by the club secretary, Les Olive, were passed through
dwards' office. The new chief executive decided to
nprove the club's affairs in matters such as legal advice,
dministration and accounting. All playing contracts were
ow negotiated directly by him with the players or, increas-
gly, with their agents rather than by the new manager,
on Atkinson. The club's activities were split into separate
epartments – playing, administration, commercial and
atering. The manager of each division was given his own
udget and told to report directly to Edwards.

Martin Edwards is a much less interesting figure than his
ther, 'Champagne Louis'. To many people Louis
dwards came across as a jolly if rather lonely person, and
f course at 17 stone or more he could not help standing
ut. Martin Edwards is dull in comparison – slim, well-
ressed, softly spoken, albeit with some charm. He is the
ypical image of a modern young businessman.

The United manager he had inherited in 1980, Dave
exton, was, superficially at least, also a rather grey figure.
exton seems in many ways an unlikely person ever to be
football manager. In his spare time he reads philosophy
ooks, studies the lives of thinkers like Wittgenstein and
Iill and reads the poems of Robert Frost. His approach to
ootball is highly scientific. One of his first acts at Old
rafford had been to buy a video camera and projection
creen so that United players could watch and analyse their
revious games. Training was largely coaching and tactics,
hereas in the Tommy Docherty days it had been mostly
ames of five-a-side football.

Sexton's period at Old Trafford had been mostly
neventful. Docherty's 4–2–4 team with Steve Coppell and
ordon Hill on the wings had been modified to Sexton's less
dventurous 4–4–2 formation. Hill was allowed to follow
)ocherty to Derby County, as it was considered that he
as too selfish and did not contribute enough towards team-

work. On one occasion Martin Buchan had clipped him
round the ear for failing to help out in defence. Stev
Coppell, meanwhile, was played further back.

Indeed, Sexton might have lost his job in 1979 had it no
been for United's remarkable FA Cup exploits that spring
While the side had found it difficult to pick up points i
the league, in the Cup they knocked out Liverpool in th
semi-final after two scintillating games at Maine Road an
Goodison Park. The final against Arsenal at Wembley prod
uced what was probably the most exciting finish ever see
in an FA Cup final. Arsenal were winning with just fiv
minutes to go. Then, in the space of two minutes, firs
McQueen scored and then McIlroy netted an equaliser
Extra time beckoned, and most thought that after such
comeback United were hot favourites. But extra time wa
never needed. In the euphoria United slackened a little
Graham Rix crossed the ball to Alan Sunderland for th
winning goal, seconds before the final whistle.

Thousands crowded the streets of Manchester to welcom
Sexton's losing team home the following day. And th
excitement of the Cup run overcame any misgivings abou
how the team had played in general. In the followin
season, 1979–80, United chased Liverpool to achiev
runners-up position – the first time they had come secon
since 1968 – though a 6–0 defeat at Ipswich just four day
after Louis Edwards' death showed that they did not alway
play championship football.

Martin Edwards formally congratulated the United man
ager for coming second in 1980. Both Dave Sexton and hi
assistant, Tommy Cavanagh, were awarded new three-yea
contracts and their salaries were increased by 50 per cen
Yet early in the following season, 1980–81, relation
between Edwards and his manager grew strained. The tear
had thrown away a money-spinning run in the UEFA Cu
by being knocked out in the first round by Widzew Lodz
Edwards was worried about falling crowd figures as Unite
struggled to match the results of the previous season. Th
team had not lost often, but there had been a succession

home draws against weak opponents. Home matches against Aston Villa and Wolves had attracted gates of barely 38,000, far below the previous season's figures.

Meanwhile, Sexton had spent £1.25 million and a £75,000 signing-on fee acquiring the England forward Garry Birtles from Nottingham Forest. Although £500,000 was immediately recovered with the sale of Andy Ritchie to Brighton, Sexton was told to raise a further £900,000 by selling players to balance the books.

Edwards' financial stringency was part of a more widespread check on the club's accounts, which included several cuts on the playing side. In future the squad would no longer stay overnight at a hotel before home matches. No overseas tours would be made unless the match fees covered the trip's total expenses. The professional squad of players would be reduced, along with scouts and coaches. And the United fourth XI – the B team – would be abolished.

In the months ahead Sexton raised only £90,000 from selling Chris McGrath to Tulsa Roughnecks and Steve Paterson to Sheffield United, just a fraction of what Edwards demanded – and Paterson's £60,000 fee later had to be paid back for medical reasons. Moreover, Garry Birtles found it impossible to score even one league goal by the end of the season. His goal in the FA Cup at Brighton gave a new meaning to the chant 'There's only one Garry Birtles'. Andy Ritchie, in contrast, scored three goals for Brighton against United in four matches that year. United fans joked that when the American hostages were finally released from Iran, their first question would be, 'Has Garry Birtles scored for United yet?'

At one point United went for five consecutive league games without a goal – a club record. The team also drew a record eighteen matches during that campaign – eight of them no-score draws, and eleven at home. It was extremely frustrating for the Old Trafford faithful, and the football was pretty unattractive. By February 1981 it did not look as if Sexton could last much longer.

The manager was asked to explain the team's highly

disappointing form before the directors. Martin Edwards quoted to him letters from supporters complaining about United's boring style and bad public relations. The directors even approached David Meek, the *Manchester Evening News* reporter, for advice on creating a better rapport with the press and public. Several journalists had complained of United's unfriendly treatment and of how Dave Sexton would not even give out his home phone number. The frosty reception at Old Trafford contrasted strongly with the warm atmosphere at Maine Road. Martin Edwards tried to soothe feelings by meeting the local branch of the National Union of Journalists.

What probably gave Dave Sexton a reprieve was a gentlemen's agreement among league chairmen reached on 9 February 1981, right in the middle of United's worst spell. Many clubs had suffered severe disruption from managerial changes in the middle of a season, with knock-on effects on a string of teams. It was agreed that in future chairmen would not poach each other's managers during the season. Martin Edwards had probably already decided to get rid of Sexton, but had he sacked him then it would have been impossible to find a replacement without breaking the no-poaching agreement almost straight away, or going outside the league. If United wanted a top-class successor to Sexton – and Edwards had Lawrie McMenemy of Southampton in mind – there was little to lose by waiting until the campaign was over.

To Edwards' eventual embarrassment, Sexton ended the 1980–81 season with seven victories in a row, a club record not achieved before or since. He was just two votes away from winning the Manager of the Month award. Yet five days after the final game, Sexton was axed.

Edwards dismissed him because of fans' complaints about United's failure to entertain. 'I felt we'd gone backwards,' said the chairman. 'It was having an effect on gates.' Average home crowds were down by 6,500 on the previous season. Without doubt another reason was Sexton's failure to understand the new financial atmosphere within the club. The £1.25 million spent on Garry Birtles was looking like a waste of money, and Sexton had not managed to recover it.

Of the six directors, Sir Matt Busby is known to have opposed the sacking. Perhaps it was because Sexton had been his recommendation. Busby felt that, because of the bad injuries the previous season and the winning run towards the end, Sexton deserved another year.

But Sexton also suffered from a team of good publicists at Maine Road. City had reappointed Malcolm Allison as their manager in 1979 and then replaced him with John Bond a year later. Whatever their failings with the team, both men were great promoters for the light blues. Similarly, Martin Edwards was himself outshone by the City chairman, Peter Swales, who would go to great lengths to publicise his club. Edwards remarked that United fans were fed up with the sports page headlines about City: 'We want a good publicist who can communicate with our supporters – a man with very special qualities.'

Dave Sexton was probably the first United manager since the war to be sacked for commercial reasons. Wilf McGuinness and Frank O'Farrell had been dismissed while their teams were facing relegation. Docherty had been sacked because of a love affair and his personal financial dealings. Sexton went because he endangered the club's profitability.

In 1979 the Annual General Meeting had agreed its first annual dividend since the rights issue. A payment of 5 per cent per share meant a total pay-out of £50,419, compared with a bill of just £321 from a 5 per cent dividend the year before, and indeed similar figures virtually every year since the late 1940s. Dividends of just over £50,000 were paid out again in 1980 and 1981, and holding the majority of shares, Martin Edwards and his relations got a total return in those three years of more than £80,000. Already the rights issue was producing much the effect that Les Olive had predicted. Such dividends in football were then unique: other clubs rarely paid any dividend, partly because so few of them ever made a profit, but largely because most football directors felt that any profit should be channelled back into the team. If other clubs ever did grant a dividend, it added up to only a few hundred pounds – much the same level United's once were. However, Martin Edwards still owed hundreds of thousands of pounds to his bank. To pay off that debt he either had to push up the price of shares by making the business more profitable, or earn more direct returns through his own salary and dividends.

Edwards was also determined to bring sympathetic new blood on to his board. Apart from himself and James Gulliver, every other director – Alan Gibson, Bill Young, Denzil Haroun and Sir Matt Busby – was beyond retirement age. In June 1981 Edwards proposed that his younger brother, Roger, then only twenty-seven, be elected too. The directors readily agreed, but they were not so keen on Edwards' second proposed co-option, Mike Edelson, the Manchester businessman who had bought 15,000 of Edwards' United shares immediately after the rights issue. Edelson, who came from a family of City supporters, had been on the playing staff of Stoke City and Oldham Athletic in the 1960s, but his career had been cut short by a broken leg and he never made either first team. Since then he had taken over his father's multi-million pound fur business in north Manchester, which in 1981 had paid him more than £127,000. Sir Matt Busby opposed the election of Edelson, but this time went along with Roger Edwards. However, for the United president both proposals were yet another sign of the meat family's tightening grip.

When Martin Edwards proposed Mike Edelson again more than a year later, in August 1982, Sir Matt Busby announced that he wished to retire from the board for 'personal and domestic reasons'. Busby was now seventy-three and neither he nor his wife Jean were well. He had suffered a cerebral haemorrhage the year before, while Lady Busby was now permanently in a nursing home. But the main reason was Busby's unhappiness at the way in which the club was now being run. It was no coincidence that his resignation came up around the same time that the latest

Edwards' nominee was being put forward to the board, and around the moment that Edwards' salary was increased again, to £40,000. In fact Edelson's election was deferred again and he did not become a director until four months afterwards.

Later Edwards moved to clear the rest of the old guard from the board, directors he felt were unsuited to the increasingly commercial world of modern football. In June 1984 Edwards persuaded vice-chairman Alan Gibson, who had served on the board since 1948, and Bill Young, a director since 1960, to resign. As compensation, Edwards explained, they would be made vice-presidents below Sir Matt Busby, who had remained club president after leaving the boardroom.

In their place were elected two younger men. Maurice Watkins was a solicitor with James Chapman and Co., the firm which advised United. Watkins had himself been legal adviser to the club since the Docherty affair in 1977. In time he had also become solicitor to Martin Edwards. Having grown up in Manchester, Watkins had previously worked for the Pilkington glass company and had supported United all his life. He agreed to buy 50,000 shares from Roger Edwards.

The other 'younger' man, though he was soon the oldest member of the United board, was the former club captain and England star Bobby Charlton. After leaving Old Trafford in 1973, Charlton had an undistinguished spell as manager of Preston North End, and later, while serving as a director of Wigan Athletic, had briefly stood in as the Lancashire club's caretaker manager. But he had enjoyed slightly greater success in helping build up several businesses – in travel, providing hampers and jewellery, and in running soccer schools in Britain, the United States, Canada, Australia and even China. Later Charlton was also involved with an organisation called Mundimex which arranged trips for supporters to the Mexico World Cup, but the venture failed to make any money. However, Martin Edwards needed Bobby Charlton as a name on the board

after the resignation of Sir Matt Busby, and for his football
experience rather than for any business ability. Unlike most
other board members elected since the rights issue,
Charlton did not have to buy a large shareholding through
the Edwards family. In time United managers would find
that Charlton was a strong influence on Edwards when it
came to football decisions.

Martin Edwards was soon making an impact in the higher
levels of English soccer. He was among a group of chairmen
of leading clubs who were pressing for changes which would
make football more commercially minded. They wanted a
smaller league and a slimmer first division to stop the
smaller clubs living off the bigger ones, as they saw it.
Other demands were that clubs should be allowed to keep
all home gate receipts, a reduction in the 75 per cent
majority required at Football League meetings, and a better
contract with the TV companies. At one point, around 1982
and 1983, Edwards was among those chairmen threatening
to form a breakaway super league of the top clubs if football
did not mend its ways. 'The danger is that if the present
situation persists,' he warned, 'there will be no alternative.'

With no dividends since 1981 Martin Edwards was seek-
ing some way to repay the debts he had built up in buying
his stake in United. He had been impressed by the recent
decision of Tottenham Hotspur to float the club on the
stock exchange in 1983. This flotation had valued the assets
of the North London club at more than £9 million. Edwards
was convinced that United must be worth more than that,
and as the owner of 70 per cent of the shares, he was
determined to see if there was any way in which he could
get his hands on some of that value.

Yet the current United share price was only about £3.
With just over a million shares in all, this valued the whole
club at only £3 million. The problem for Edwards was that
there was no proper market in United shares. The only
people interested in buying them were a few hundred supporters who generally wanted them only for sentimental
reasons. Shares could be bought only through one or two

Manchester stockbrokers, such as Joe Stephens and Derek Wall, and even then people who wanted to buy them had to wait until somebody wanted to sell. But if a free, competitive market were established in United shares, Edwards felt that his holding would greatly appreciate in value.

The 3.8 million extra shares that Spurs had issued in football's first stock market flotation in September 1983 had sold out within minutes of coming on to the market. After that the price had initially risen above the opening £1 mark. The operation had made Tottenham's existing shareholders much richer, and in particular Irving Scholar and Paul Bobroff who had bought a majority for just £600,000. It had also raised nearly £3.5 million for the club to spend as it saw fit.

In late 1983 Edwards and his solicitor, Maurice Watkins, arranged for Kleinwort Benson, the merchant bank that had supervised the 1978 rights issue, to investigate the possibility of United taking a public share listing like Tottenham's. They considered both a full listing, like Spurs', and a much simpler listing on the Unlisted Securities Market (USM). A USM listing had in fact already been considered briefly in December 1981, but rejected as being too costly. Yet with a proper market in the shares, prices could more exactly reflect the total assets of the company, the regular annual profit figures and the team's prospects, which after the 1983 FA Cup win against Brighton were looking good.

Kleinwort Benson examined the Spurs flotation and on that basis tentatively valued Manchester United at between £6 million and £8 million. The difference between United and Tottenham was accounted for by the fact that the London club had more than £2 million worth of land at their Cheshunt training ground. Kleinwort's valuation must have been somewhat disappointing to Martin Edwards. Even so, if the club could be floated at a total value of £8 million – including the issue of £1.5 million worth of new shares – existing shares would be valued at £6.50 or so each. Between them his family might then make £500,000 without having to give up control. But if the family were prepared to reduce their share to 40 per cent and take the risk of losing control, it might be possible to make more than £1 million.

Before Edwards could proceed further with the idea, however, he had an even better prospect – a bid to buy United from the multi-millionaire publisher Robert Maxwell. At the time Maxwell's own club, Oxford United, were only in the third division, with division one still a long way off. It was well known that Maxwell had other football ambitions, and in particular was eager to acquire a first-division team. Martin Edwards' version of events is that a gentleman came to see him one afternoon in January 1984 and said that a bid of £10 million was on its way. Then Maxwell phoned in person and, without mentioning money, fixed a meeting in London for two weeks ahead.

It seems that one person acting as a middleman was Andrew McHutchon, a businessman based in North Yorkshire, who specialised at that time in buying football clubs. Later the Football League banned McHutchon from any involvement in clubs after his work for the notorious Anton Johnson, who had acquired control of three different league sides. McHutchon put out feelers towards United in the middle of 1983, well before Maxwell's bid became public, through the former United goalkeeper Harry Gregg.

Once in contact with each other, however, Edwards and Maxwell appointed as their go-between Professor Roland Smith, the man who advised the Edwards family on the 1978 rights issue and who also had one of the expensive table seats in the Executive Suite at Old Trafford. The publisher never seemed short of money and might have been the answer to the Edwards' money worries – problems which were illustrated by the United chairman's comment at the time: 'I was going to have to do something about my financial situation very soon anyway. The involvement of my brother, Roger, and I in the rights issue five years ago was very costly. . . . We are still very heavily committed at the bank and need to improve our position. So there was going to have to be some kind of flotation in the near future.'

The news that 'somebody' was bidding for United quickly became public through Derek Potter in the *Daily Express* on 1 February 1984. Having been tipped off about the proposed deal, Potter had a private meeting with Edwards before publishing. A figure of £10 million was soon mentioned in the papers. It was another week, however, before Maxwell's name became firm, but there is no evidence that the publisher ever offered this sum. It would have been a rash thing to do straight away for, unlike his Oxford United team, Maxwell claimed to see Manchester United as a financial opportunity. 'I am not a member of the Salvation Army. Football clubs can be a commercial proposition, yielding 10 per cent a year,' he argued.

As might be expected, Maxwell arranged for his own advisers, the accountants Coopers and Lybrand, to look closely at United's finances and make their own serious assessment of what the club was worth. United gave them several years' annual accounts and valuers' reports on the club's properties. But Maxwell's interest soon aroused considerable opposition from ordinary United supporters. An offer to match any Maxwell bid soon emerged from a consortium of wealthy Manchester businessmen, United season-ticket holders and share-holders, led by Peter Raymond who worked for an American chemicals company. Martin Edwards' comment that 'we will listen to any genuine offers as long as the parties prove themselves *bona fide*' seemed to indicate that his interest in Maxwell's approach was more than simple curiosity.

On the morning before meeting Maxwell for lunch in London, Edwards met James Gulliver at the Savoy Hotel and then went with his solicitor, Maurice Watkins, to see Kleinwort Benson in the City. The United men presumably wanted to know if there was any way of increasing the low valuation the bankers had put on the club. Edwards and Watkins then spent two and a half hours with Maxwell over lunch at his London offices. The United chairman

reportedly asked Maxwell for £15 a share, a total valuation
for the whole club of £15 million. It is not known how
much Maxwell was prepared to offer, but it seems unlikely
that his own advisers would have valued the club at much
more than £8 million. Given his stated desire to run United
on a commercial basis, he probably offered a lot less than
the widely quoted £10 million, if indeed he made an offer
at all.

For the United chairman to have taken less than £10
million, though, after all the speculation in the press, would
have made him look silly. Maxwell publicly stated that he
was not prepared to haggle over the price of an institution
like United. One report has it that the publisher was rather
annoyed by Ron Atkinson's comment on television after
United's 5–0 victory at Luton the day before, that each
goal would increase United's price by £1 million.

Edwards rang Peter Raymond to say that he was now no
longer interested in selling his stake in the club to anybody.
But the idea of a public flotation was still pursued for
several months. Kleinwort Benson eventually concluded
that if the club were floated like Spurs, Martin Edwards
would gain very little if he wanted to retain a 50 per cent
shareholding.

From then on Martin Edwards had to concentrate on
other means to reduce and service his large bank overdraft.
Fortunately for him, Football Association regulations had
eased the limits on the dividends clubs could pay – to 15
per cent of capital per year, so United could now pay out
annual dividends of £150,000. The club made a record
profit of £1,731,000 in the year to 1984, and the directors
proposed just such a 15 per cent dividend to the Annual
General Meeting that November. It produced a total pay-
out to shareholders of £151,284 – three times greater than
any previous United dividend, and by far a record pay-out
for a football club. Martin Edwards received £77,319 of
that money. Les Olive cannot have failed to notice that the
sum was in fact a few hundred pounds *more* than the figure

e had warned about six years earlier, only his prediction
ad probably come true even sooner than he had feared.

As for Robert Maxwell, his interest turned towards
uying the *Daily Mirror*. Subsequently he boosted his foot-
all assets by purchasing Derby County, and in 1987 he
nsuccessfully tried to buy Watford from Elton John.
hortly afterwards Maxwell was linked with a 5 per cent
hareholding in United owned by a mysterious nominee
ompany, Lancashire & Yorkshire Nominees Ltd. Rumour
ad it that Maxwell owned the shares. This seems unlikely
ince the company is represented by Biddle and Co., solici-
ors who acted *against* Maxwell in his recent attempts to
top publication of a biography of him. Furthermore, it
eemed unlikely that Robert Maxwell was about to launch
nother bid for the club, because 20,500 United shares that
Maxwell definitely did own, through his company Publish-
ng and Databank Consultants Ltd, were sold between 1986
nd 1987.

The only arrangement Martin Edwards ever did strike
vith Robert Maxwell involved the publisher's helicopter.
After buying the Mirror Group, he made several flying
isits to his newspapers' print plant in Manchester. There
vas no available landing site in the centre of the city, so
United agreed to let Maxwell land on the No. 1 car-park
pposite the ground – an area which, it so happened, was
ne of those property assets Edwards had hoped might
nake United more financially attractive to wealthy inves-
ors.

9
Chief Executive

'Should the United get into the first League they
will speedily become one of the richest and most
powerful clubs in the competition.'

The Book of Football, 1906.

His £65,000 suite of offices high above the entrance t
United's ground overlooks the Manchester to Liverpoo
railway. On the corner of the building a sitting-room is fo
relaxation and entertaining visitors. It is furnished wit
luxurious white leather arm-chairs, a matching convertibl
two-seat sofa, chrome and glass occasional tables, large po
plants, and mirrors stretching from floor to ceiling an
concealing a television, video recorder and drinks cabinet

The main office next door, again fitted out with furnitur
imported from Italy, is dominated by a large desk and, t
one side, a highly polished conference table for holdin
business meetings. A glass bookcase holds volumes o
United programmes dating back to the war, together wit
virtually every book that has ever been written about th
club. Along one wall, blinds open to reveal a window look
ing out on to the Old Trafford pitch and the inside of th
stadium. Next to this window hangs a portrait of the ma
simply referred to as 'father': Louis Edwards, the chairma
whose ambition created this office, but who did not liv
long enough to enjoy it. And, symbolically perhaps, behin

the picture is a safe. Just inside the office, a side door opens on to a bathroom – with a personal WC, wash-basin and a shower unit. The distinctive United crest is embroidered on each of the red towels.

On the ground level below, next to the entrance to United's Red Devil Grill and the Trafford suite, electronically controlled shutters conceal a double garage. Inside is housed a gleaming company car. The driver, Martin Edwards, enjoys a very different life-style from the directors and part-time chairmen who presided at Old Trafford in the days when it had only tiny offices and big debts.

The £95,781-a-year chairman and chief executive of Manchester United Football Club runs a business that had a turnover of more than £9 million in the year ending July 1989. His 160 or so employees include some of the highest-paid sportsmen in Britain; three of them, Bryan Robson, Mark Hughes and Brian McClair, reputedly earn more than £100,000 a year. His football ground is not just host to the million or so people who come annually through the turnstiles. Its directors' box, private boxes, executive suites and window tables are occupied by top businessmen such as Professor Roland Smith and James Gulliver, and former Cabinet ministers such as Stan Orme, the Salford MP, and Lord Barnett, deputy chairman of the BBC.

Martin Edwards stands at the centre of one of the most famous institutions in the sporting world. Around him is a complex interlocking network of businessmen and financial deals that have made him a paper-millionaire. The duties of the chief executive of Manchester United are far more glamorous and rewarding than those he once had liaising with Woolworth's store managers in the £11,000-a-year management job in his family meat business.

The man who enabled Edwards' transformation from meat-firm divisional managing director to football tycoon is James Gulliver, a businessman of international stature who had himself risen rapidly during the early 1980s. Both men are children of the Thatcher years, whose rise to power has coincided with the Conservative prime minister's period of office. Like many businessmen of the 1980s they seemed to know more about making money multiply on paper than producing concrete achievements. Yet James Gulliver resigned from the United board in the autumn of 1985, just as his Argyll Group was about to mount its famous and unsuccessful bid for Distillers. The intense scale of his other business activities, and the fact he was now based in the South of England, meant that Gulliver had little time for United matches or board meetings. During his six years on the board Gulliver managed to attend only about a third of the meetings, even though they were monthly not weekly. The Scotsman nevertheless suggested to Martin Edwards that he might like to sell most of his shareholding to him, while carrying on in the job of chairman and chief executive. Gulliver insisted that he himself was not interested in becoming chairman.

Gulliver's offer was rejected, and instead he agreed to sell his 102,000 shares back to Edwards, or rather to Edwards' wife Susan, at £4.05 each. It was not one of Gulliver's most profitable deals, the price being just £1 more than he had paid the Edwards family for the shares six years before: allowing for inflation, they had dropped in price. Part of the arrangement was that Gulliver would be a vice-president of the club, in the same way Alan Gibson and Bill Young had become.

The food tycoon's resignation from the board may partly have been prompted by unhappiness at the way the club was being run, in particular over Ron Atkinson's commercial dealings. 'I think Ron Atkinson's been a good buyer,' Gulliver told *Business* magazine shortly after his resignation, 'but he's a man with no knowledge of the use of money. He's got a blinkered approach. . . . I think he's quite a talented manager, but he needs controlling. . . . I think Mr Edwards has got some toughness, but he's just not able, for various reasons, to handle Ron Atkinson.' Gulliver wrote to apologise to Martin Edwards afterwards, saying that the quotes were highly selective and that he denied having any misgivings.

Martin Edwards admits that he failed to get as much out of James Gulliver's presence as he and his father had hoped when they invited him on to the United board. Above all, the businessman had failed to find a way of creating a fluid market for United shares that would help the Edwards family make money by selling some of their holding. The process of replacing Gulliver on the board, and disposing of his own former shareholding, took Martin Edwards several months.

Earlier in 1985 Edwards had come into conflict with a local twenty-seven-year-old Arab businessman called Amer Mouaffac Al Midani. The cause of the trouble was Edwards' decision to purchase the Warrington Vikings Basketball Club, an episode described in Chapter 12 of this book. Midani was the owner of the rival Manchester Giants team, but the conflict soon turned to an agreement to merge the two basketball sides. Martin Edwards and Amer Midani became good friends and, in time, business allies.

Though he was brought up in war-torn Beirut, where he claims to have been the Lebanese junior table-tennis champion, Amer Midani actually carried a Saudi Arabian passport until he took out British citizenship in 1985. Midani studied at Stockport College of Technology, and in 1978 attended a part-time course at Manchester Business School.

The key point about Amer Midani is his father, Mouaffac Al Midani, one of the richest men in the world. A Syrian who made his money in textiles, Midani senior later took Saudi citizenship, and now owns a series of franchises in electricity and telecommunications in Saudi Arabia. He caused a great stir in Britain in the late 1970s when he led an Arab consortium which bought the Dorchester Hotel – they later sold it in 1985.

Mouaffac Midani tries to avoid any publicity, but enjoys powerful political connections. When Ronald and Nancy Reagan returned to California in early 1989 after eight years in the White House, the official 200-guest 'welcome home' party was not hosted by any of the wealthy west coast millionaires who had backed Reagan's political career, but by Mouaffac Al Midani. The celebrations took place at the Arab's secluded nine-acre estate in Beverly hills, where his mansion had recently undergone a $40 million renovation. The evening was said to be an extravagant affair, even by the standards of Ronald and Nancy Reagan.

That Midani should have hosted the party surprised many close to the couple, but Midani senior had enjoyed close relations with the Reagan White House. In 1986 he presented the First Lady with a personal cheque for her anti-drugs campaign. It was made out for one million dollars.

Amer Midani, assisted by a small share of his father's money, set up a string of companies in the North-west in the early 1980s, operating in various fields. As well as the Giants basketball club, he was involved in property, travel and even racehorses.

Midani's companies belong to one parent body, the AMM Group of Companies Ltd. Until recently this was itself owned by a parent company in Amsterdam, called AMM Development bv, which was believed to belong to Midani's wealthy father. But, judging from their annual reports, none of Amer Midani's British firms shows any sign of the 'highly successful business career' Martin Edwards wrote about in 1987. The AMM Group lost between £320,000 and £390,000 in each of the four years between 1984 and 1987 and £124,000 in 1987–8.

In May 1986, around the time he agreed to merge the Manchester Giants basketball club with United, Midani agreed to buy 100,682 of the Manchester United shares James Gulliver had sold back to Susan Edwards. In fact they were actually purchased by an organisation based in Lichtenstein called the Philen Establishment. This organisation again belongs to Midani's wealthy father, and Amer Midani is described as the firm's British representative. The Philen Establishment's only known UK address is 73 South Audley Street, London W1, at the rear of the Dorchester Hotel in Mayfair, the offices of Gibson, Dunn and Crutcher,

Midani's American firm of solicitors. The 100,682 shares represented precisely 10 per cent of United's share capital. The price was £700,000, and so Susan Edwards made a profit of almost £300,000 in the six months since buying the stock from Gulliver.

Amer Midani was not actually elected to the Manchester United board until February 1987, some months later. (Coincidentally he was replacing a director, Denzil Haroun, who died in 1985, who also had Syrian ancestry and a background in textiles.) But Midani's share ownership did not become publicly known until Martin Edwards revealed it in answer to a query about the Philen Establishment at the Annual General Meeting in December 1987, eighteen months after the deal with Midani had been agreed. No mention had been made in the 1987 accounts of this link between Midani and the Philen Establishment.

For those who knew him well, Midani's sudden involvement with one of the world's great football clubs came as something of a surprise. Until then he had shown little interest in the game. Midani owns a house in Bramhall, but spends much of the year abroad and visits Manchester irregularly. He has a home in Geneva, and often stays at one of the two luxury sporting hotels his family own in Marbella in Spain – the Puente Romano and the Marbella Club both of which are members of the leading Hotels of the World group.

Midani is also well liked by the players, many of whom have visited the Marbella Club. In the summer of 1988 Martin Edwards was also a guest at the Midani Hotels during the period when Tottenham Hotspur clinched the transfer of Paul Gascoigne.

Bobby Charlton's election to the United board in June 1984 was portrayed as an attempt to improve the club's public relations. It was an area which Martin Edwards had always found difficult, particularly since the resignation of Sir Matt Busby two years earlier, and Edwards felt that his manager Ron Atkinson did not always project the right kind of image for the club. Since then Charlton's influence at Old Trafford has been stronger over playing matters than that of any of the other directors, including at times Edwards himself. The United chairman has been known to defer to Charlton's judgement on issues such as player transfers, and Charlton reportedly had an important role in Atkinson's eventual sacking in 1986. The former United captain was also behind the appointment in 1988 of Manchester Polytechnic lecturer Les Kershaw as chief scout to replace Tony Collins. Charlton's major business interest, of course, is his soccer coaching school, and the tour facilities of Old Trafford are used extensively by the school's weekly batches of summer pupils.

Roger Edwards resigned from the United board in February 1985, after less than four years as a director, and was made a Vice-President of the club. He sold his United shares and decided that with that money, together with the proceeds from his Argyll shares, he was now rich enough to emigrate to Majorca and live in semi-retirement as a tax exile. Roger Edwards' own businesses had not been particularly successful, in spite of help from United. His company, Dawn Print Ltd, produced leaflets for the club Development Association, but according to the accounts the business never made much profit.

Martin Edwards arranged to sell 50,500 of Roger Edwards' United shares to an accountant with Price Waterhouse, Oscar Goldstein. It was much the same kind of arrangement that had been struck with the solicitor Maurice Watkins. Like Watkins, Goldstein was not only an adviser to United, but was also employed in a personal capacity by Martin Edwards and became a close friend. Like Watkins, Goldstein was promised a seat on the United board, but the accountant's purchase agreement with Edwards in 1984 also included an arrangement that he could become United's company secretary when Les Olive eventually retired. Goldstein was given two seats in the directors' box in 1984, and he began to accompany the team on foreign tours.

However, the deal was never carried through. In September 1985 Oscar Goldstein pleaded guilty in a Manchester court to falsifying an Inland Revenue form. He was accused of setting up a ring of friends who had all made deeds of covenant to each other in order to cheat the Inland Revenue of hundreds of pounds in tax. Goldstein had originally told the tax men that the deeds had not been made as part of a reciprocal agreement. He was fined £1,000 by the court and subsequently expelled from the Institute of Chartered Accountants. Goldstein had resigned from Price Waterhouse only a few weeks earlier, presumably in anticipation of the court case, and set up in business on his own as a tax adviser. Though Edwards now felt unable to install Goldstein in the United boardroom, the former accountant continued to advise both Edwards and United about tax matters.

A much more recent recruit to the board has been Nigel Burrows, elected in June 1988. Like Mike Edelson, Maurice Watkins, Oscar Goldstein and Amer Midani, the deal was that Burrows would earn his directorship by first buying a substantial shareholding. The 50,000 shares Burrows says he bought were those previously held by Oscar Goldstein. When it was clear that Goldstein would not become secretary on Les Olive's retirement in 1988, he took advantage of a clause in his original share purchase contract whereby Edwards had to buy Goldstein's shares back for a minimum of £3 each. It appears, however, that the price Edwards subsequently received from Burrows for the returned shares was more than £5 each. Certainly it was widely known for some time in Manchester that 50,000 surplus shares had been offered to a select group of United's wealthy supporters for £250,000. And the carrot to buy was a place on the United board. Whether Goldstein received any more than the minimum £3 per share is not clear.

Burrows was only thirty-four when he joined the board. He is the co-founder and director of Analysis Financial Services, a firm based in Harrogate, Yorkshire, and now taken over by the British and Commonwealth Group for whom he is employed on a three-year consultancy fee.

Martin Edwards came into contact with him as a member of United's Executive Suite, and a regular patron of the club's Luncheon Club, which has operated since 1986. The two men had been negotiating their deal since late 1987. Since then Burrows has arranged to take over the name and operations of Delta Sports, the company which used to organise United's corporate hospitality. Burrows claims to be a former Stretford Ender, and described his election to the board as a 'dream come true'.

Being a United director in the late 1980s is a very different proposition from what it was in times gone by. In 1902 United's four new directors had to pay £500 each to save the club – a considerable sum at that time – and the United president, J. H. Davies, donated £3,000 of his own money for new players. Again, in the 1930s, the club had been saved by funds from the pocket of its latest president, James Gibson. Under FA rules clubs were not allowed to pay directors until 1981, when one paid board-member was allowed for the first time – Edwards, of course, in United's case.

The rewards of being a director come not only from the substantial business contacts one meets at such a large club, but also through generous expenses. United directors get these while carrying out club business, such as attending matches, when in reality of course they are simply furthering their hobby. In 1984 directors' allowances to away matches were as follows: first-class fare and cost of taxis; or if travelling by car 28p per mile up to a maximum of £70; meals if not eaten at the team hotel, £20 for dinner and £15 for lunch; an overnight allowance to cover drinks etc. of £15; and an additional allowance of £15 to cover drinks etc. when attending functions.

Since 1984 the expenses have almost certainly been increased. The mileage allowance is now 30p, for example. Directors also get a £20 per day expense allowance while on foreign tours. United fans who spend several pounds on coach and rail fares travelling to Old Trafford, and another £3.50 to stand on the Stretford End, may be surprised to learn that some of the wealthy businessmen who serve as United directors actually claim mileage for games at Old Trafford.

After becoming chairman in 1980, Martin Edwards continued to pursue outside business interests. Not only did he remain a director of Argyll Foods until November 1983, but there were other activities too. For instance, he served for several years on the board of Russ Evans Contracting Ltd, a company managed by a Manchester businessman, Ernie Kearns, but which has since gone into liquidation. Much more lucrative was a relationship Edwards began with a firm called Exclusive Cleaning in 1980. Exclusive was the name of several companies, in fact, a part of the multi-million-pound Brengreen Holdings built up by David Evans. Evans, once a reserve player with Aston Villa FC, is also a former Gloucestershire county cricketer, and in 1980 had just recently been elected a director of Luton Town where he later became chairman. He was also embarking on a career in Conservative politics that saw him serve as a councillor, make rousing speeches at the Tory Party conference and in 1987 secure election as a Conservative MP.

In the summer of 1980 Martin Edwards became a non-executive director of David Evans' firm, Exclusive Cleaning and Maintenance Ltd. It was a period when Edwards had no full-time job, and Evans agreed to pay him an annual retainer, an arrangement which lasted until 1985. According to sources inside the company, part of the deal was that Edwards would get commission on all business that he introduced to Photravel Ltd, an Exclusive subsidiary which Manchester United had already been using for some years for most of its club travel.

Photravel's agent, Peter Johnson, the man United usually dealt with, left the company in 1981 to set up his own travel business. At first the United directors voted to move with Peter Johnson, as they felt his service had proved to be 'very satisfactory' in the past. In the following month, February 1982, however, the board changed their minds

and agreed that Exclusive could carry on tendering for
United's travel.

Martin Edwards also earned commission on cleaning
work he introduced to Exclusive. Among his lucrative contacts and contracts were Greenall Whitley, the brewers,
Rackham's stores in Leicester and Sheffield, and various
branches of both the Midland Bank and the Abbey National
Building Society in Manchester and Cheshire. Quite how
Edwards went about setting up cleaning contracts for individual building society and bank branches is not clear.

It was a very rewarding sideline for the United chairman.
The man who generally liaised with Martin Edwards was
the general manager of Exclusive's northern division,
Danny McGregor. McGregor, it so happens, had played as
a centre-forward in the mid-1950s for United's junior teams
and had later appeared briefly for Accrington Stanley before
the club folded in 1962. McGregor even sent Martin
Edwards a commission payment for work that Exclusive
had carried out for United at Old Trafford. So Edwards
was actually getting a percentage of the money on work he
himself was ultimately responsible for commissioning for
the club. United's annual reports regularly state: 'No director, either during or at the end of the Financial Period, was
materially interested in any contract that was significant in
relation to the Group's business.' Clearly United's Exclusive
cleaning and travel business cannot have been considered
'significant'.

In July 1985 Martin Edwards advised the United board
that the commercial manager at Old Trafford, John Lillie,
should be given notice to terminate his contract. Some
United directors had been unhappy for some time with
Lillie's work, which he combined with running his own
business, and it had long been clear that he might have to
go. Lillie's replacement as commercial manager turned out
to be a former United junior player by the name of Danny
McGregor.

Today, from his office at the front of the new administration block, McGregor hustles and haggles for new busi-

ss for United. The contacts and methods he built up er the years as managing director of Exclusive's northern mpany provide excellent background for this work. ithin United, McGregor is a powerful figure. Yet in an rangement even more extraordinary than the deal dwards once had with Exclusive, McGregor was allowed have an outside arrangement with an organisation called e Delta Group which earned him at least another £600 a onth. What is particularly strange about the arrangement that Delta were responsible for selling advertising space ound the ground, and until 1988 also arranged United's rporate hospitality packages.

For Martin Edwards, much more important than outside rectorships and commissions are his substantial invest-ents on top of his majority stake in Manchester United. hese include both large shareholdings and property. He wns a luxury flat in Marlborough Road, Sale, which he ught in 1981, and property in Florida in the United tates, near to where both his sister, Catherine, and his ncle, Douglas Edwards, now live.

Most of Martin Edwards' share investments were for any years handled by a Manchester securities dealer called icholas Baldwin, who lives in the same road as the United airman – Oak Road in Mottram St Andrew, a pretty llage near Wilmslow. In 1985 Baldwin's firm, Harrison aldwin, ran into considerable financial difficulties, but he anaged to conceal these from Edwards and his other cli-ts. By the middle of 1987 Harrison Baldwin was £1 illion in debt, and Black Tuesday in October 1987 finally nt the company over the edge. Harrison Baldwin went to liquidation in January 1988 with debts of around £4 illion. Of that, the Edwards family accounted for more an £500,000 between them. Martin Edwards was owed nly £33,000 of the total, but his mother, Muriel, was wed £383,000 and the trustees of Louis Edwards a further 136,000. Martin Edwards might eventually have expected inherit a third of the last two amounts.

Since his appointment as chief executive in 1981 on a

salary of £30,000 a year, Martin Edwards' income from
United has risen rapidly. In 1985–86 he was taking £75,46
and by 1988–89 this had steadily risen to £95,781.

By July 1989 Edwards had been paid £535,000 by th
club in the previous six and a half years. The paymen
included annual bonus awards, which were decide
officially by the United directors. In 1983 the bonus wa
agreed as 2 per cent of the previous year's profits – £12,70
In 1985 it was agreed that half the bonus would b
accounted for by 1 per cent of whatever profits were mad
on transfer dealings. When this provision became public
known, there was an outcry. It was argued that Edward
had a direct interest in selling players and not buying then
and the awarding of a bonus on transfer profits wa
dropped.

But Martin Edwards' remuneration has continued t
include a bonus award, fixed by the directors each year. I
1986 the bonus was £25,000 but because of the earli
revelation relating to transfer profits, the awarding of
bonus was a sensitive matter. The ideal solution, of cours
would be for Edwards' earnings to be lumped together a
an aggregate salary. Possibly because of the fear that th
would be seen as a massive percentage increase of aroun
50 per cent, United still appear to be saddled with th
bonus problem. At the annual general meetings of 198
and 1988, the United chairman stated that his salary ha
only increased in line with inflation and at the same rate a
the income of his staff – around five to six per cent.

On top of his salary and bonuses, Edwards has benefite
from the large dividend payments over recent years. The
were dividends of £50,432 in 1979, 1980 and 1981. Ther
after two years with no dividend, he proposed a payme
of £151,284 in 1983 and it was followed by dividends
£100,424 in 1985 and £100,464 in 1987. Altogether, b
1987 the 1978 rights issue had cost around £500,000 i
extra dividend payments. Of that Martin Edwards had bee
paid £233,684, and his family, of course, many thousand
of pounds more.

Some shareholders had argued that the 1987 dividend payment, which cost £100,464, was in fact issued illegally, against the expressed wishes of the 1987 Annual General Meeting. When Edwards put the proposed dividend to a vote, it was rejected overwhelmingly on a show of hands. Edwards then said that he wanted the matter put to a poll whereby votes are assessed according to shareholdings. At that point a shareholder declared that a poll would be unproductive since everybody knew that the dividend would inevitably be accepted because of Edwards' controlling shares. The meeting therefore voted overwhelmingly to reject the idea of a poll, but without rescinding the previous decision by a show of hands against a dividend. Amid the confusion the dividend remained unapproved. Yet shareholders received their dividend cheques only a few days later.

One shareholder, a solicitor called Stephen Elder, who had once worked for Amer Midani, even wrote to United pointing out the irregularity and claiming his was a 'serious breach of company legislation'. Elder received a phone call from Maurice Watkins in which the latter stated that his was the only complaint that had been received, and he tried to persuade Elder he was mistaken. Yet several other shareholders recall events at the 1987 AGM in just the same way Elder did. When the matter was raised at the 1988 AGM, the board not only refused to accept a proposition that the details be accurately recorded in the company's minutes book and that the original proposal be put to the meeting again, but Martin Edwards denied that any complaint had been received during the intervening twelve months.

In 1988 no dividend was declared since the club made a loss of £1,296,000. This had been turned into a pre-tax profit of £1,767,000 by 1989, but again no dividend was awarded, possibly because Martin Edwards felt unable to sustain the outcry it would have caused.

In his nine years as United chairman Martin Edwards has used the very size of his own club to become an important figure within English football. Unlike his father and Sir Matt Busby, however, he has never served on the Football League Management Committee, preferring instead to act within an elite group of clubs that have wielded power by their sheer financial muscle. The Big Five, as they refer to themselves – United, Liverpool, Everton, Tottenham Hotspur and Arsenal – accounted for around 20 per cent of league home attendances in 1987–88. Since 1982 representatives of the Big Five have met secretly at regular intervals to plan how to further their own interests. The Five usually get together at the Park Lane Hotel in London's Mayfair before important meetings of the League or negotiations with the television companies.

Martin Edwards is particularly close to the Tottenham Hotspur chief executive, Irving Scholar, one of the men behind the London club's stock exchange flotation in 1983. Scholar and Edwards meet regularly and the United chairman has often visited White Hart Lane to gather new ideas. In 1988 the relationship was such that Tottenham's publishing subsidiary, Cockerel Books, brought out the official club history of European football, *Red Devils in Europe*. And even United's match-ticket computing system is an offshoot of a Spurs subsidiary. The software is supplied by Synchro Systems, a company which is 75 per cent owned by Tottenham.

Over the last eight years the Big Five have successfully pressed for changes in the League's structure that would give them more power and money. This has inevitably been at the expense of the minor sides within the League. 'The smaller clubs are bleeding the game dry,' Martin Edwards argued. 'For the sake of the game they should be put to sleep.' Among the important changes the Five have successfully lobbied for was the decision in 1983 to end the system whereby away teams got a share of league gate receipts. In 1986 all the first-division sides were given greater voting power and at the same time it was agreed that first-division clubs would in future receive 50 per cent of all sponsorship and television money.

Throughout the period the Big Five have not been afraid to apply their ultimate sanction – breaking away to form a 'Super League'. The Liverpool chairman, John Smith, warned of this in 1982. Everton's Philip Carter revealed in 1986 that they had actually carried out a feasibility study. But it was in the summer of 1988 that the Super League warnings by Martin Edwards and his four colleagues from the football elite became most serious. At a meeting of the Big Five at the Park Lane Hotel on 16 June 1988 the clubs' chairmen decided to reject the Football League's arrangements for televised football with the BBC and the new satellite station, BSB (British Satellite Broadcasting). Greg Dyke, director of programmes at London Weekend Television and chairman of the ITV Sports Committee, offered each of the Big Five £1 million every year to allow their games to be televised on ITV. The agreement would run for four years from 1989. This compared with £70,000 they could expect from the proposed deal with the BBC and BSB.

On top of that Dyke wanted to offer five middle-ranking first-division clubs the sum of £2 million to share between them, to join in with the Big Five. The arrangements he proposed would involve twenty live games a season, at least one and a maximum of three from the home ground of each team. Clubs would also receive £50,000 when a match was broadcast live from their ground.

Clause 11 of the ITV proposals was the most explosive. It ran:

> Finally should the ten clubs ever break from the Football League, ITV would be extremely interested in becoming the sponsor of the ITV Super League. We understand this gives you problems with players' contracts but if this could be achieved we think it would be in both your and our interests. In these circumstances it would certainly be in our interests to promote the new League to the best of our ability.

A trawl through the records shows that arguments over

television contracts and Super Leagues are nothing new for
Manchester United. As long ago as 1947, when only a few
thousand people in Britain owned TV sets, the Old Trafford
directors told the League that the question of televising
games was a matter for the whole League, not individual
clubs. A decade later, in 1957, the BBC complained when
United sold the TV rights for the European Cup semi-
final to ITV for £2,500 without offering them to the BBC.
Moreover, the United board had supported the idea of a
Super League of top clubs way back in 1960. The club
wrote to the Conservative MP and former Olympic runner
Chris Chataway when he suggested the idea at the time.

But the proposals to the Big Five in 1988 are the first
signs of the inevitable consequence of the commercialisation
of the national game into a profit-making business designed
to benefit individuals. Martin Edwards came under considerable attack from United supporters in the pages of the
Manchester Evening News and in phone calls to the club.
Edwards and the other Big Five chairmen rapidly had to
backtrack, arguing that it was never their intention to form
a breakaway league. However, the evidence is that they
would have been quite happy to go it alone, and indeed
may well do so yet. The hostility shown by the fans in the
summer of 1988 reveals how these club chairmen could
easily kill, or at least seriously maim, the goose that still
lays many of their clubs' golden eggs – the supporters who
trudge faithfully through the turnstiles.

10

The Building of Old Trafford

'Old Trafford is the only ground where you can walk out to the centre circle when the place is deserted and it still oozes atmosphere.'

Tommy Docherty.

Edgbaston, the famous cricket ground in Birmingham owned by the Warwickshire county side, is not the first place one might expect to find leading officials from a football club, especially in the middle of the soccer season. Yet on the afternoon of Friday, 30 March 1961, the Manchester United chairman, Harold Hardman, along with Louis Edwards, Les Olive and Matt Busby made what proved to be a decisive journey to Warwickshire's home ground. It was a financial visit. They wanted to learn how the men at Edgbaston had, over the previous decade, managed to make so much money. Moreover, they were funds raised not from cricket but, indirectly, from football.

In the early 1950s Warwickshire had realised that the days of great individual cricket patrons, men prepared to subsidise the English county teams, were drawing to a close. The era of company sponsorship, however, had not yet arrived, and the county's officials searched for alternative sources of income. A football pools competition was the answer they came up with, and soon it was producing an annual turnover of more than £500,000 and a yearly profit of £70,000. Warwickshire's army of 4,700 agents looked after a third of a million pools customers, each of whom paid a minimum stake of a shilling a week. With the profits new stands for spectators were erected. Indeed, the ground was improved so much that in 1957 Edgbaston regained its status as a test match venue, after a lapse of twenty-eight years.

Until the 1960s, the finances of English football teams had been fairly simple. Any club knew that its expenditure would be limited by the players' maximum wage of £20 a week. So, according to the number of staff on the books and the level of overheads, it was fairly clear how much any club had to raise every match at the turnstiles. But the 1950s had seen increasing agitation from the Professional Footballers' Association to abolish the maximum wage, a reform that Matt Busby himself supported. By 1960, with footballers under the skilled leadership of Jimmy Hill, it was obvious that limits on players' earnings would not last much longer. Clubs would have to start competing with each other in the money they were prepared to offer. For many clubs it was clear that new sources of income might be needed if they were to stay at the top.

After Munich, Matt Busby and his new director, Louis Edwards, decided that they wanted to develop Old Trafford into the kind of great football stadium they had visited on their Continental travels. Busby's ideal model was a ground at which Manchester United had not in fact played: Barcelona's magnificent Nou Camp stadium in Spain. The United manager admitted at the time, though, that 'we could never pay for it on our gates'.

Five days before Christmas in 1960 the United directors decided to ask the Football Association for permission to run a football pools competition. Without waiting for the FA's reply, they then agreed to go ahead with enquiries: at the following meeting, in January 1961, 'Mr Busby was asked to obtain further information.' Hence the trip to Edgbaston.

Matt Busby and Louis Edwards were keen on copying

the Warwickshire pools scheme, but the United chairman, Harold Hardman, felt uneasy. As a Methodist he thought pools were a form of gambling, and he managed to overcome his doubts only when his colleagues promised to shoulder full responsibility. Les Olive made a second trip to Warwickshire, and United tried to persuade the main organiser of the county's pools, Winnie Crook, to come to Old Trafford. She declined. Instead the club took on her assistant, Bill Burke. A former gas board employee, Burke had started off as one of Warwickshire's collectors only a few years earlier, working part-time on commission before joining the operation full-time. United gave him a three-year contract on £1,500 a year.

In July 1961, equipped with nothing more, he says, than 'paper clips, rubber bands and a bottle of ink', Burke set up in a small office formerly occupied by United's assistant secretary. He saw Manchester United as something of a challenge. Could the kind of sudden transformation he had helped bring about at Warwickshire's ground be repeated? He was exited by the thought that at Manchester United any new stands would be filled every other week, instead of only once a year at Edgbaston, whenever they hosted a test match. Burke became secretary and organiser of the new Manchester United Development Association (MUDA), a body which had its own directors – all chosen from the United board – and which had been set up with the object 'wholly to raise funds for the development of amenities for Manchester United Football Club and support of athletic games'. Legally it was a totally separate organisation.

The new man at Old Trafford simply established a football pool modelled on Warwickshire's. The football club lent him £1,000 to get things going, and it was made clear that the Development Association's finances should be run separately from those of the club. Burke recruited his part-time agents by sending out a letter to members of the supporters' clubs and to all season-ticket holders. Within two years 1,000 United supporters were engaged as agents,

earning commission on stakes they collected from the pool's
20,000 customers. As an incentive, agents were also given
their own regular prizes. They occasionally received free
match tickets too, and priority in the allocation of season
tickets. Whenever United were involved in a cup match
where tickets were scarce, agents' names would go into a
draw for an allocation. In later years the 'winners' of the
cup ticket draw were almost always those agents whose
work was producing the most revenue.

The United pools competition was fairly complicated. In
the big national football pools, such as Littlewoods and
Vernons, customers have to predict which matches are
likely to produce draws, or various alternatives such as
selections of home or away wins. But for United to do that
would have involved a large amount of work in checking
each coupon, and might have annoyed the traditional pools
companies. Instead, Burke's pools customers were allocated
four numbers corresponding each week to four different
Football League or Scottish League matches. Whether
people won or not basically depended on the scores in those
games. Officially customers could ask to select their own
four numbers, but in practice it was difficult to do so, and
in effect the contest was one of pure chance. In time the
absence of any skill in the contest would cause Bill Burke
considerable problems.

In the early 1960s United's new commercial venture was
probably unique among English football clubs, though Rangers and Celtic had long run football pools in Scotland.
Partly because United enjoyed a monopoly in English
soccer, Burke was quickly successful. Many of the quarter
of a million members he eventually attracted had no real
interest in football and did not identify with Manchester
United. Burke says the majority of customers were women
who wanted 'a small, regular flutter'.

Under existing pools law, a third of the stake money
went in pools tax (nowadays – 42½ per cent) while another
third had to be distributed in winnings. After the expenses
of running the operation, United aimed for a return of

about 12 per cent. By April 1962 Burke had built up a surplus of £5,103 and was able to repay the football club's £1,000 loan. That summer saw the first benefit of the Development Association's work when 1,700 wooden seats were installed at a cost of £5,000 in what became known as E stand at the back of the famous Stretford End terraces. In recognition of their work, development agents were allocated some of the seats in the new stand. Meanwhile, the Development Association's work had grown so much that its offices were soon enlarged.

But the most dramatic innovation arising from Bill Burke's work was the new cantilever stand, on which work began in 1964. Until then the popular side of the ground, opposite the main stand, had consisted of standing terraces which were only partly covered. The ambitious plans for this area – the most up-to-date football stand in Britain – ensured that the FA awarded three games in the 1966 World Cup to Old Trafford instead of Manchester City's Maine Road. Since the war City's stadium had arguably been a better ground than Old Trafford; soon United would undoubtedly boast Manchester's top venue.

The new development was inspired by the cantilever north stand at Sheffield Wednesday's ground, Hillsborough, which had been built in 1961. But United's stand, opened in August 1965, was much more impressive as a structure, and it contained a totally new feature in British football. Bill Burke had arranged for the United directors to visit a similar cantilever stand built by the same architects, Mather and Nutter, at Manchester racecourse. In particular he invited them to sit in one of the new private boxes at the top. But the directors did not like the glass barrier which separated them from the action. To convince them, when United's stand was half-built, Burke took the board members up the unfinished concrete terracing to a spot where he had set out a few kitchen chairs. Yes, they agreed, it was a magnificent view out over the pitch. They promptly gave approval for a row of glass-fronted private boxes to be installed above the rows of ordinary seats. The directors decided that the boxes should cost £250 or £300, depending on location, for which the box holder and his four guests would be admitted to every game during the season, but separate arrangements had to be made for the World Cup. Holders were also allowed to add their own television sets and telephones. A bottle of champagne awaited each holder on the day when the boxes opened in September 1965.

Burke hoped to tap a new market for football – local businessmen and companies who wanted to impress clients or reward their staff. One of United's new boxes even housed Albert Finney briefly, during a scene from a famous film of that era, *Charlie Bubbles*, released in 1967. As they sat with their unobstructed view, box holders could order drinks or a simple meal. So as not to lose the crowd atmosphere behind the glass, noise was relayed through a speaker system on which the volume could be adjusted. The boxes not reserved by the directors were so oversubscribed by outsiders that Stretford council had to wait five years before getting one.

The board's initial scepticism about the boxes seemed to disappear completely, for, according to the minutes of one of their meetings, 'each director was allocated three boxes at £300, and one at £250 for disposal to his friends'. The directors' allocation of twenty boxes accounted for nearly half the total. In most cases the directors simply sold the boxes to friends or acquaintances. In spite of the heavy demand, when three boxes were given up by their owners in 1966, one of them was assigned 'for the personal use of the club chairman' who by then, of course, was Louis Edwards. Edwards was allocated yet another box in 1975, though, of course, he actually sat in the directors' box.

When the £325,000 bill came through for the construction of the new stand, most of it was paid directly by the Development Association rather than by the football club. This meant that nearly all the improvements to Old Trafford were being paid for by the surplus from the pools competition, in accordance with MUDA's rules. Consequently, the club's own profits could be devoted to football

and acquiring new players. The 1961 Warwickshire trip
had provided rapid and impressive results.

A vast new gymnasium had also been constructed by
the Association for £30,000 at The Cliff, United's training
ground in Salford. About one per cent of the Association's
funds was also donated to local sporting causes, which,
of course, did much to help United's public image. The
Development Association continued to accumulate large
levels of funds, waiting for the day when United needed
them for ground improvements. And Bill Burke, according
to a colleague, was 'a financial wizard' at investing the funds
to squeeze out the best return. Money was often placed on
overnight markets to earn the last bit of interest.

The pools operation reached its peak around 1969 and
1970, after the excitement generated by the European Cup
triumph. A staff of twenty was now employed in the Association's offices by the railway bridge next to the entrance to
the ground. A team of 6,000 agents looked after a quarter
of a million clients. There were attractive prizes of £4,000
or £5,000, and sometimes Mini cars were awarded to agents.
Moreover, both agents and customers were constantly
encouraged by the fact that the profits were going towards
substantial ground improvements.

In 1970, though, the whole future of Burke's work was
put in jeopardy. After a long legal test case, *Singette Ltd
and others* v. *Martin*, the House of Lords confirmed the
verdicts of lower courts that small pools competitions such
as United's were illegal. The deciding factor was that
because customers effectively had their numbers chosen for
them, no skill was involved. The pools were, in effect,
lotteries, and so subject to the much stricter limits then in
force on lottery competitions, such as a top prize of only
£100.

What initially seemed bad news for United was, however,
eventually turned in the club's favour. Fortunately the
police seemed to be in no hurry to prosecute. Manchester
United quickly banded together with Rangers and Warwickshire and, more importantly, with charities such as the

Spastics Society, whose Top-Ten competition ran along similar lines. They lobbied ministers and wrote to every MP. As a result the Government passed the 1971 Pool Competitions Act to help the worthy causes that stood suddenly to lose income. The 1971 Act allowed the existing small pools schemes to continue for another five years, but no new competitions could be established by rivals. From 1976 until 1987 the Act was annually extended by successive home secretaries.

So Burke's successful pools operation was not only allowed to continue, but also, at a time when football was waking up to commercial possibilities, the new law meant that other clubs could not copy the idea and compete. As far as English football was concerned, the Government had granted United a virtual pools monopoly. Bill Burke could give out much higher prizes and turn over much more money than the traditional lottery schemes, and these advantages far outweighed the 33 per cent pools tax that was levied then. A measure of Burke's achievement was the number of officials from other clubs who came to consult him about his work. The biggest compliment of all was an enquiry from Everton, the club belonging to the Moores family, the owner of Littlewoods Pools, though funnily enough the Moores brothers had actually begun their vast empire by distributing pools' coupons outside Old Trafford in 1923.

The Home Office made it clear, however, that it would not carry on renewing the 1971 Act indefinitely, and the exempted organisations were expected to devise alternative money-making ventures. In 1973 the Development Association began a spot-the-ball competition in conjunction with Ladbrokes which, in the brief time it operated, proved to be a bigger money-spinner for United than the pools. Ladbrokes, however, found it not worthwhile and abandoned the venture.

The new 1976 Lotteries and Amusements Act greatly relaxed the previous restrictions on lotteries, allowing much bigger prizes than before. Soon most football clubs and many local councils had set up their own lottery schemes. Bill Burke decided not to jump in straight away, not totally convinced at first that a lottery would be worthwhile. In 1978, however, the Manchester United Lottery was established and it became a sub-division of the Development Association's work. The club sold the familiar scratch cards both on sites at Old Trafford and through association agents. In fact several different lotteries were run at once, some short-term, lasting only a week, and others, with bigger prizes, lasting much longer. But even with the new lottery rules, and free of the 33 per cent pools levy, lotteries could never match the income United's pools competition had once generated.

Yet the old pools were by no means as lucrative as they had once been. Unlike Rangers, for instance, United failed to increase pools stake money in line with inflation. Income therefore declined in real terms. So too did the prize money, and people naturally lost interest. Moreover, the Irish Customs had prevented the large team of agents in Ireland from receiving pools literature, because Irish law is much stricter on such matters. And successive increases in postage rates also added to MUDA's costs.

When Burke retired as organiser of the Development Association in 1981, after twenty years, it was estimated that his work had raised £4 million for United. Most of it had been channelled into paying for the new cantilever stands, which today cover three sides of the ground. Two thirds of that money had come from the work of the Development Association, the rest from other activities initiated by Burke since his appointment as overall commercial manager in 1973. Already, by the time Burke retired, the Association had become much less important as a source of income, and there was much more competition from other clubs' lotteries. Moreover, no proper plans had yet been made for the day when the exemption of the 1971 legislation ended, and United's pools became illegal.

In 1982, shortly after Burke's retirement, United went into partnership with Glasgow Rangers, a club with a

brilliant record in the field of prize competitions. Rangers
in fact made the first approach; the organiser of their pools,
Hugh Adam, was also worried about what to do when the
competitions became illegal. The Glasgow club's pools were
by then five or six times larger than United's even though
they employed no more staff, and they enjoyed dominance
in Scotland among soccer club competitions. Rangers hoped
that by going in with United they could take a step further,
and gain entry into the much larger market in England.

The result was a contest called Spaceshot, which was
designed to use the vast team of agents employed by both
clubs. Essentially it was based on the idea of spot-the-ball.
Photographs were taken of Rangers and United players
against a goalmouth, pretending to take penalties. Customers had to predict where the ball would hit the net, as
decided by a team of judges which included Denis Law,
Bobby Charlton, the Rangers player Sandy Jardine and
the Scottish referee 'Tiny' Wharton. Because the contest
involved skill, in as much as customers had to anticipate
the judges' verdict, Spaceshot could not be deemed a lottery. This meant that it was not subject to any restrictions
in turnover and prize money. A joint company was formed
to run Spaceshot, Rangeman Promotions Ltd, and at the
time it was widely predicted that the venture would bring
both United and Rangers vast wealth.

This did not happen. Spaceshot flopped. Firstly, the
competition turned out to be far too complicated for both
agents and customers to follow. It was based on two separate photos that had been taken specially – one with a United
player and one with a Rangers man – showing them shooting at goal with no goalkeeper or other opponents. People
entering the contest had to work out coordinates – 15–27,
21–33, or whatever, on a master grid – to show where in
the goal they thought the ball would end up. Customers
were then expected to enter both sets of coordinates on a
duplicate form. It was so easy, though, for customers to
get the photos, and the numbers for the vertical and hori-
zontal axes, mixed up; it would have made things a little

simpler if numbers had been used on just one axis and letters on the other. Even Denis Law and some of the staff administering it did not understand Spaceshot fully. Matters became yet more complicated when, at around the same time, agents were allowed to pay cash directly into the MUDA and Rangeman accounts through the Girobank transcash system. This just made it harder to keep proper records.

Secondly, when Spaceshot was launched in February 1983, it seems that it failed through hostility to operating the scheme, and even religious bigotry, among some of Rangers' agents. Manchester United are regarded as a Catholic club and traditionally have enjoyed close ties with Rangers' arch rivals, Celtic, who, incidentally, were furious about the link-up. Many agents and customers preferred to concentrate on the previous competitions. Some people even tried to enter only one half of the Spaceshot competition and insisted the money went solely to whichever of the two teams they supported.

The third reason for the failure of Spaceshot, according to Development Association staff, was that there was even coolness among some senior personnel at Old Trafford to the scheme.

The outcome was that Spaceshot was dropped after just two months, and each club lost £74,000 on the venture. Rangers, however, later ran a modified and much simpler version of Spaceshot. It made what the Glasgow club regarded as a modest £250,000 a year, more than United now earns annually on all its competitions. So an excellent financial opportunity may have been lost. Had United run the scheme with Celtic, and made it simpler to enter, it might have made money for Old Trafford too. But then it was Rangers' idea.

As United's competitions – the pools and the lottery – slowly declined, the Development Association found it harder and harder to keep within the rules laid down by the Betting and Gaming Board. In particular the expenses on a lottery must not exceed 25 per cent of the income. In other words each lottery has to achieve an income which is four times greater than its costs. To get round these regulations, lottery expenses were gradually transferred to the football club. Development Association staff suddenly found that they were no longer MUDA employees, but worked directly for Manchéster United, though few had any reason to complain. The club was also paying more and more of the Association's administrative costs, such as postage, stationery and staff meals. It meant that the claimed expenses of United's lotteries, as set out in regular returns to the Gaming Board, were increasingly understated and false.

With many different lottery competitions all launched during the course of a season, income from a popular lottery would often be reassigned to an unsuccessful lottery which would otherwise not have met its income target. By juggling with the figures like this, using good lotteries to subsidise the bad ones, it was possible to ensure that the expenses stated on returns to the Gaming Board never went above 25 per cent of the income. On one occasion a lottery for the basketball club, with a car as the first prize, failed to meet its expected sales target of £30,000. So the Development Association's printers, Dawn Print, were asked to provide a false invoice. This meant that the basketball lottery's apparent expenses could then be reduced to the permitted level.

Things reached the stage, however, where few of the existing lotteries were making enough money to meet the spending limits, even though they were still just about profitable. Staff in the Development Association offices were spending vast amounts of time playing around with the figures rather than promoting the lotteries themselves. Life was constrained by the fact that Gaming Board returns had to be submitted within six weeks of a lottery finishing. 'At the end,' one former employee recalls, 'it reached a point where there were no longer any good lotteries to pinch money from. So we just pinched money from the lottery that was furthest away in time.'

ABOVE Norman Whiteside scores the second goal against Brighton in the 1983 Cup final replay – becoming the youngest player ever to score in a Wembley FA Cup final. (*Manchester Evening News*)

BELOW United players posing for the FA Cup winners' traditional photo after beating Brighton 4–0. (*Syndication International Ltd.*)

LEFT Club president Sir Matt Busby and his former right-hand man Jimmy Murphy. Over for years ago they set about the ta of building Manchester Unite into football's most famous cl (*Harry Goodwin*)

BELOW Decision time as the directors meet for their month board meeting in 1984. On th agenda this time is a warm welcome for the newest mem Maurice Watkins and Bobby Charlton (far right). Others in attendance are (left to right) I Edwards, Denzil Haroun, sec Leslie Olive and chairman M Edwards. (*Manchester United Supporters Club*)

ᴛ Ron Atkinson with his
ᴅd batch of signings, in
▪ – Jesper Olsen, Alan
▪il and Gordon Strachan.
▪il says he was not suited to
▪ving crosses from the two
▪ men. (*Syndication Inter-*
nal Ltd.)

LEFT Peter Beardsley was
signed for £250,000 by Ron
Atkinson, but played only one
match before being trans-
ferred back to Vancouver.
(*Manchester United Supporters
Club*)

ᴛ United chairman, Martin
▪ards, in front of the stadium
▪ather built into one of
▪in's top football grounds.
▪*nchester Evening News*)

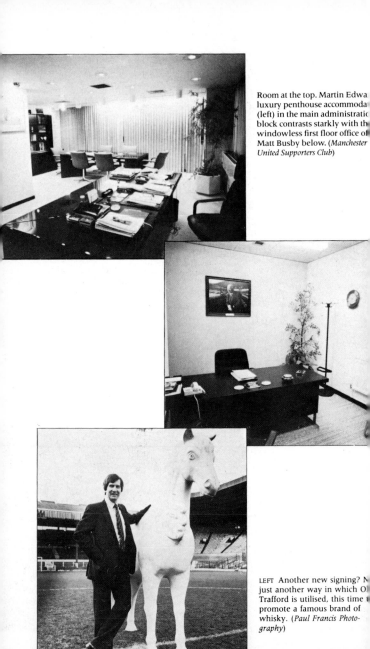

Room at the top. Martin Edwa[rds']
luxury penthouse accommoda[tion]
(left) in the main administratio[n]
block contrasts starkly with th[e]
windowless first floor office of
Matt Busby below. (*Manchester
United Supporters Club*)

LEFT Another new signing? N[o,]
just another way in which Ol[d]
Trafford is utilised, this time [to]
promote a famous brand of
whisky. (*Paul Francis Photography*)

Martin Edwards and
Mitsuda of Sharp Elec-
s conclude another
sion to the club's sponsor-
eal with the Japanese
whose contracts since
have brought United over
0,000. (*Manchester United
rters Club*)

LEFT A whole new ball game saw United branch
into basketball when they took over the
Warrington Vikings on New Year's Eve 1984. It
proved a financial disaster and was sold three
years later. (*Manchester United Supporters Club*)

United's 'Red Devils'
etball team is launched at
tretford Sports Centre in
, (left to right) Rick Taylor
eral manager), Maurice
ins, Ron Atkinson, Joe
ton (coach), Martin
ards and Bobby Charlton.
chester United Supporters

ABOVE FA Cup winners 1985. Eighteen months after winning his second FA Cup in three years, Ron Atkinson was sacked. (*Manchester United Supporters Club*)

BELOW Fergie's Furies. Alex Ferguson and his players pose for a new team photograph shortly after his arrival as manager. Of the twenty-two players pictured, only five were still with the club three years later. (*Manchester United Supporters Club*)

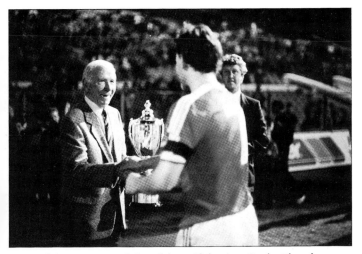

Sir Matt presents captain Bryan Robson with the winners' trophy at the end of the Manchester international tournament, held at Maine Road in August 1987. In the background is Dennis Roach, the agent who organised the competition and has been involved in many of United's deals. (*David Smith Sports Photography*)

BELOW Shortly after Norman Whiteside's transfer request was announced in 1988, this poster appeared on a billboard in the centre of Manchester. (*David Smith Sports Photography*)

LEFT Jim Leighton and Mark Hughes were signed in the summer of 1988 for £2,000,000. (*David Smith Sports Photography*)

BELOW Match-day host Vince Miller (centre) presents United's senior officers to members of the Europa club at the beginning of the 1988-89 season. From the left are club directors Nigel Burrows, Bobby Charlton, Amer Midani and Maurice Watkins, Martin Edwards (chairman), Sir Matt Busby (president), Danny McGregor (commercial manager) and director Michael Edelson, (*Manchester Evening News*)

It got so bad that the absurd situation occurred where United were actually buying their own lottery tickets! To boost the stated income levels on several lotteries Martin Edwards and other club officials actually agreed that United would purchase £11,000 worth of tickets at face value from the Development Association. The money then had to be accounted for. One suggestion was that the £11,000 bill should be presented in United's accounts as a part of the club's expenditure on promotion and advertising. It is not clear whether Martin Edwards and the United staff actually sat down together and rubbed the tickets off to see how much the club had won from itself!

In January 1985 the pools competition, as permitted by the 1971 legislation, was officially closed down. The Government had finally warned that the exemption of the act would not be extended beyond the next general election. In effect, United's pools operation, with variable prizes depending on the level of stakes and the number of winners, was simply transformed into two linked lotteries with fixed prizes. To most customers it would have looked much the same as the old pools contest.

Since 1978 the Development Association has also been involved in a scheme for agents to sell Christmas hampers. Weekly payments are collected from customers as agents do their competition rounds. Initially the distribution was chaotic, and once several customers had to be reimbursed after their hampers were not delivered in time for Christmas. The hampers were provided by Bobby Charlton Promotions and despatched from a site on an industrial estate in Ormskirk. In 1986 the firm was paid more than £40,000 for hampers. Bobby Charlton's company has also provided jewellery for the Development Association, which was sold to pools customers via agents in a similar way, though it produced much less trade than the hampers.

In 1986 the Development Association's competitions officially made a profit of £350,883 on ticket sales of £942,851. But the figures badly overestimate the true return, since the accounts do not include those large areas of expenditure that are now met by the football club to keep within the Gaming Board's restrictions. Allowing for the subsidy from the club, the 1986 surplus of £350,883 was in fact reduced by more than half to only £158,258. For the same reasons the accumulated development profit of £4,040,000 between 1961 and 1989 must also be an exaggeration. A more accurate figure might be about £3 million.

Today the Development Association runs a whole series of lotteries – two based on the pools idea, others based on scratch cards – and it continues to sell hampers and jewellery. But the organisation is nothing like the force it was in Bill Burke's day. Burke's successors – John Lillie, the commercial manager from 1981 to 1985, and Barry Moorhouse, who ran the Development Association until 1987, have lacked Burke's ideas, drive and ability. Under Barry Moorhouse, petty rivalries built up between staff involved with the pools competition and those working on lotteries. Morale also fell badly after a series of thefts which lost £8,000 over a four-year period. One Development Association employee was convicted of a small theft and sacked, but afterwards money still continued to go missing.

As Moorhouse failed to find any culprit, all his staff fell under suspicion. At one point the assistant manager, Tony Woodward, was arrested by the police, questioned at length, and then cleared completely. Woodward was nevertheless sacked from his job on the grounds, said Martin Edwards, that it would have been intolerable for him to carry on working with Moorhouse. He eventually received £10,000 in compensation following months of legal argument. The money was paid only on condition that Woodward would not take legal action against Moorhouse for defamation of character. He was also obliged to sign United's usual confidentiality clause not to disclose the secrets and internal affairs of the club.

The Development Association, bringing in around £250,000 a year, now accounts for only a small fraction of United's non-football income. Today, with many soccer clubs running lotteries, United faces stiff competition. The 6,000 agents Bill Burke had on the books at the Association's peak in the early 1970s have been reduced to around 1,800.

The absorption of MUDA into Manchester United's financial affairs, which was carried out officially in the early 1980s, means that the relationship between the money MUDA raises and ground improvements is now obscured. The visual incentive that agents and customers once saw growing up all around them in the form of newer stands has now become blurred.

The phenomenal success of Rangers in prize competitions helped pay for the £10 million redevelopment of three sides of their Ibrox ground between 1978 and 1981. The Glasgow club's competitions in Scotland are probably three times larger than United's. In generating more than £700,000 a year, they have helped make Rangers by far the wealthiest football club in Britain.

In the 1960s and 1970s Bill Burke and the club directors were determined that as each area of the Old Trafford ground was redeveloped, it should contain ventures that would in themselves generate further income. The private boxes had set a precedent and uncovered further potential. In 1975 a further phase began when the Executive Suite was opened in the main stand for supporters who wanted to eat before matches but could not afford a whole box and might have wanted only a couple of seats. The building contract was awarded to John Lee and Sons, one of whose directors, David Lee, was Louis Edwards' son-in-law, though both Louis and Martin Edwards left the board meeting while the decision was being taken.

By 1987 United's catering facilities had produced more than £600,000 surplus over the previous nine years, making them one of the most profitable parts of the club's business. Old Trafford has two main restaurant areas which during the week cater for the general public, and six different suites which can be hired by individuals and organisations who want to hold dinners, wedding receptions or meetings.

They employ forty full-time and sixty more part-time. On match days 600 members use the Executive Suite for a fee of £730 each a season. This gives them access to the restaurants and bar, and a seat in an area behind and to the side of the directors' box. The catering staff have been known to prepare more than 800 meals on some days. Less wealthy supporters can use the less luxurious facilities of the Sir Matt Busby Suite next to the ticket office, which provides a cafeteria service.

Twenty years after their installation, the private boxes cost between £4,000 a season for five seats and £15,000 for eight seats, while a four-place window table brings in £6,325 a year. The idea of boxes has been copied at most major football grounds; Arsenal, for instance, have built forty-eight boxes at Highbury's famous Clock End. Both the Arsenal boxes and those constructed by Spurs in their controversial development of The Shelf at White Hart Lane have been sold on leases which last several years, while United still prefer to let the Old Trafford boxes annually. In the prosperous South-east the business potential of boxes is now far greater than in the North-west, and for both the North London clubs the recent sale of long box leases provided capital sums of several million pounds. Manchester United still boast more boxes than any other club, however – 103 of them around three sides of the stadium – and in 1987 only two became vacant at the end of the season. But the demand is not as great as it once was, and nowadays United have to go out in search of new occupants.

The area of the large private boxes, restaurants and Executive Suite along the top of the main stand is now filled every match day with businessmen and rich supporters from all over Manchester and the North-west. It is often said that the only way to get hold of the British Aerospace chairman, Roland Smith, is to ring his table at Old Trafford when United are at home. Some occupants of the boxes and the suite use the club's facilities as an extension of their offices. They spend time on the telephone or meeting friends and business contacts, entertaining and impressing commercial clients, and making money.

The terrace supporter on the Stretford or Scoreboard End or in the United Road Paddock, however, has benefited little from the money generated by Bill Burke and the Development Association. The concrete he stands on and the barrier he leans against are much the same as they were thirty years ago. The refreshment and toilet facilities are spartan in comparison to the executive facilities, and in some sections as poor as ever. Even the argument that the ordinary fan has benefited by way of relatively cheap admission to Old Trafford had now lost ground in the wake of United's recent membership scheme. This means that the Stretford End supporter has to pay more than he has had to for many years to support his team from his usual vantage point. And with season and league match ticket-book holders now forced to become members of the controversial scheme, the cost being incorporated in their substantially increased renewal fee, United have made it clear that loyal supporters are no longer exempt from the drive for profit.

Most of the ground improvements paid for by Bill Burke have benefited a very different class of supporter. The Old Trafford his work helped build is the United of the private box and the Executive Suite: a football ground which, like the club itself, has become a forum for making business deals.

11
Player Politics

'It's a rat race, and the rats are winning.'

Alex Ferguson on football agents, 1988.

On Saturday, 11 January 1986, there was great excitement among the press corps at the Manor Ground, the tiny home of Oxford United. But it was not the kind of interest normally associated with a visit by Manchester United. The talk among journalists, which began about two hours before the kick-off, revolved around rumours that Manchester United were involved in a multi-million-pound deal that would mean the departure of their star striker, Mark Hughes.

By the time Hughes volleyed home Gidman's cross in the seventy-fourth minute for yet another of his remarkable goals, the telephone lines between Oxford, London and Manchester were carrying the first reports of his pending transfer, soon to be splashed over the back pages of the Sunday morning papers. The speculation would have severe repercussions for United. After winning the FA Cup the previous May, they opened the 1985–86 season with an extraordinary ten consecutive wins and established a ten-point gap at the top of the first division. And Mark Hughes had played a leading role in United's brilliant start. But then form dropped dramatically, and injuries hit the team. Nevertheless, after beating Oxford that day, they still seemed to have some chance of winning the title for the first time in nearly twenty years.

Within days of the Oxford match it was revealed publicly that Mark Hughes' five-year contract with United, signed less than a month earlier, had stipulated that if he left Old Trafford he would cost any buying club £1.8 million. Then it became known that the contract also stated that Barcelona had the right of first refusal if Hughes did choose to leave. When rumours circulated that he had indeed already signed for the Spanish club, United refused to confirm or deny them. The speculation became intense. Eventually, in late March 1986, Old Trafford announced that Hughes was indeed going to Spain.

It had been a delicate situation for United. Until 1985 Mark Hughes had been badly rewarded by the club. His income had not yet been adjusted to take account of his swift two-year rise from youth team to first team, and he was earning only £250 a week. Had Hughes refused to sign a new contract, he would have been free to seek rich sums abroad. The complicated UEFA multiplier system, based on a player's age and earnings, would have awarded United a meagre transfer fee of around £400,000 just as it had undervalued Joe Jordan when he went to AC Milan in 1981 for £250,000.

For United the near £2 million price tag seemed the only way to guarantee adequate compensation if Mark Hughes chose to leave. Moreover, when the deal with Barcelona was agreed, the Spaniards insisted that it was kept secret, since Hughes' arrival would affect the position of their existing foreign players. So United were unable to put an end to the intense speculation, yet the uncertainty, and Hughes' marked drop in form, seriously undermined the campaign for the league title. The pressure on Hughes only worsened a long-standing drink problem. 'My last few months virtually turned into a one-man beer festival. I was on the town most nights of the week.' In the first half of the season Hughes had scored eleven times. His scoring touch only returned when the speculation about Barcelona

was resolved, but by then it was too late. United finished
a disappointing fourth for the third time in three years,
after a season that had promised so much.

Hughes' contract in Spain was worth around £2 million
over five years, but he struggled there as a player. His
partnership with the England striker Gary Lineker did not
work out, and by the end of his first season he had been
demoted to the reserves. When Terry Venables was sacked
as Barcelona manager in 1987, Hughes' playing future
looked bleak. Only going on loan to Bayern Munich in
West Germany revitalised his form and career.

Just over two years later, Hughes' return to Old Trafford
proved to be almost as remarkable as his departure. On
Thursday, 23 June 1988, again after months of press guess-
work and gossip, he rejoined Manchester United. The £1.6
million fee was only £200,000 less than United had received
when they sold him to Barcelona. As the talks had progressed, and as United fans' anticipation had increased and
thus the price of disappointment had grown ever greater
for Martin Edwards, Barcelona's asking price was reported
as having crept up from £1.1 million to £1.3 million, then
to £1.5 million and finally to £1.6 million. The figure mentioned publicly, though, was £1.8 million.

Never before in post-war football had any player ever
left Manchester United and then returned. Normally those
who had left the club in the past found their career going
rapidly downhill thereafter: Johnny Giles being perhaps the
most notable exception. Equaly remarkable was that before
his two multi-million pound transfers, Mark Hughes had
spent barely two years in the United first team and had
made just eighty-nine league appearances.

The 1988 agreement with Barcelona was confidently
assumed to have made Hughes the highest-paid player at
Old Trafford, far better off than Brian McClair who had
just become the first player since George Best to score
twenty league goals in a season, and better rewarded than
even the England captain, Bryan Robson, whom most
would consider a much better player. Robson's earning

power, though, is supplemented considerably by his outside activities.

'Sparky' Hughes said he was delighted to be back, but many believed that he had never wanted to go in the first place. A former United reserve player, Joe Hanrahan, recalled Hughes saying to him before he left: 'Has it ever occurred to you I might not want to go?' A similar impression emerged from other remarks Hughes made that winter – one newspaper quoted him as saying that he was being forced out. Later, when he had joined Barcelona, Hughes told guests at Norman Whiteside's wedding that he had never wanted to leave United. Such statements only reinforced the widely held opinion that Martin Edwards and Dennis Roach, who claims he is paid a set fee on any new contract Hughes signs, were more interested in the transfer than the player himself.

For ordinary Manchester United fans the Hughes affair greatly increased disillusionment with Martin Edwards and the Old Trafford administration. 'Sparky' was one of their favourite players. After his tremendous partnership with Norman Whiteside in United's youth team, and his introduction to the first team in 1984, he had played a major role in the 1985 FA Cup success, scoring one of his extraordinary goals in the semi-final replay against Liverpool. The details that leaked out in 1986 about Hughes' new contract with United seemed only to anger fans who believed Martin Edwards was simply out to make money for himself. Such opinions were reinforced by the revelation that Edwards received bonuses based upon one per cent of any profit made on transfers during a season.

In the spring of 1988 it was Martin Edwards and Dennis Roach who carried out the negotiations to bring Mark Hughes back to Manchester. And Roach could have expected to be rewarded with around £80,000 for his 'set fee' (based on a modest five per cent) from United, on top of any money from Hughes himself. Remarkably, within a few days of the striker's return in July 1988, the Italian club Juventus offered £2 million for him. Even Martin

Edwards would have known that, if the offer were accepted, such a move would be difficult to explain to the fans and would devastate the player. Yet the United chairman may have been tempted by the Italian offer since the money would have been useful in the competition with Spurs to buy Paul Gascoigne from Newcastle. Bobby Charlton's admiration for Gascoigne was common knowledge and he was reported as having been involved in trying to persuade the Newcastle star to come to Old Trafford.

Martin Edwards' close relationship with the agent Dennis Roach leaves him open to criticism of a conflict of interest. For Roach has not just negotiated on behalf of several United players – including Mark Hughes, Gary Bailey, Peter Davenport, Norman Whiteside, Paul McGrath, Jesper Olsen and Johnny Sivebaek – he also works as Manchester United's own agent in arranging overseas tours and friendly matches against foreign opposition. Roach's firm, the Professional Representation Organisation Ltd (PRO), is based in a small office near the cathedral at St Albans in Hertfordshire. It boasts the former Arsenal manager Bertie Mee and the BBC commentator Bob Wilson as its consultants.

United's relations with Dennis Roach go back more than ten years. In 1979 he arranged for Dave Sexton to buy the Yugoslav international defender Nikola Jovanovic for £350,000. Roach's company at that time, the Euroach Agency, registered in Cyprus, had actually bought Jovanovic's registration from his club in Yugoslavia, Red Star Belgrade, and it claimed to own the player. Roach proposed that United should pay his Cyprus company both a transfer fee and a regular service fee while Jovanovic was at United, as well as the player's salary. The Football Association, however, refused to allow such a deal because it involved paying an agent, which was then against the rules of both the FA and the world football body FIFA. When an alternative deal was finally arranged to bring Jovanovic to Old Trafford, he was not a great success, and played only twenty-four games for the club in three years – a cost of well over £15,000 a game.

Another football agency that emerged around the same time was Circle Sports Ltd, based in Essex, which tried to fix United up with two Peruvian internationals – Juan Oblitas and Percy Rojas – from Sporting Cristal of Lima. The proposal came to nothing, but in time United would begin fruitful relationships both with Circle Sports and its owner, Eddie Buckley, and with Dennis Roach and PRO.

After Ron Atkinson succeeded Dave Sexton as manager of United in 1981, the club's relations with Roach began to flourish. He had once played against Atkinson in the Southern League when the United manager was at Kettering and Roach captained Bedford Town. Roach says that he acted as the United manager's personal agent in commercial deals. He had formerly owned a furniture company but in the late 1970s slowly moved into the job of representing star international footballers interested in prospering overseas, including Johann Cruyff, Trevor Francis and Liam Brady.

In 1984 Martin Edwards struck an exclusive agreement with PRO to arrange money-making pre-season foreign tours and friendly matches. In subsequent years Roach has made United hundreds of thousands of pounds from such fixtures, and himself earns 10 per cent on each deal. Until recently most United friendly games against foreign opposition were organised by Roach. The 1987 summer tour to Sweden and Denmark, for instance, made £36,000 for United and £4,000 for PRO. A match in Bahrain in December 1986 made £13,500 for the club and £1,500 for the agent. Roach also organised the Manchester tournament at Maine Road in August 1987 involving United, City, Atletico Mineiro of Brazil and PSV Eindhoven, for which United received a guaranteed payment of £30,000. It was planned to repeat the contest at Old Trafford in 1988, with Gothenburg and Atletico Bilbao as guests, though City would have received a guarantee of only £20,000 compared with United's £30,000. The idea was dropped at a late stage because United said that the newly restored Old Trafford

pitch would not be ready in time, but then the club proceeded to arrange another home friendly with Hamburg
instead, through another agent. The affair is known to have
caused some controversy and it is believed that at one
stage Manchester City were even looking to United for
compensation.

Dennis Roach is just one of the many football agents who
now inhabit top-class European football. His PRO agency
is probably the biggest of them all and Manchester United
have, at various times, been involved in several other of
Roach's money-making ventures.

Nowadays nearly all United's first-team players employ
agents of their own to negotiate with the club. Up until
about a decade ago players would talk directly with the
manager about contracts and salaries. Now the discussions
are between the chief executive and a player's personal
representative who, in some cases, may receive 20 per cent
of what he agrees for his client.

Three other developments in the last thirty years have
radically changed the relationship between a top league club
and its players, and have had a particularly far-reaching
effect on United's affairs. First came the abolition of the
maximum wage in 1961. Until then most United first-team
players would be on the maximum wage, which before
abolition was £20 a week during the season and £17 in the
summer. Benefits on top of that were few. Players might
receive occasional bonuses if they won a trophy, and at the
end of five- or ten-year periods they would get a lump-sum
benefit payment of a few hundred pounds. Because of the
restriction United could not use its wealth to attract top
stars since they would get no more at Old Trafford than
elsewhere. It meant that Matt Busby's early dealings with
his players had been relatively simple.

The second development was the introduction of freedom
of contract in the late 1970s. Until then players remained
on the books of a club even if their contract came to an
end and they no longer had any wish to play for the side.
This meant that clubs had a considerable hold over players.

Now, though, when a contract finishes, a player is free to move as he pleases. His previous club is compensated only by a transfer fee agreed between the sides or, more often, fixed by an independent tribunal which is rarely generous in its estimates. It is therefore in a club's interests to keep all its players on contracts so as not to lose them without much compensation. But this inevitably costs teams like United more in higher and longer lasting wage agreements, and involves the club constantly in negotiating contract renewals.

The third important change has been the destruction of foreign barriers to transfers over the last ten years. The process began in a marked way with the arrival of the Argentinian World Cup stars Osvaldo Ardiles and Ricky Villa at Spurs in 1978. Since then United have taken on several foreign stars – Nikola Jovanovic, Arnold Muhren, Jesper Olsen and John Sivebaek – and have negotiated for many others. Yet foreign clubs have also succeeded in luring away top United players at the peak of their careers – Joe Jordan, Ray Wilkins and Mark Hughes. Until the late 1970s it was unknown for a top player to leave United until the club had decided that he was no longer of much further value.

At Old Trafford these trends have been responsible for a marked shift in power away from the manager. In Matt Busby's day he would have conducted any negotiations over players, though the board would have taken a close interest. Now his successors as manager have neither sufficient time nor enough business experience to do all the work; nor could they commit the club to the large sums of money involved. Instead players' contracts are now largely the responsibility of Martin Edwards, who will often be assisted and advised by Maurice Watkins.

The financial climate for top British footballers began to change radically in the late 1970s. It was exemplified perhaps in the summer of 1980 when Dave Sexton tried to sign the Arsenal player Liam Brady. Arsenal wanted £1.5 million for him, but Brady himself was also demanding an

annual salary of £90,000, guaranteed bonuses of £20,000
and a signing-on fee of £50,000. The figures were extraordinary by the standards of the period. The United board
would offer Arsenal only £1 million and Brady a salary of
just £50,000 plus a £100,000 signing-on fee spread over
three years. Even though the payments were much less
than the Arsenal player wanted, they were far higher than
any United player received at the time – Steve Coppell, for
instance, was earning only £33,800 a year. But the terms
were not enough to stop Brady going to Juventus of Italy
instead.

When Garry Birtles joined United from Nottingham
Forest in October 1980, his contract involved a £1,250,000
transfer fee, wages of £800 a week (£41,600 a year), and a
signing-on fee of £75,000. Meanwhile, negotiations to keep
Joe Jordan at United collapsed the following summer when
the Scottish striker refused a £15,000 fee to sign a new
contract and turned down wages of £750 a week, and higher
in subsequent years. Jordan left for AC Milan after demanding sums that would have brought him £97,000 a year –
almost £2,000 a week. But Jordan would have been happy
to stay at Old Trafford if United had been a little more
flexible and at least discussed a compromise.

The UEFA multiplier system awarded United only
£250,000 for losing Jordan, while the replacement signing
by Ron Atkinson – Frank Stapleton – not only cost the
club £900,000 (a fee fixed by the League tribunal which
Arsenal considered absurdly low) but he was also paid
around £1,000 a week. Bryan Robson was given a similar
salary on joining United a few weeks later.

The era of players' agents, high wages, arguments over
contracts and high signing-on fees had truly begun. Sometimes players' agents managed to negotiate into their contracts limits on the amount the club could get if the player
was subsequently transferred again. Jesper Olsen, who cost
£800,000 from Ajax of Amsterdam in 1984, insisted that
United could ask for no more than £450,000 if they wanted
to get rid of him, and that if he chose to return to Denmark

they would get no fee at all. By the time Dennis Roach negotiated his transfer to the French club Bordeaux in November 1988, the fee was only £375,000.

Brian McClair was promised a signing-on fee of £100,000 when he joined United from Celtic in 1987, though it was to be paid over four years. The Scot joined the club only after long, secret negotiations over the previous season. Alex Ferguson and Martin Edwards met McClair secretly in both Glasgow and Carlisle before they managed to secure his transfer, and Ferguson's successor as Scotland manager, Andy Roxburgh, even complained about them holding a meeting with the player in the Scotland team hotel.

The rewards for players and their agents are made all the more complicated by United's sophisticated bonus systems which become more lucrative every season, though some might argue that they have little effect on results. When bonuses began in the 1950s and 1960s, they generally involved payments simply if the club finished at a certain position in the league. In 1965, for instance, the players shared £6,500 between them when they won the league championship. One United bonus agreement, made just after the abolition of the maximum wage in 1961, even offered players extra amounts according to the home crowd figures. During the post-Munich period when gates at Old Trafford fell badly, the players were promised £1 each for every 1,000 spectators above 37,000 and £2 for every 1,000 above 45,000.

By the early 1980s the bonus systems was even more complex, with extra money for each league point won, and progressively more money as more points were accumulated. But United's system of reckoning was particularly confusing in that the club continued to award only two points for a win, even after the league itself introduced three points for a win in 1981. In the 1986–87 season players received £100 per point for the first thirty-five points, £200 for each of the next ten points, £300 for the next ten and £400 for any points thereafter. It was difficult for the players to understand on a week-to-week basis, but once the last threshold had been passed in the latter stages of the season, each subsequent victory was worth £800 to each player.

The inadequacy of this system was highlighted in the last ten matches of the 1987–88 campaign when United claimed eight wins and two draws. Based on the previous season's bonuses, those who played in all ten games would have received an extra £5,200 each. Such was the absurdity that the team's 2–1 win over Wimbledon in the last match of the 1987–88 season would have awarded each player an £800 bonus, including substitute Lee Martin who was then earning around £130 a week in basic wages. The result would have cost the club £10,400 in bonuses, yet the match itself was almost completely meaningless. United were already assured of being runners-up, and the official gate was only 28,040 – the real attendance was lower still. In contrast, had the players beaten Liverpool in the highly important match at Old Trafford earlier in the season, instead of drawing 1–1, they would have earned only £100 each on bonus money, because the season had not yet reached the high levels of bonus payment.

Some would attribute the famous end to the 1980–81 season – the seven successive victories which were followed by Dave Sexton's controversial sacking – to such cumulative bonuses. Yet the argument that players perform well only with such incentives seems unconvincing. More often United have squandered vital points at the end of a season, and it does not account for the tremendous start in 1985–86 which would have earned only meagre bonuses.

Since 1988 United have operated a much simpler bonus system, paying £100 for each actual league point won. There is no progressive element, but the system is slightly more generous overall than before, and the £50,000 extra bonus for winning the title has been doubled to £100,000.

In terms of basic wages the spread among the United first-team squad is surprisingly wide, and probably wider than ever before. Long-serving defenders have often been badly rewarded in comparison with star forwards. In his last season, for instance, Kevin Moran was paid a basic

salary of only £41,600 after ten years' service with the club.
The 1986–87 basic salaries for Bryan Robson (£98,000),
Gordon Strachan (£78,000) and Jesper Olsen (£85,000)
reflected their star quality and high transfer fees, though
in Strachan's case his contract was renegotiated when he
threatened to move to France just before the 1988–89
season. Norman Whiteside (£45,000) and Paul McGrath
(£39,000), who did not arrive via expensive transfers, got
relatively small rewards. Perhaps the most surprising figure
was that of Brian McClair who, with his signing-on fee,
was receiving only £65,000 a year before bonuses in 1987–88
– the season he scored thirty-one goals. His salary may have
reflected his previous pay at Celtic who are notorious for
how little they pay their staff. In November 1988 McClair's
contract was renegotiated to bring him in line with Mark
Hughes.

Life on the fringes of the team seems particularly unre-
warding. Salaries earned in the 1986–87 season by Liam
O'Brien (£13,000), Gary Walsh (£9,100), Billy Garton
(£18,200) and Clayton Blackmore (£20,800) reflected the
fact that most ordinary footballers cannot expect vast
incomes even in the modern era, though Walsh received an
additional £75 in appearance money for first-team games.
The sums may still be higher than what most people earn,
but in comparison with the rest of the entertainment industry, and allowing for a footballer's short career span, being
an ordinary player, even at Old Trafford, does not make
you a rich man.

On top of their salaries most of United's first-team squad
have club cars. The club meets insurance and tax on the
vehicles, but the players are expected to service them. And
in the past, ten of the top players had the extra perk of
living in club houses for which they paid a rent of £1,000
a year – well below the economic charge. They could also
buy their homes at any time during the period of their
contract, at a cost of just 5 per cent in excess of the original
purchase price, which normally meant a good bargain.
United have always provided club houses for players,

though as time has passed the club's modest suburban semis in Sale, Davyhulme, Old Trafford, Urmston and Chorlton have been replaced by much larger properties, worth £150,000 or more, in the leafy Cheshire lanes around Bowdon, Hale and Wilmslow.

Manchester United's elaborate system of rewards for its players and officials was perhaps an obvious case for scrutiny by the tax authorities, especially at a time when the Inland Revenue is meant to be gunning for big names to set an example to the ordinary public. When the tax men launched an investigation into United in late 1987, it was dismissed by Martin Edwards as routine. 'This is not a big concern for me or Manchester United,' he said when news of it reached the press in February 1988. But four months later a different story emerged when it was revealed that the club had confessed to avoiding tax on payments to players, and the Inland Revenue accused United of holding 'sham' board meetings.

The investigation looked into a string of tax-free, lump-sum amounts that United had made to players and club officials dating back to 1980. Most of the payments had been made on advice from Martin Edwards' close associate Oscar Goldstein while he was a partner with Price Waterhouse.

United admitted that the sums of £25,000 to Lou Macari, £10,000 to Martin Buchan and £4,000 to Mickey Thomas had been wrongly declared as tax-free 'ex-gratia' payments. The Revenue also queried the tax liabilities of £60,000 paid to Arnold Muhren when he left United, £60,000 of a £104,750 insurance payment to Steve Coppell when he was forced to retire, and £15,000 to Garry Birtles.

The inspector, Mr Tillmanns, made reference to other examples (£50,000 to Sammy McIlroy and £25,000 to Jimmy Nicholl) of compensation having been first negotiated and then dressed up with such phrases as 'ex-gratia' and 'mark of personal esteem' in what he called 'prima facie, sham letters' and board meetings.

Payments made to Frank Stapleton through an off-shore

trust account were also under investigation and it was
revealed that former manager Ron Atkinson was paid
£115,000 when he was sacked, with his assistant, Mick
Brown, receiving £45,000. Aberdeen were given £60,000 as
compensation for losing Alex Ferguson when he replaced
Atkinson as manager.

In March 1988, possibly in response to the tax inquiry
at Old Trafford and similar investigations at other clubs,
the Football League, the Professional Footballers' Association and the Inland Revenue issued new guidelines about
tax-free payments to players. All such payments linked with
transfers are now clearly liable to tax, though amounts paid
in the case of injury or retirement which are not part of a
contract are not always taxable. The agreement also granted
clubs an amnesty over most previous payments, though
United did not reach a settlement with the Inland Revenue
until late 1989.

Player transfers too have become a complex business
nowadays. It should be stressed, though, that the figures
given in the press are in fact only estimates of the fees that
change hands. In most cases the figures are pretty accurate,
but not always. When the Scotland goalkeeper Jim Leighton joined United from Aberdeen in May 1988, a decision
may have been taken to exaggerate his price. The figure
quoted in the press was £750,000, but the real amount was
only £450,000, and United have done nothing to correct any
newspaper's mistake. It was perhaps in United's interest to
make out that they spent more than they did, and in Aberdeen's to let their supporters think they received more than
they did. Similarly when Ray Wilkins joined United in
1979, the price was only £700,000, though the figure most
often given in public was £825,000. In contrast, when
United signed the seventeen-year-old Torquay player Lee
Sharpe in May 1988, the official fee was £65,000, yet
journalists talked of £30,000. Sixty-five thousand pounds
was a large sum for a teenager who had appeared only
fifteen times in the Torquay first team. Moreover, United
agreed to pay Torquay a further £60,000 when Sharpe made

a first-team competitive appearance – which occurred in
September 1988 – and another £60,000 after thirty first-
team competitive games, which was achieved by the end of
the 1988–89 season – £185,000 in all. A further condition
was that United would play a friendly match at Torquay,
for expenses only, at some future date and this took place
in September 1989.

The most complex deal of all must be that which brought
John Sivebaek to Old Trafford from Vejle Boldklub of
Denmark in 1986. At one point it looked as though the
move had collapsed because of fears about a pelvic injury
that had shown up on the player's medical examination,
but United eventually agreed to pay the sum of £285,000
in three separate instalments. An initial fee of £150,000 was
to be followed by a further £75,000 eighteen months later,
and another £60,000 twelve months after that, so long as
the player was passed fit to play a minimum of twenty-
five matches during the 1986–87 season. Had the playing
conditions of the agreement not been met and Sivebaek
chosen to return to Denmark, there would have been no
fee involved and only if he was then transferred to a club
outside Denmark would United have been able to claim
back their initial £150,000. As it happened Sivebaek made
a total of 31 appearances in 1986–87 before being transferred to St. Etienne at the beginning of the 1987–88 season
for £227,000. United also agreed to play a friendly against
Vejle at Old Trafford or to pay £10,000 if the game could
not be arranged.

Friendly fixtures are a common aspect of transfers nowadays, especially for players from lower-division sides and
foreign clubs. United played St Patrick's Athletic in 1983
after buying Paul McGrath, and Brandon United in 1988
after acquiring Paul Dalton from them.

Alex Ferguson, the United manager at the time of going
to press, has long been worried, however, by the extra
burden that meaningless friendly games arranged as part of
some financial deal, or by agents such as Dennis Roach,
place upon players. He argues that the fans rightly expect

their players to be fresh. The reduction of the first division
to twenty clubs and the disappearance of four league fixtures
should help a little.

When Alex Ferguson arrived at Old Trafford in November
1986, he inherited a squad from Ron Atkinson that was
demoralised and indisciplined. In fact the lack of discipline
among the players was one of the reasons why Ron Atkinson
was sacked after being the longest-serving manager since
Sir Matt Busby. Atkinson had not been the first choice for
the job in 1981. Lawrie McMenemy, Bobby Robson and
Ron Saunders all rejected Martin Edwards' approaches first
– a sign partly of how difficult people realised the United
job to be and partly of disquiet at the way in which Dave
Sexton had been sacked. Atkinson was the first of Busby's
successors not to have been chosen by Sir Matt himself,
although Busby did suggest that the appointment be kept
in-house and recommended Harry Gregg for the job.

Atkinson's first season, 1981–82, saw more than £3
million spent on new players – including £900,000 on the
striker Frank Stapleton from Arsenal and £2,000,000 on
the midfield players Remi Moses and Bryan Robson from
West Bromwich Albion. Robson was to become the most
complete English footballer of the 1980s, and soon assumed
the England captaincy from his injured United team-mate
Ray Wilkins. In his all-round ability Robson had everything
– tackling, passing, running, vision, stamina, goal-scoring
and sheer domination of a game. He would perform
superbly in defence if needed, and yet could be relied on
to score almost as frequently as the forwards. The only
drawback for both United and England was that, throughout the Atkinson years, Bryan Robson suffered persistent
hamstring and shoulder injuries and was absent for long
and important periods.

Under the leadership of Atkinson and Robson, United
reached three Wembley finals – the FA Cup finals of 1983
and 1985, and the Milk (League) Cup in 1983. Twice the
FA Cup came back to Old Trafford with red and white

ribbons. In 1983 beating Brighton required extra time in the first game, which ended 2–2, and a Wembley replay before United marked up a 4–0 victory. Two years later the reds prevented Everton chalking up a remarkable treble of league championship, FA Cup and the European Cup-Winners Cup. Norman Whiteside scored in extra time when United were down to ten men after Kevin Moran had rather unjustly been sent off.

The Atkinson years also saw the resparkling of United's old European tradition. In the Cup-Winners Cup in 1984 Barcelona, one of the strongest teams on the Continent, were beaten 3–0 on an incredible night at Old Trafford after United had gone down 2–0 in the first leg in Spain. But Atkinson's injury-striken team were defeated by a last-minute goal from Juventus' Paolo Rossi in the second leg of the semi-final in Italy.

Yet United never managed to emulate their exciting cup success in the league championship. Season after season the club seemed within reach of Liverpool or Everton, the two sides that had now come to dominate the English game, and yet, after chasing the leaders throughout the campaign, never managed even to finish runners-up. In 1983 United came third. Then three years running, in 1984, 1985 and 1986, after being in serious contention each time, they had to settle for coming fourth in a two-horse race! Something was badly missing from the United make-up, as seen so dramatically after the collapse that followed ten consecutive opening wins in the 1985–86 season.

Frequently the United players displayed their best form only against top teams. Liverpool secured just one league victory over United during Atkinson's five seasons, while United went unbeaten at Anfield. Against lesser sides, however, the players often struggled. After a 3–0 defeat at Southampton, the United manager threatened to put 'kids in place of the international stars if their application isn't 100 per cent all the time. . . . I consider it an honour to be manager of Manchester United,' Atkinson complained; 'I think players should have that same pride. . . . If you're getting well-paid for it, you've got to sweat blood and tears sometimes. All we're sweating at the moment are tears.'

Apart from United's extraordinary inconsistency, Atkinson, like Dave Sexton before him, was ultimately condemned by several unwise financial moves during his last two seasons. Not only had he brought the future England striker Peter Beardsley to United and then let him return to Canada after only half a first-team game, but he spent vast sums on other forwards who seemed overawed by Old Trafford. Alan Brazil cost £700,000 from Spurs but never got a proper chance in the first team and quickly lost confidence. Atkinson later swapped him, together with £350,000, for Coventry's Terry Gibson, who proved an even greater failure, scoring just one goal in twenty-three games. Neither Brazil nor Gibson was the type to make use of the balls sent across by Atkinson's two wing-men, Jesper Olsen and Gordon Strachan. Another striker bought by Atkinson, Peter Davenport from Nottingham Forest, also found it difficult to hit the target. In the new profit-and-loss world of Old Trafford, a manager cannot afford to make such mistakes, or to throw away comfortable leads at the top of the first division. And Old Trafford attendances were slowly dropping.

The United manager found himself increasingly in conflict with Bobby Charlton on the United board. Ron Atkinson attended fewer board meetings than any previous post-war United manager except Wilf McGuinness who was not invited. In his absence Martin Edwards would often defer to Bobby Charlton. Atkinson, for instance, wanted to buy the England defender Terry Butcher from Ipswich for £700,000, but Charlton argued that he would not be a worthwhile investment.

Atkinson's final season at United began badly when he fined seven players for an after-hours drinking session on a pre-season trip to Holland. Then Jesper Olsen was involved in a fight with Remi Moses that ended with the Dane needing eleven stiches in hospital, missing a Littlewoods Cup match and causing big headlines. Initially Atkinson

denied that there had been any trouble, calling it simply a
'clash of heads'. When the truth came out, it only undermined Atkinson's credibility. Moses was also in trouble for
getting medical treatment in Holland without club permission and then presenting United with a bill for several
thousand pounds.

Such incidents only hastened Atkinson's departure. So
too did his failure to achieve much of a rapport with supporters, who considered him too 'flash' and would sing,
'He's big, he's round, he's worth a million pounds,' in
derision rather than admiration. The axe finally fell after
a 4–0 defeat in the Littlewoods Cup at Southampton in
November 1986. Before sacking Atkinson, however, Martin
Edwards made sure that there was a good replacement.

The story told by Martin Edwards and his new manager,
and accepted by the official United history published in
1988 by David Meek and Tom Tyrrell, is that Atkinson
and his assistant, Mick Brown, were dismissed first, and
then Martin Edwards flew to Aberdeen to persuade the
Aberdeen manager, Alex Ferguson, to replace him. Ferguson himself told one of the authors that the call from
Edwards after Atkinson lost his job came as a complete
surprise. The Aberdeen chairman, Dick Donald, was convinced, however, that the deal had been arranged before
Martin Edwards phoned him officially to ask permission to
come and talk to his manager. One would give Edwards
and Ferguson the benefit of the doubt had not the United
chairman made secret arrangements for himself and Maurice Watkins to meet the Aberdeen manager at Glasgow
Airport on the evening *before* Atkinson was dismissed.

The new man found Old Trafford a much harder job
than he had expected. Results did not improve much and
the disciplinary problems continued. Four players, Gordon
Strachan, Billy Garton, Paul McGrath and Kevin Moran,
were fined heavily for arriving late for the team bus in
Dublin in March 1987. Then, on a tour to Malta in May
1987, Norman Whiteside and Paul McGrath were reported
as having spent all night drinking, and arrived late at the

airport the next day. They were fined a week's wages. The club's troubles continued on a mid-season visit to Bermuda in December 1987, when Clayton Blackmore was accused of raping a woman. The resulting legal bill was sent to Blackmore himself.

In Alex Ferguson's first full season, 1987–88, the team finished second, nine points behind Liverpool. It was only the second time since 1968 that United had even been runners-up. Although the number of league defeats – five – was the lowest since 1906, and Brian McClair scored more than twenty league goals, United did not look likely champions. Ferguson was unhappy with the attitude of many of his squad. Indeed, by the end of the season there were few players who had their manager's full confidence. Apart from those he had bought – Brian McClair, Viv Anderson and Steve Bruce – the only players he seemed content with were Mike Duxbury and Peter Davenport, though he later sold Davenport to Middlesbrough. Following United's FA Cup defeat at Arsenal in February 1988, the reds' manager admitted: 'The players are playing for their futures. They have a duty to perform with total commitment in every game, with every kick, until the end of the season.' Secretly, Ferguson was looking to replace Chris Turner, Gordon Strachan and Jesper Olsen, and by March had drawn up a list of priority signings, which included Jim Leighton, Mark Hughes, Trevor Steven, Gary Pallister and Paul Gascoigne. As back-up, names like Paul Stewart, Craig Johnston, Kevin Drinkell and Colin Clarke were also mentioned.

So when two of United's top stars Norman Whiteside and Paul McGrath publicly asked for transfers in April 1988, Ferguson told the board that they should be allowed to leave. A fee of £900,000 was expected for McGrath and £1.5 million for Whiteside. Publicly Ferguson's stance was that United could not afford players who did not want to play for the club, but privately the reasons behind the requests were more complex. In fact, Ferguson is thought to have long considered selling Whiteside because of worries

about the player's behaviour, and McGrath had asked for
a transfer as long ago as the previous October. In January
1988 McGrath was banned from driving for being found
drunk after a crash, but alcohol was only part of his problem. The biggest concern was his persistent knee injury.
Whiteside too enjoyed a drink, and reports from the changing rooms at The Cliff that alcohol could be smelt on his
breath each morning at training did not endear him to a
puritanical manager who greatly admires teetotallers like
Viv Anderson.

United were even said to be prepared to get rid of the
biggest player of them all, the England captain Bryan
Robson, who was also banned from driving after being
caught over the alcohol limit. Indeed, when Martin
Edwards spoke to Newcastle United in April 1988 about
Paul Gascoigne, he said that they could consider any United
player in exchange for Gascoigne, including Robson.

While the United manager wanted to clear out most of
his first-team squad, long contracts signed before his arrival
prevented him from doing so. Eventually, though, Turner
moved to Sheffield Wednesday early in the 1988–89 season
and Olsen to Bordeaux. Gordon Strachan signed for Leeds
United in March 1989, having almost joined the French
club, Lens, the previous summer.

Ferguson's problem was that, unlike Terry Venables, a
manager in a rather similar position at Spurs, he was heavily
restrained by his chairman in what he could spend on new
players. Martin Edwards recalled only too well the costly
transfers of Ron Atkinson's last two years when almost £2
million had been wasted on Alan Brazil, Terry Gibson,
Chris Turner and Johnny Sivebaek. Ferguson was not
helped either by the presence of Atkinson's much cheaper
acquisitions. Players such as Mark Higgins and Peter
Barnes had restricted the progress of the club's own promising youngsters, and also commanded high wages. Ferguson,
on a four-year contract, clearly had more immediate priorit-
ies than Edwards, who might own the club for life. The
financial tensions between the two United men were

revealed publicly after Ferguson had been at Old Trafford for about a year. The United manager stated after one board meeting:

> If we buy now it will mean going into the red. I am not saying we can't buy but we have got to be prudent. We cannot afford to get it wrong. We got £1.8 million for Hughes, but that money had already been spent on new players before we had even received the fee. . . . We still have a big squad on high wages, so there are limits to which we should go.

For Ferguson the resources he had been allowed at Old Trafford clearly did not match his expectations:

> I came here thinking I would have the luxury of buying players. I have done a lot of hard work at youth levels but to win the league we need to buy. I'm disappointed I haven't had that kind of money. Liverpool have bought the best and what sticks in my gullet is the difference between us and them. I respect them but I don't like being second.

He was hardly veiled in his criticism of Edwards:

> He is now facing two very tough choices between having a very good team and balancing the books. It is impossible to have both at present. All I can say is that at Aberdeen I bought twelve players and had just one failure, and I felt that badly. I have a respect for money.

The best example of the financial tensions between Ferguson and Edwards, though, came in the summer of 1988 over Paul Gascoigne, the young midfield player who had made it clear that his horizons lay beyond Newcastle United. United had originally met Gascoigne's advisers at Old Trafford in late 1987 to discuss possible transfer arrangements.

To have met Paul Gascoigne's extraordinary personal terms would have required a vast outlay – far more than was being paid to either Bryan Robson or Mark Hughes. Firstly, Gascoigne wanted a £100,000 signing-on fee. Then his required salary on a four-year contract would have averaged out at £125,000 a year. On top his new club would have to pay £5,000 for every England cap he won. The Football Association would not have been too pleased to learn that the club that acquired Gascoigne had a considerable interest in his *not* playing for England. He was to get a £15,000-club car, a £200,000-new house and a huge slice of any transfer profit at the end of the period. They were among the most demanding terms ever made in the history of English football – higher in some ways than what Liam Brady had requested in 1980 – and particularly bold for a twenty-one-year-old player who had yet to play for his country.

For Martin Edwards, the majority shareholder whose dividend payments are dependent upon his club's finances, it would have been difficult to sleep at night with a £4 million overdraft, a figure which might easily grow to £5 million by the end of the 1988–89 season after high interest payments. Edwards must have doubted that the club would ever get the money back, particularly since nobody seemed to be showing interest in the transfer-listed Whiteside and McGrath. Even Manchester City's transfer debts in the early 1980s had never been greater than £3 million.

Gascoigne's transfer took place, or rather did not take place, while Alex Ferguson was on holiday in Malta. With Tottenham about to complete the deal, Edwards went for a week's holiday at Amer Midani's Marbella Club and the player agreed to join Tottenham Hotspur. Early the following season he won his first cap for England.

Edwards subsequently stated that he could not understand what had happened, and claimed, 'The indications were he would join us. We did table a bid which we believe was as good as Tottenham's.' But Alistair Garvie, Gascoigne's adviser, totally refuted the suggestions, insisting: 'Martin Edwards is talking a load of rubbish and he knows it. It was in their power to match Tottenham's offer and the fact is they didn't.'

By the end of 1988 Alex Ferguson knew that after spending more than £4 million on Anderson, McClair, Leighton, Hughes and the Norwich defender, Steve Bruce, any further big deals would have to be financed by sales. He was increasingly anxious for unwanted players to leave United, in order to replenish his transfer account and ease the wage bill. Moves were set up for Graeme Hogg, Clayton Blackmore and Peter Davenport, but all three men were initially reluctant to go, even if staying at Old Trafford meant reserve football. Hogg did eventually join Portsmouth in 1988, and Davenport went to Middlesbrough. Ferguson used the money raised to bring the Irish defender Mal Donaghy from Luton, and to buy Bristol City's Scottish winger, Ralph Milne.

But few clubs seemed very interested in buying Whiteside or McGrath, two men who might raise much more substantial sums. Potential buyers seemed worried about both players' physical condition. One deal for McGrath to join Spurs involved a complex scheme whereby United would receive an extra £100,000 each time he fulfilled a certain number of appearances, but the transfer fell through. Only in the summer of 1989 did McGrath eventually join Aston Villa for £450,000, and Whiteside go to Everton for £750,000. Both sums were around half the amount the United directors had originally hoped for.

After achieving the runners-up spot in 1988, Ferguson's second full season at Old Trafford proved to be a severe disappointment. Mark Hughes played extremely well on his return from abroad, displaying a much less selfish attitude. He seemed to have cured his excessive drinking, and eventually won the Professional Footballers' Player of the Year award, but his fellow-striker Brian McClair had suddenly lost his previous scoring touch. A succession of nine league games in October and November 1988 summed up the season's frustration. They produced eight draws and one defeat, mostly against average opponents who should

have been easy prey. And in no fewer than eight of the
matches United had actually been ahead at one point, only
to throw their lead away.

The only consolation was a run to the FA Cup quarter
finals, assisted by some stirring performances from a batch
of young players brought in when several senior men were
injured. Defenders Tony Gill and Lee Martin; midfielders
Russell Beardsmore, Lee Sharpe and David Wilson; and
forwards Mark Robins and Deiniol Graham, had all yet to
celebrate their twenty-first birthdays. They inevitably
invited comparisons with the Busby Babes, since they were
all home-grown, with the exception of Sharpe. Yet unlike
Matt Busby's deliberate youth policy, Ferguson was only
picking his young players because of injuries and financial
stringency. Moreover, once the senior stars recovered, most
of 'Fergie's Fledglings' returned to the reserves.

United finished the 1988–89 season in eleventh place.
Ferguson had completely failed to eradicate the inexplicable
inconsistency that plagued the Atkinson era. Form would
slip still further the following season, 1989–90, bringing
the side close to relegation, yet United's poor record on the
field would once again be overshadowed by extraordinary
developments off it.

12
A Different Ball Game

'Manchester United had the opportunity to become one of the top basketball clubs in Europe, and it didn't happen. It was a missed opportunity.'

Rick Taylor, General Manager
Manchester United Basketball 1985–87.

The seven men who gathered in October 1907 to sign the memorandum of association of Manchester United Football Club Ltd clearly had high ambitions for their new company. Article 4, item 2 of the memorandum set out the sporting objects of Manchester United: 'To promote the practice and play of Football, Cricket, Basketball, Lacrosse, Lawn Tennis, Hockey, Polo, Bowls, Cycle and Motor Riding, Running, Jumping, the physical training and development of the human frame . . .' For a further eight lines details were given of the club's possible sporting activities.

For nearly eighty years Manchester United confined itself to the very first of the sports laid down in the company's memorandum, football. Then, towards the end of 1984, Martin Edwards began negotiations for United's involvement in the third sport on the list, basketball. It wasn't the first occasion on which interest had been shown in extending the club's activities in this direction. In 1980–81 there had been tentative discussion about taking over the Manchester Giants basketball team. The deal eventually fell through and the Giants were in the end bought by an Arab businessman called Amer Midani.

In November 1984 the new United director Maurice Watkins was approached by the FSO Warrington Vikings Basketball Club. They were having financial problems, and wanted to know if Manchester United might be interested in buying the club. United's directors were certainly interested. Watkins had been to one or two Vikings games as a guest of one of their directors, Nigel Roden. Martin Edwards had played basketball at Cokethorpe. His friend Dennis Roach was the owner of the Polycell Kingston club in London, one of the country's top sides, and had taken him along to see several matches. Edwards was also aware that many leading European football clubs, such as Real Madrid, Barcelona and Bayern Munich, also ran strong basketball teams. He soon had what he calls the basketball 'bug'. A meeting was arranged with the Vikings' directors on the evening of Tuesday, 27 November 1984.

FSO Warrington were one of the country's top basketball sides, and near the top of the first division of the National Basketball League. At the time of the approach to United they had also been playing in European competition, and were already in the semi-finals of basketball's national cup competition. They had run into money problems, however. Their home ground, the Spectrum Centre in Warrington, held only 1,200 spectators. The venue could not cope with the public demand, yet the club was losing money.

It was a time when Manchester United's football future was looking extremely rosy. After four years with Ron Atkinson in charge, the team looked set to add more trophies to the FA Cup they had won in 1983 and they were regularly playing in Europe. Edwards saw a basketball team as a natural step forward. With weekly television coverage on the new Channel 4, basketball looked as if it might enjoy an explosion of popularity in the same way that snooker had done. Martin Edwards was also keen to be seen to further relations within the local community.

His interest aroused, the United chairman quickly began

going to local basketball games and, in particular, to Vikings matches. He met officials from the English Basketball Association, who soon agreed for the basketball club's name to be changed to Manchester United. Trafford Council were happy to let the team use the main hall at Stretford Leisure Centre on Chester Road, only a few hundred yards from the Old Trafford football ground. But the Stretford hall was barely larger than the Spectrum Centre in Warrington and could hold only 1,550 people. For future years Martin Edwards hoped that he might be able to use the new Greater Manchester Exhibition complex, the G-Mex Centre, which was currently being built on the site of the old Central railway station in the city centre. In the meantime, other ways would have to be found to stem the basketball team's continuing losses.

Sharp Electronics, which had sponsored United's football team since 1982, were approached for a similar deal on the new basketball operation. An extension to the existing Sharp agreement was due shortly and it was felt that they might agree to include basketball in the new sponsorship deal. Edwards met representatives of Warrington's existing sponsors, FSO, at the Royal Lancaster Hotel in London and they were happy to support the new club for the time being. With the likely prospect of Sharp taking over sponsorship in the long term, a contract to buy Warrington Vikings was finally signed on New Year's Eve 1984. The new FSO Manchester United Basketball Club was officially launched at a press conference on 3 January 1985.

United invested £7,000 to acquire a 75 per cent stake in their new enterprise, and it is thought that they paid off £40,000 of the Vikings' debts. A new company was set up, Manchester United Basketball Ltd, whose board comprised both United directors and two former members of the Vikings board who had agreed to transfer their bank guarantees to the new operation. Almost immediately, though, United's plans hit a problem. Top-class basketball was, of course, already being played in the Greater Manchester area, just 6 miles along the Chester road in

Altrincham, by the Manchester Giants. The Giants' owner
and chairman, Amer Midani, was not happy about United
transferring the Warrington club to Manchester. He
regarded it as the Giants' catchment area for basketball
support and fund-raising. In view of his father's wealth,
Midani would be a tough opponent.

The Arab businessman quickly issued a writ against
United. Rather than get involved in a long, expensive,
legal tussle, Edwards and Midani met to try to resolve the
differences. Midani dropped his action on the understanding that United would not organise any basketball fund-
raising activities, such as lotteries, for the next fourteen
months. The two men also agreed to consider the idea of
jointly building a brand-new sports arena to house both
basketball clubs and to promote other events. United would
assist the Giants in trying to secure equal television rights
over the coming year, and there would be two pre-season
friendly matches between the rival sides.

The Vikings had actually been purchased through
United's Development account, MUDL, referred to inter-
nally as 'Muddle'. It was the same account that had been
used two years earlier for the disastrous Spaceshot project
with Glasgow Rangers, an inauspicious move perhaps.

Officially, United's full involvement was not due to start
until the beginning of the 1985–86 basketball season, but
the team's success in winning the 1985 basketball championship play-offs was seen as the first trophy for the new
Red Devils. With the regular television coverage Sharp
Electronics happily agreed to pay £250,000 to sponsor the
club for three years.

Martin Edwards was delighted at the success of his new
team. He had watched most basketball home games up to
the end of the season and witnessed the basketball side's
triumph at Wembley, which preceded the football team's
FA Cup triumph there only a few weeks later. Edwards'
enthusiasm was similar to that of a small boy with a new
toy. Indeed, there were some who wondered whether his

nterest was now greater than it was for the United football
ide.

Overall, Manchester United basketball matches attracted
 very different kind of audience from the football club.
Families often went together, and a survey has shown that
7 per cent of British basketball spectators are female. At
Stretford Leisure Centre there was little of the aggressive
hostility towards opposing fans seen at soccer matches.
Supporters of both teams happily sat side by side, egged
on by the young American-style female cheer-leaders, and
 running commentary. Very few of those who went to
watch Manchester United basketball went to the football
oo. Many United football fans resented their club's
nvolvement in the new sport, arguing that it detracted
from the soccer side. The basketball team, now called Sharp
Manchester United, won the National League in 1986 and
o qualified for the European Cup – at a time when United's
football team were banned from Europe after the Heysel
disaster.

Meanwhile, Edwards was also keen on building a new
activity centre' to cater not just for basketball but other
ports too, as well as pop concerts, exhibitions and religious
vents. This idea had indeed first been mooted by his father
n the late 1970s. It would be built on the No. 3 car-park,
and United had bought opposite the scoreboard end of the
Old Trafford ground. In August 1985 the club's architect,
Ernest Atherden, attended a United board meeting with
plans he had prepared for a building with 9,000 seats on
wo tiers and which would cost £3½ million. But now
Edwards was beginning to have doubts about the idea. The
European football ban, together with the Football League's
failure to reach a deal with the TV companies over television
ights in the coming season, would mean that United could
xpect to lose a substantial amount of income. The club
ould make £200,000 from each round of European compe-
itions, and as much as £1 million from a good European
eason. Without television United lost not only a share of
he money from the TV deal itself, but also large sums

from ground advertising. A decision on Atherden's plans
was deferred, but the directors allowed the architect to
carry on with a feasibility study at no extra cost.

The basketball venture turned out to be a considerable
drain on United's finances. At the 1985 Annual General
Meeting Martin Edwards admitted that basketball had lost
£107,000 in just the first six months, and by the following
year the accumulated loss had reached £253,000. This was
despite the fact that the basketball club's general manager,
Rick Taylor, was raising more than £100,000 a year in
sponsorship, on top of the £83,000 coming annually from
Sharp Electronics. Taylor claimed that the basketball
team's overall contribution to United was underestimated,
since some of the sponsors he had originally signed up for
basketball went on to sponsor the football team instead.

Edwards' friendship with Amer Midani grew to the stage
at which, in May 1986, the two men agreed to merge their
two basketball teams. The result was one of the strongest
basketball sides in Europe. Although the Giants had lost
around £½ million in recent years, United paid nearly
£100,000 for the operation. Martin Edwards told his fellow
football directors that he would nominate Midani as a director of United, though an opportunity to do so at the 1986
AGM was passed over and he did not finally join the board
until February 1987.

The United chairman had not abandoned his plans for
the club to move into other sports. Edwards, Danny
McGregor and Bobby Charlton made several visits to the
big European clubs to develop their expansionist ambitions;
Edwards visited Real Madrid after a European Cup basketball tie between United and the Spanish club in the autumn
of 1986; and Bobby Charlton and Danny McGregor made
a special trip to Barcelona in October 1986. They reported
that the 109,000 members at Barcelona each paid about £32
a year, for which they got free admission to basketball and
handball matches and could use several sports facilities
including an ice-skating rink. Members could even obtain
preferential rates of interest at local banks and book ticket

or matches over the bank counter. So great was the club's popularity that Barcelona also had a waiting list to join.

At the same board meeting at which the directors heard about the Spanish visits, Martin Edwards reported that he had also been involved in negotiations with Salford City Council, who wanted to use the Manchester United name on many of the sports teams they ran. United had recently become involved in a scheme being tried out by the Professional Footballers' Association called 'Football in the Community'. Run by the former United forward Brian Kidd, this programme was designed to allow members of the public in the Manchester area to use the facilities of six local league teams at times when they were not required by the clubs themselves. Professional footballers were also involved in coaching in local schools and at youth clubs. The Salford scheme, however, offered a much wider opportunity than the PFA scheme. Moreover, Salford provided a much simpler option for United than copying the big Continental clubs by building brand-new facilities, which would have been expensive. In April 1987 the then Sports Minister, Richard Tracey, helped Edwards launch a scheme in conjunction with Salford, with the clumsy name of Manchester United Salford Sports Systems. In future 10,000 Salford schoolchildren would participate on a team basis in soccer and eight other sports – athletics, gymnastics, swimming, basketball, volleyball, handball, trampolining and even artistic roller-skating – playing under the name of Manchester United Salford. A joint trust was set up between United and Salford Council, and a company was established to administer matters. Sponsorship worth £40,000 was arranged with Homeowners Financial Services.

Because of legal complications in setting up the joint trust, the venture started slowly, and it was almost a year before the Salford 'Triple S' scheme as it was called, was even mentioned in United's match-day soccer programme. The theory was that sports once organised solely by Salford Council would now receive considerable back-up from Manchester United. Leading United players were designated as presidents at each of the six Salford sports centres, and occasionally they used to go along to hand out prizes. Soccer training sessions were held at The Cliff for Salford schoolboys, and United players sometimes helped with coaching. Salford volleyball and handball teams have competed abroad under the Manchester United name, but the whole venture has been a poor substitute for the multi-sports activities of the great Continental football clubs.

By 1987 the basketball club's losses were becoming intolerable. Sharp Electronics had made it clear that now that basketball was no longer getting regular television coverage, they were not prepared to renew their sponsorship when the current three-year contract ended. The main cost was wages. Although no players were full-time, the basketball wage bill was £131,000 a year – including £110,000 for the players – and Edwards decided that he had either to trim the squad or cut their pay. The chairman reconciled himself to the idea of having a much weaker team if it meant cutting losses and United basketball surviving a few more years. The team's general manager Rick Taylor was told that he could spend no more than £80,000 each year on players' wages.

The finances of the Manchester United basketball team were tiny in comparison with those of the football side. The operation involved both amateurs and part-time professionals. Even Alton Byrd – the most entertaining player in the league – earned only £22,000 a year. In spite of attempts to cut the wage bill, no way could be found of balancing income with expenditure. By November 1987 Martin Edwards was having strong doubts about whether to carry on with basketball. The losses for 1986–87 had worked out at £67,000, more than twice as much as the United chairman had promised shareholders the year before, and he was no longer a regular attender of matches. In an effort to save the venture an alternative venue was sought and at one stage it seemed that it might be possible to move matches to Eccles, where Salford would make

available a hall seating 3,000 at a cost of just £50 a game,
compared with £450 at Stretford.

But at the 1987 AGM Edwards, a man who hates the
slightest criticism, got just what he had feared. A shareholder called Anderson, who had protested at the basketball
losses in 1986, continued his attack:

> I think we agreed at the meeting last year, you and
> I, that this money is coming out of the pockets of the
> people who pay at the turnstiles to watch football.
> Now in view of the fact that the manager has said
> publicly very recently he is not able to get all the
> money he wants to buy necessary players, do you
> think it's right we should continue to throw money
> down this bottomless well?

Martin Edwards, having to defend a policy he no longer
believed in, announced that the club would persist with the
venture for one more year. He argued that there were no
basketball teams anywhere in Europe which made a profit
and said that it was seen as a promotional thing.

Having experienced shareholders' hostility for the third
year running, Edwards immediately took steps to rid himself of the club. What had made matters worse was Rick
Taylor's decision to accept a lucrative and secure job in
America as assistant director of athletics at San Diego University. Taylor says that his main reason for leaving was
not being allowed to extend his commercial activities into
the football side of United, as Edwards had initially suggested to him. 'There was nowhere for me to go up in the
organisation,' Taylor explains. 'I got the results but for
some reason they didn't follow through.'

Yet Edwards knew it would now be almost impossible
to find anybody as good as Rick Taylor at raising money
for basketball. He referred to Taylor's expertise as 'selling
fresh air'. The club was no nearer getting a basketball
sponsor to replace Sharp, and finding one would be even
harder now that it was known United might be involved
for only another year. What made the situation even worse

was that after recent modifications, the possible new Eccles venue could hold no more spectators than the Stretford Leisure Centre.

Coincidentally Edwards had been involved in discussions on football matters with David Kay, a Manchester business-man, who ran a sports agency with the former England rugby union captain, Richard Greenwood, called People Management Ltd. The company employed the star United basketball player Alton Byrd, and had heard about Edwards' problems with basketball. Kay and Greenwood saw a good opportunity and offered to find a new sponsor for Edwards. But as United's commitment to basketball became less certain, this quickly grew into an agreement around Christmas 1987 for the company to buy the whole basketball venture.

In January 1988 People Management Ltd agreed to pay United £50,000 – in three instalments – for their 75 per cent shareholding in the club. No credit was given to People Management to allow for the remaining sponsorship money United had already received from Sharp. The individual directors who had guaranteed the club's bank account set-tled the overdraft.

The People Management director Richard Greenwood argues that soccer and basketball were 'uneasy bed-fellows', and that British sport is not familiar with Continental-style multi-sports clubs such as those of Barcelona and Real Madrid. He also felt that United had treated basketball very much as a 'sideline'. It is true that after attending nearly all his team's early matches Martin Edwards' interest soon waned, and big United names like Bobby Charlton and Bryan Robson were seen far less frequently at Stretford Leisure Centre.

People Management stated initially that they expected the basketball team to be breaking even within a year. By the spring of 1988 this looked fairly improbable. It was obvious that with United's name no longer linked with basketball many of the sponsors would choose to end their

ssociation with the team, and this largely seemed to
appen.

Edwards' very public decision to drop basketball cannot
ave been welcome news to his close friend Dennis Roach.
Roach was actually trying to sell his own Kingston Polycell
eam to Tottenham Hotspur, at the very time United were
howing that basketball was not the wisest investment for
football club. When Manchester United moved into the
ame three years earlier it had been predicted that several
op soccer sides would adopt what was widely seen as an
up-and-coming sport. Portsmouth, in fact, were the only
ther English league side to do so.

The sale was not just a financial humiliation for the Old
Trafford club. The team soon restored the name of Amer
Midani's old side, becoming the Manchester Giants again.
A name change had in fact been part of the agreement to
ell the club, but David Kay and Richard Greenwood
rgued that it was necessary anyway. The name of Manches-
er United, they said, conjured up the wrong kind of image.

13
Selling United

'You can see the changes. Business people come in, not many with any experience of football. It has become a business organisation.'

Sir Matt Busby on United, 1986.

'Attention please!' the loud-speakers boomed out before each game. 'Will somebody please remove Read's sausage van from outside the players' entrance.'

'My dad was no fool,' Al Read, the Manchester comedian who died in 1987, often told his audiences. Having deliberately parked his meat van right outside Old Trafford, 'he knew damned well that sooner or later' the announcement would come. Often he might wait for a second request before actually going out to move the van. Two messages like that, Read calculated, broadcast to the 25,000 or so who watched United in the period around the First World War, were excellent free advertising for his sausages. And it cost no more than a few pence turnstile money. Herbert Henry Read was, perhaps, in his own small way the first man to appreciate the true commercial potential of Manchester United Football Club. It would take the son of another Salford butcher to exploit it fully.

Right up until the late 1960s few football directors paid much attention to making money beyond the ordinary turnstile and transfer receipts. In 1948, for instance, Oxo

offered to pay Manchester United £20 a season for the right
to run refreshment bars selling their famous hot drink at
reserve games played at Old Trafford – the first team were
still playing at Maine Road. The United directors were so
keen, however, that supporters out on the largely uncovered
terraces should be able to warm themselves with steaming
Oxo that they asked for only a 'nominal rent of £5', a
quarter of what the company had offered. The United board
was similarly generous the following year. When the new
British Railways Board asked for an advertising hoarding
alongside their station next to the main stand, the directors
allowed them to put one up for nothing.

Even in the era of the 1968 European Cup win Manchester United did practically nothing to exploit the club crest
and name commercially. At that time anybody could use
United's club badge to sell their own products, without fear
of legal action. When United looked into the matter, they
found that the existing crest, based on the City of Manchester coat of arms, could not be copyrighted, and eventually
designed a new one on which they declared a copyright and
so could sue anyone who breached it.

Today, however, few areas of Old Trafford are not
exploited to full commercial advantage. Home match gate
receipts of around £5 million a year account for only two
thirds of United's total income – the rest comes from a
whole range of other activities. The ultimate aim is to get
that outside income up to 50 per cent.

The best-known of Manchester United's current commercial arrangements, though actually not the most lucrative, is with Sharp Electronics, the Japanese company
which has its British headquarters in East Manchester,
within only a few yards of the site where United began
playing as Newton Heath more than a hundred years ago.
Sharp's relationship with United began in 1982, shortly
after Martin Edwards became chief executive.

United had in fact been rather slow to acquire a club
sponsor. Liverpool and Everton, for instance, had arranged
sponsors as early as 1979, and wore the logos on their

shirts. One drawback initially had been that the television companies refused to allow shirt advertising in televised games, and a high proportion of United games were on TV. At its launch in 1982 United's three-year contract with Sharp was described as the biggest sponsorship deal in soccer, and was worth £750,000. By the time the current fourth contract expires in 1990, United will have earned nearly £3 million from Sharp. Officially much of the money has been allocated to specific development projects, such as the new administrative block at the northern end of the main stand. In reality it simply boosts United's total income.

The sponsorship deal agreed in March 1987, was worth £800,000 to the club. Publicly neither side ever reveals the amount paid, though both sides have been happy to let others refer to the slightly underestimated figure of £750,000, £50,000 below the true amount. For their large outlay Sharp get their name on United's shirts and tracksuits, especially attractive now that the TV companies allow shirt displays. It particularly helps that United's red shirts are the same colour as Sharp's corporate red. But the club are also expected to provide Sharp with considerably more than the prominent logos on the team members' chests.

Indeed, the extra benefits Sharp get are themselves worth well over £100,000 a year. United provide an eight-seat box for Sharp's guests at every game, together with meals. They are also given twelve seats at the back of the directors' box, and twenty-four seats in the Executive Suite for every home match. Then, for two matches every season which are chosen as Sharp family days, the firm is given a further 2,500 seats. On top of that they automatically get 100 ordinary seats for every game, as well as 100 extra places in the Executive Suite for four matches during the course of a season. In addition United must provide Sharp with ten seats at every away game, 100 seats for every cup semi-final the team is involved in, and 200 tickets if United reach any cup final.

In terms of extra advertising, Sharp get the back cover

of every match-day programme, and their logo on the front cover. There are regular announcements on the electronic scoreboard and the public address system, two advertising hoardings outside the ground, and six boards around the pitch. The latter are in the most prominent positions – by the half-way line directly opposite the television gantry, behind the goals and next to the corner flags.

United players are also meant to promote Sharp and its products. Photos showing members of the squad with Sharp microwave ovens and photocopying machines are taken each season and used in the firm's advertising. Two players are expected to have a drink with Sharp's guests after each game and pose for photos with them. Under Ron Atkinson, deciding who was going to fulfil the unpopular Sharp suite chore became something of a ritual. Names would be drawn from a hat at the team hotel before the match, or on the coach during the ride to the ground, and the unlucky 'winners' were derided by the rest of the party. Players are also expected to make regular promotional visits to Sharp's factories in Manchester and Wrexham.

Sharp's former UK chairman, Toshi Mitsuda, became a fervent United fan, but rather than use his firm's private boxes he preferred to go out in the rain and mud to take photographs by the touchline.

The company believes that the United association has helped get the Sharp name recognised in Britain. At times, though, Sharp have been strict, and United are not allowed to take any sponsorship or advertising from Sharp's electronic competitors. When their Japanese rivals, Canon, began sponsoring the Football League Championship in 1983, Sharp expressed concern. Canon's sponsorship of the competition was barely mentioned in the match-day programme thereafter and, unlike other league clubs, United did not give Canon a full-page advertisement. Similarly, in 1982 Sharp were very angry with a photo on the front of a programme showing a United game against Arsenal. The problem was that Sharp's logo could barely be seen anywhere in the picture, but the logo on the Arsenal shirts was quite prominent – and it belonged to Sharp's rival, JVC.

Commercial operations at Old Trafford did not really get going properly until 1973, when Bill Burke, the man who had set up the Development Association, was appointed commercial manager as well. One of his first moves was to end Shell and BP's monopoly of advertising boards around the edge of the pitch, for which they paid just £10,000 a year, a sum that also covered a full-page advertisement in each programme. The petrol companies were getting a remarkable bargain at a time when around two thirds of United's home matches were shown in recorded highlights on television. Within a year of terminating Shell's contract, Burke was receiving £22,000 from perimeter advertising, and the figure rose steadily thereafter.

Of course, advertising boards have been a feature at English soccer grounds for as long as Oxo has been drunk, but recently at Old Trafford the boards have moved upwards. Today on the roof above the Stretford End is a 'Wonderful Gas' sign; the money British Gas paid in the first year went towards new lavatories at that part of the ground. In direct competition, two neon signs at the other end of the stadium state 'This is a . . . Plug for Electricity'. Previously a clever sign for the Mortgage Point changed from red to white to yellow to green and back to red every few seconds and made £2,500 in 1986–87. The new corner Family Stand, for children accompanied by parents, proclaims that it is sponsored by Panini Stickers – the football stickers children collect and put in special albums – and earned £10,000. In recent years boards around the field have encouraged spectators to fly with three different airlines and drink two brands of whisky.

In 1986 the selling of advertising around the edge of the pitch was contracted out to Delta Sports Ltd, based in Bolton and run by Harold Hassall, the former Wanderers and England international. United received 85 per cent of all the revenue from the perimeter adverts and from the posters on six huge hoardings on the number one car park.

Nowadays this work is contracted out to Bermitz Farmer Ltd, based in Hull, who bring in even more money from ground advertising as a result of new television agreements with ITV and the BBC for live coverage of league and cup games. Even more lucrative, though, are those matches that are now shown live in Scandinavia on a regular basis. United have always enjoyed strong support in Denmark, Norway and Sweden and when chosen as the 'live' match, hoardings in the various languages are erected around Old Trafford. The money to be earned from ground advertising on these occasions can sometimes be almost twice that received for matches broadcast to a home audience – a reflection perhaps of the current state of English football.

From 1985 Delta Sports also sold corporate hospitality packages for United and what is known as 'match sponsorship'. From this work the club received a guaranteed £50,000 a year, or 50 per cent of Delta's gross income after expenses, whichever was the greater. These corporate hospitality packages were designed for the new breed of business football supporter. They included a night's hotel accommodation, tickets to the match, a champagne reception beforehand, a tour of the ground, lunch, entertainment hosted by former player Pat Crerand, free drinks, travel and even a photographer to record the occasion, all for £98 a person. Since 1988, however, United have organised the hospitality packages themselves. Matches are now graded into 'A' games, 'B' games and 'C' games, depending on the calibre of the opposition, and each costs a different price.

Alternatively firms can 'sponsor' a particular match, a different thing from Sharp's sponsorship of the club over several years. For a fee of £5,750 upwards match sponsors can buy 'hospitality' at a game for forty or more guests, as well as advertising in the match programme, on the electronic scoreboard and over the public address system. They also get several advertising displays, including two 20-foot boards by the pitch, positioned near corner flags to catch television cameras. United's ventures into the world of corporate hospitality are, of course, part of the growing trend in British sport. From Wimbledon to Cheltenham, Wembley to St Andrew's, companies use sporting occasions to reward staff and entertain clients – though often, it seems, customers have little interest in the events they are invited to.

The most blatantly commercial of all their arrangements, however, must be the one United have for their playing strip with the world-famous sports manufacturer Adidas. Exploiting the popular Manchester United kit was one of the first moves made by Bill Burke when he became commercial manager, at a time when manufacturers were beginning to realise the potential. Until then one red and white football outfit was much the same as another – United's plain red shirts with white trimmings, plain white shorts and plain red socks were identical to several other league sides'.

Burke first agreed a deal with the manufacturers, Umbro International. Umbro would design a distinctive United kit with a club badge and enjoy the right to produce it under licence. This meant that replicas could be made and sold in shops, and United were granted a royalty of 10 per cent on each kit. In 1975 United's kit contract was switched to Hurst and Cooke of Leicester, who later became Admiral. The new suppliers guaranteed United a minimum of £15,000 a year for three years, although the overall royalty was only 5 per cent. Admiral also agreed to pay extra bonuses if the team achieved certain playing targets – £10,000, for instance, for reaching the FA Cup final, and another £6,000 if they went on to win the Cup. For Admiral the extra television exposure and prestige of a Wembley appearance would make the money worthwhile.

In 1980 Admiral signed a new four-year contract with the club, but then went bankrupt within only a few weeks – the two events were unconnected, it seems. A new deal for a similar period was quickly agreed with the German firm Adidas, who, after Admiral's demise, had become the main manufacturer of English league kits. As part of the arrangement the players received £15,000 to share between them. The Adidas contract was renewed in 1983, ahead of schedule, and again in 1987. But on the second occasion United actually received a more favourable offer from Hummel, the kit manufacturer that is a subsidiary of Tottenham Hotspur. Hummel promised a minimum of £1.6 million over four years, while Adidas was offering only £1.5 million over the same period. Martin Edwards went back to Adidas and they agreed to improve their bid.

United's present deal with Adidas is worth a guaranteed £350,000 a year and lasts for five years, not four as originally proposed. United get an extra 10 per cent royalty once sales go beyond £750,000 in any one year. Adidas enjoy sole rights to manufacture and market the strip, which sells for about £40 in the shops. It brings Adidas an annual turnover of about £1 million, so United can expect some royalties on top of their guarantee.

Nowadays the design of football strips is a fine, calculated business. Each set of shirt, shorts and socks is carefully planned to generate the maximum revenue for the sole manufacturer and the club. As part of every kit deal since 1973, including the current five-year contract with Adidas, the two parties agree to change small details of the strip every two years, a deliberate move to regenerate demand at regular intervals. And each part of the kit – shirt, shorts and socks – has to be changed. In 1984, for instance, white bands, looking like shoulder-straps, were added to the shirt; red pinstripes appeared on the white shorts; and white bands were added on the top of the black socks. 1986 saw equally small changes. The white shoulder-straps were replaced by two white stripes down each arm of the shirt; the shorts' red pinstripes gave way to three black and red stripes down the side; and the white bands on top of the socks fell to half-way down. The new strip introduced in 1988 included the letters 'MUFC' subtly marked in the texture of the fabric, rather like a watermark on paper. Few adult supporters notice or care about such small details, but their ever-demanding children certainly do. United's deal with Adidas is the more lucrative commercial arrangement of all at Old Trafford. Sharp actually guarantee a larger annual payment, but allowing for the cost of the numerous extra benefits Sharp get, such as free boxes and hospitality, the Adidas deal is in fact more profitable.

United's match-day programme, the *United Review*, is another major source of income. Carrying advertising copy from all the club's major sponsors, it plays an important role in the commercial operations. The programme is among the most popular in the league. It used to sell to around 96 per cent of every home crowd, partly because of the tokens inside which fans collect to get priority for tickets for big matches. At 70p the programme is also among the cheapest in the country and, helped by a small amount of advertising that actually pays, it generates a profit of well over £100,000 a season – as high as £190,241 in 1986 for instance.

A much less successful publication was *Man-U-News*, a newspaper launched by Danny McGregor in September 1987. It was based on monthly newspapers which had already been successfully produced for Chelsea and Portsmouth by Hayters, a sports news agency run from Fleet Street by Frank Nicklin, a former sports editor of *The Sun*. Hayters hoped to finance the paper through advertising, and United received 50,000 free copies each month to sell at 30p each. But distribution through major outlets was unsuccessful. Poor circulation hit advertising revenue. Nicklin could not make the publication pay and it folded after three issues.

A quite profitable activity in the last few seasons has been the sale of video tapes of United games. Dave Sexton originally bought the club's video equipment in the late 1970s to film every match for analysis in coaching. It has since developed into a business and fans can buy compilations of matches and goals, and there have even been plans to sell the videos in the shops of away teams that have come to Old Trafford and won! United were also expected to earn lucrative royalties on the BBC video, *The Official History of Manchester United FC*, released in 1988.

Diaries and books bring in further revenue. The *Man-*

chester United Diary, published every year, makes United a guaranteed £2,500. Other money is earned from in-house events, such as the club's own version of the *Miss Manchester United* contest, which, together with fashion shows, was budgeted to realise £4,000 in 1986–87. Charity Dinners and Fun Day events, an extension of another successful venture first initiated by the supporters' club, were expected to earn £4,000. The original fans' 'Family Day' was run in conjunction with the Variety Club of Great Britain and helped provide a mini-bus for underprivileged children.

There are limits, though, to the extent to which matches at Old Trafford, space inside the stadium and the United name can be sold commercially. Bill Burke's latest successor, Danny McGregor, believes that those limits have nearly been reached. He sees his task now as finding new ways of exploiting the magic of the Manchester United name beyond Old Trafford. Already that has meant United joining projects involving other British clubs.

One of the most controversial recent ventures was Red Devil, supposedly United's own lager, which caused a minor outcry when it was launched in 1987. The scheme, set up with a firm called Team Advance, also involved Liverpool and Everton. Red Devil drinkers who collected a certain number of ring-pulls from the cans could obtain tickets and team souvenirs. A total of 640 ring-pulls could be exchanged for one ticket to Old Trafford, though after that amount of lager the police might not allow one into the game. For John Smith, chairman of Liverpool and the Sports Council; Philip Carter, chairman of Everton and the Football League; and United's Martin Edwards to launch a club lager was perhaps a little strange when alcohol is banned from football terraces and drink is blamed for much football violence. But such considerations – and indeed the unhealthy linking of alcohol and sport – came second to the expected profit. In fact, Team Advance failed to market the lager successfully, and the scheme seems to have folded. As far as is known, nobody ever collected the necessary 640 ring-pulls!

Red Devil lager failed despite the publicity generated by the controversy. The launch even warranted an edition of the Manchester United Club-Call, a daily recorded telephone message put out by British Telecom's Supercall department. Fans can dial for the latest information about United – scores, match reports, interviews, ticket news and so on. A team of journalists in London, backed up by stringers in Manchester, keeps the service up to date. United guarantee to give the Supercall journalists reasonable access to players and officials for interviews. In return United expected to earn £20,000 in 1986–87. Today it is probably worth nearer £100,000.

Club-Call's editorial standard is quite high, though overall it contains little you could not find in the press. But costing 44p a minute at peak hours and 29p off-peak, up to a maximum of three minutes, the service cannot endear itself to the parents of young fans who could spend £5 a week if they called every day. Manchester United's is among the most popular of all Supercall's forty soccer lines. Around 1,000 calls are received daily, averaging a minute and a half in length, and the figure rises to 2,400 when United are playing a distant away game. Calls reached a peak on the day Ron Atkinson was sacked in 1986; and so, with the subsequent extra royalties, United recovered a little of Atkinson's £100,000 severance cheque!

Supercall even introduced its own 'man of the match' award at the end of the 1987–88 season. They hoped that fans would actually be keen enough after a game to pay for the privilege of phoning to nominate their best United player. The award was quickly dropped.

The Red Devils Souvenir Shop next to the railway bridge on Warwick Road is United's most public commercial enterprise. For more than twenty years it has sold pens, underpants, lampshades, mirrors, cigarette lighters and hundreds more items all sporting the Manchester United badge. After opening in 1967, it quickly became the most successful souvenir shop at any league club, with a range of more than 200 items. On match days the trade was once so heavy that there were long queues outside an hour and a half before kick-off. The people had to be marshalled by a commissionaire, and smaller branches were opened around the ground.

Yet the fact that Sir Matt Busby had owned the lease on the shop became widely known only in 1979 when somebody asked a question at the first large-scale Annual General Meeting of the club, though a previous revelation in a Sunday newspaper had passed almost unnoticed. By then Sandy Busby had in fact taken over the day-to-day running of the business. The shop proved to be so successful over the years that by 1986 it had an annual gross profit of around £100,000 and employed eight staff. The £5 rent that Sir Matt Busby originally agreed to in 1968 had been increased voluntarily to £75 a week by the mid-1980s.

Almost since becoming chief executive in 1982, Martin Edwards had been trying to persuade Sandy Busby to give up the lease. In particular he was keen to include shop profits within the club accounts at a time when he wanted to make United more attractive for public flotation. It was only in 1987, however, when the lease had nearly expired anyway, that Sandy Busby agreed to sell the remaining two years. Busby knew that if he stuck it out until the very end, United would take the freehold back and he might end up with nothing.

The price was reported as being more than £200,000. It seems a generous sum but Martin Edwards admitted at the 1987 Annual General Meeting that it included over £100,000 worth of stock that Busby had bought over the years. And a large proportion of the money was paid by way of an annual consultancy fee to Sandy Busby, but on one important condition. He had to agree not to reveal to outsiders any information about the souvenir shop or United as a whole, or indeed anything learnt about the club even after he left. Busby also had to agree not to run a business selling sports souvenirs within 10 miles of Old Trafford for the next five years.

Sandy Busby would have been happy to continue running

the shop, even on very different terms from those his family had previously enjoyed – as a United employee, for instance. Instead the shop was leased to Circle Sports Promotions Ltd, part of Maybank Press Ltd, based in Ilford, Essex, and run by Eddie Buckley. United had enjoyed various dealings with Buckley over the previous ten years, including the publication of six *Manchester United Annuals* between 1977 and 1982 and the production of other items such as club calendars, a poster magazine, duvets and bed-linen, on which the club received various royalties.

The new Circle Sports management, however, ran the operation somewhat less efficiently and attractively than the Busbys. Their window displays were drab, dusty and full of rubbish dropped by customers. In January 1988 the window still showed a poster for a programme fair that had occurred two months earlier. In the spring of 1988 Circle Sports went into liquidation, and in August that year United began direct management of the Red Devils Souvenir Shop.

The summer of 1988 also saw the club launch out in a new retail venture – leisurewear. This involves selling simple everyday clothes in modern designs – shirts, trousers, pullovers, jackets and so on, from a new fashion shop next to the Red Devils Souvenir Shop. But unlike previous garments sold by the souvenir shop, many do not display the United name prominently, and few are in club colours. Some carry United's small, distinctive, stick-man logo, made up from the letters MUFC. A glossy catalogue showing United players modelling the new leisurewear was sent out to all club members, and the intention is that many of the sales will come from mail-order business.

The takeover of the souvenir shop from Sandy Busby in 1987 was perhaps symbolic of a process that had been going on at Old Trafford for twenty-five years. It marked the final phase in the transfer of power at Manchester United from the Busbys to the Edwards. Sandy Busby, the son earmarked by the creator of the modern United to continue his influence at Old Trafford, had finally been evicted by

Martin Edwards, the son of the man Busby had brought to United, who had purchased the club for next to nothing and started his own dynasty.

14
The Man Who Didn't Buy United

'I was never in it for the fast dollar, ever.'

Michael Knighton, on his deal to buy United.

Sixteen castles once dotted the twenty miles of the Girvan Valley in Ayrshire – monuments to the bloody battles that raged in this part of South West Scotland in medieval times. Three miles up the valley from the coastal town of Girvan, about twenty miles south of Ayr, is Killochan, built in 1586 on a site first owned by Robert the Bruce in the early 1300s. Every Christmas for hundreds of years, the laird of Killochan had to deliver three spears to the Bruce seat, Turnberry Castle, five miles to the north. In the seventeenth century Killochan housed secret Presbyterian services, and its thick walls still hold concealed rooms where the persecuted dissenters once hid from English troops.

One Friday evening in late July 1989 Killochan Castle saw history unfold in very different circumstances – its grand rooms were the setting for probably the most controversial deal ever agreed in the long, sorry history of British football.

The final details were settled over dinner. Killochan's 37-year-old owner, Michael Knighton, a property speculator, assured Martin Edwards he would instigate no revolution when he took over Manchester United. The directors and staff at Old Trafford would stay put, he promised, while

Edwards himself would remain on the board as chief executive for three years, on a salary of more than £80,000.

Shortly before midnight the two men shook hands and the deal was struck. Martin Edwards, expecting to be ten million pounds richer, stayed overnight at Killochan. Knighton had arranged the next day for a helicopter to ferry Edwards from the castle grounds to Glasgow Airport, and the plane back to Manchester. A great burden had been removed from his shoulders, or so the United chairman must have thought as he flew home.

Yet only a few weeks earlier there had been little sign that Edwards was on the point of selling up. One evening shortly after the 1988–89 season ended, the United chairman had in fact discussed his position with his fellow-directors over dinner. Did he intend to sell, they all wanted to know. Edwards pointed out that when he took the chairmanship in 1980, he had planned to give the job ten years, and then consider whether to carry on. That was still his intention, he assured them, so any questions about his future would not be resolved until the full ten years were up, at the end of the coming season, 1989-90. Then, Edwards said, he would ask himself whether he was doing a good job, whether the fans still wanted him, and assess how the club was doing on the field, and financially.

By the summer of 1989, however, the answers to those questions were already looking more unsatisfactory for Martin Edwards than at any time during his nine years at Old Trafford. After United had fallen 1–0 to Nottingham Forest in the FA Cup quarter final, the previous season had fizzled out. More worrying than the team's final mid-table league position was the evaporation of the famous red support. The official crowd at home to Everton in mid-May was only 26,722 – an appalling figure for such local and relatively attractive visitors. And 23,368 against Wimbledon was the club's worst home league crowd since 1966. Moreover, the real figures were, of course, much lower – probably about 15,000 – because of the way United count season-ticket holders who don't attend. Old Trafford's aver-

age home crowd for the 1988–9 season, 36,247, had been
the worst since 1962.

The man due to assume Martin Edwards' responsibilities,
Michael Knighton, was born in Belper, Derbyshire, in
October 1951. His father, Albert Knighton, held a series
of jobs: he was a baker and a driver, and worked in
the Derbyshire mining industry, both at the coal-face
and on the surface. A great-grandfather on Knighton's
mother's side, William Layton, had played 361 games
for Sheffield Wednesday between 1898 and 1909, mostly
at full back, and had helped the Yorkshire side win the
league in 1903 and 1904, and the FA Cup in 1907. A
specially commissioned portrait of Layton hangs alongside
Knighton's collection of nineteenth-century paintings at
Killochan.

Michael Knighton, too, had once shown promise as a
footballer: he signed originally as a schoolboy apprentice for
his local Derby County, and in the 1967–8 season became a
professional with Coventry City who'd just won promotion
to the first division for the first time. Among the biographi-
cal details Knighton would distribute to reporters in 1989
was a photo of himself in the Coventry 'B' side – the fourth
team. His team-mates included the future Aston Villa captain, Dennis Mortimer, and goalkeeper David Icke, better
known nowadays as a BBC sports presenter and spokesman
for the Green Party. Icke is one of the few Coventry colleagues who remember much about him. Knighton was a
'character', Icke says, had a 'very broad South Derbyshire
accent', and was known as 'Elvis' because of his hairstyle.
'He was always standing in front of the dressing-room
mirror,' Icke recalls, 'combing his hair and flexing his
muscles.'

The young Knighton was apparently 'football crazy', certain that one day he was destined to be a superstar. But
Knighton's hopes of fame in league football were destroyed
after only a few months at Coventry, by a ruptured thigh
muscle.

In later years Knighton played amateur soccer for two

Derbyshire non-league sides, Ilkeston and Heanor Town, but forced into a new career, he chose teaching. A physical education course at Durham University eventually led in 1976 to a job teaching PE and geography at St David's, a private school in Marsh, a suburb of Huddersfield, West Yorkshire. Within two years Knighton was deputy head, and in 1980, at the age of only 28, he was appointed headmaster. By 1983 he had actually bought the school.

Knighton has explained how his career might easily have been confined to teaching had it not been for the birth of his first child, Mark, in 1977. Because of a lack of oxygen during the delivery the boy was partially paralysed and almost deaf. 'It had a profound effect on me and I decided right then to become financially self-sufficient,' Knighton says. 'I was a teacher, had no money and could have lost my job.' Mark Knighton did recover considerably, though today he still has only twenty per cent hearing and some paralysis. But the event had a strong motivating effect on his father.

That year Knighton sold the family car for £750, and used the money as a deposit to buy a four-storey building in Marsh for £12,000, containing florist and greengrocer shops on the ground floor. The following year Knighton sold the two shops, together with their business and goodwill, for £24,000 – twice the amount he had paid for the whole building. The profit bought further buildings in West Yorkshire and Edinburgh, his wife's home town. Thus his property business had started, Knighton claims, with no financial help either from his parents or his wife's family.

Knighton says he is not a developer of property, only that he has accumulated wealth through shrewd buying. 'I bought period properties or properties of architectural merit and allowed the capital growth to accrue.'

By the mid-1980s, Knighton had done so well from property dealing that he felt able to return to his first love. 'You know, I'm going to spend this money we have made on a football club,' Knighton recalls telling his wife Rosemary late one night as they settled down in bed. He wanted to contribute to a game he still felt passionate about.

His first target was fourth-division Halifax Town, not far from Huddersfield. One of the least distinguished sides in the League, with possibly the worst stadium of all 92 clubs, Halifax had debts of around half a million pounds, and were about to fold. After quite extensive discussions in late 1987, Knighton lost interest when the local Calderdale Council would not sell him the freehold on Halifax's ground. Knighton considered owning the land vital to developing the club, but also felt the new investment Halifax needed – around £6 million – was 'sheer madness' for such a small club.

Early in 1989 Knighton's sights were set much higher – on third-division Bolton Wanderers, founder members of the league, and four-time winners of the FA Cup. Quiet negotiations went on for more than four months, but the Bolton directors could never take seriously Knighton's offer to inject £1.5 million into the club.

While the Bolton talks were progressing, Knighton was introduced to a former Wanderers' chairman, Barry Chaytow, by a Manchester City director during a game at Maine Road. The two men quickly struck up a close friendship, but rather than help in acquiring Bolton, Chaytow was more useful in advising Knighton on other possible targets, among them Manchester United.

Press speculation in May 1989 that Martin Edwards might be on the point of selling United to Amer Midani prompted Knighton to ask Chaytow whether it would be worth approaching Edwards. Chaytow rang the United chairman to suggest a meeting, without explaining on the phone what Knighton was interested in. Chaytow recalls that the subsequent lunch in the Manchester United restaurant lasted about three hours. In the weeks ahead Knighton and Edwards continued talks together without Chaytow's help.

Edwards told Knighton he wanted £10 million for his 50.2 per cent stake in the club – around £20 a share. 'When

Martin mentioned the figure he wanted I didn't quibble,' Knighton explained later. 'I agreed straight away. There was no haggling.' Knighton appreciated what Edwards didn't – that he was getting a bargain. 'It's a snip,' Knighton would boast, 'I can't believe I got the club for £10 million. There are people, I know, who would have paid twice that amount.'

Under the Stock Exchange take-over rules Knighton would have to make the same £20-a-share offer to every other United shareholder. In theory that might add another £10 million to Knighton's bill, though of course many United shareholders would not sell whatever the price. But what impressed Edwards was that Knighton was also prepared to spend £10 million more on completing the development of Old Trafford as a modern cantilever stadium. From their table in the restaurant they would have seen how cantilever stands now encircled three quarters of the ground, but that the Stretford End was still covered by an old-fashioned steel roof which was now more than thirty years old. Edwards had long feared that with the constant pressure to buy new players it might never be possible to rebuild the Stretford End, the traditional home of United's most vociferous fans. It seems to have been Knighton's promise to develop the area which persuaded Edwards it wasn't worth also approaching the many others he knew were interested in buying his shares.

Martin Edwards mulled over Michael Knighton's proposal during a month's holiday with his family in the Greek Islands. The secret Friday night trip to Killochan was arranged on his return to Manchester.

The clandestine nature of the negotiations between Knighton and Edwards may partly have caused the trouble that arose later. Had Edwards been more open, more questions might have been asked. Had they known about it, fellow directors would have tried to counter Knighton's bid; indeed interest in one day buying the club had long ago been expressed to Edwards by Amer Midani and Nigel Burrows.

Maurice Watkins, United's solicitor, and in the past also
a legal adviser to Edwards, knew very early on about the
deal, which incidentally stood to bring him a million
pounds. Nigel Burrows found out accidentally while the
team were on tour in Japan in early August. Burrows'
suspicions were aroused when he overheard Edwards and
Watkins discussing at the breakfast table Susan Edwards'
plans to buy a house in the Lake District for a million
pounds. Sceptical that the family had that kind of cash,
Burrows asked whether Edwards intended to sell United.
In his hotel room at 4.00 am the next morning, Martin
Edwards confirmed that this was so, assured Burrows it
was too late to make a counter-offer, and yet overcame
Burrows' disappointment to make him promise not to tell
the other directors. So the rest of the board didn't know
until much later. Indeed Bobby Charlton and Michael Edelson only found out minutes before the news broke on 'News
at Ten' on the night of Thursday 17 August.

Who exactly the buyer was did not emerge publicly until
the following day. The newspapers had speculated about a
consortium of Scottish businessmen. The Celtic shareholder, Michael Kelly, was mentioned; so was Gerard
Eadie, owner of Celtic's sponsors, C. R. Smith. The man
the press were looking for though was much more obscure.

So obscure in fact, that Martin Edwards accidentally
introduced Knighton at the press conference as 'Michael
Whetton' – the name of United's catering manager. People
were immediately suspicious about how someone so
unknown could raise the money on his own. '£30 million
is not a lot in commercial terms. I am certainly not, if he
will forgive me, a Robert Maxwell,' Knighton responded.
'This is the age of the enterprise culture and I have been
lucky.'

Yet in his keenness to deny rumours about a Scottish
consortium, Knighton insisted it was a 'one man bid' – a
statement which proved to be misleading to say the least –
though he did mention the possibility of bringing in minor
partners later on. 'In business I'm a one-man band and

there are no major consortiums, or even small ones, in this with me,' he told the *Daily Mirror*. 'The money is all mine or my backers',' a somewhat contradictory statement which suggested that indeed he was not alone. More revealing still, he said that while it was not a massive outlay, he still expected 'to make a profit'. Quite how wasn't clear. Knighton said he wouldn't take a salary from United, but did expect 'consultancy fees' if his work for the club merited them.

The announcement seemed to mark the end of an era at Old Trafford. The Edwards family were ready to step down after nearly a quarter of a century in charge. 'The fans will, in all probability, say good riddance,' Martin Edwards lamented. 'I felt after nine and a half years I had taken the Club as far as I could.'

Never can Manchester United have enjoyed such an extraordinary opening to any league season as they did the following day. Martin Edwards had appeared on the Old Trafford pitch only rarely – indeed on the previous occasion he was booed. But Knighton's sudden emergence from the players' tunnel, dressed in United training kit, met with loud cheers. The prospective owner, who only the previous day had described himself as 'shy', delivered a two-fisted salute to the Stretford End, blew kisses, juggled with the ball from foot to foot and knee to knee, and fired shots into an empty goal. 'The boyhood dream got the better of me,' says Knighton, explaining why his shyness had suddenly gone. 'I wanted to identify with the people on the terracing.' And certainly Knighton's dramatic entrance and instant gesture towards the fans seemed very much in keeping with United's flamboyant traditions.

So too was the match that followed. The visitors, Arsenal, were the reigning league champions, having clinched the title on goal difference over Liverpool, in injury time of an incredible final game at Anfield the previous May. Yet within two minutes at Old Trafford Steve Bruce's header had put United in the lead. Three excellent goals from Mark Hughes, Neil Webb and Brian McClair in the last

half-hour made it 4–1. In one afternoon the team had
achieved something not managed in any league game the
previous season – scoring four times.

Yet it was soon clear that Knighton himself was not rich
enough in terms of personal assets to pay the £30 million
he had committed to the club.

Quite how much Knighton was worth would not be
established until some weeks later. His own accounts,
leaked to the *Manchester Evening News*, put his assets at
between £3.2 and £12 million. They were based largely on
his property around the British Isles. The most valuable
item was the 100-year-old St David's school. A co-edu-
cational establishment with around 420 pupils, it occupies
an old Victorian building, and charges fees of about £2,000
a year. With an annual fee income of around £850,000, the
school's value was put at somewhere between £2 and £5
million.

Killochan Castle was valued at between £750,000 and
£2.5 million. Other assets included farms in Yorkshire, a
150-acre estate on the Isle of Man, a hotel in Edinburgh,
various other houses in Scotland and Yorkshire, and his
fine art collection. But Knighton also owed banks nearly
two million pounds.

Knighton's take-over was actually being mounted
through a company, MK Trafford Holdings Ltd, recently
registered in the Isle of Man, where he had gone to live as
a tax exile early in 1989. In fact the company had only
changed its name from Appeal Holdings the very day the
deal was announced – the 'MK' presumably representing
Knighton's own initials. Though several questions were
asked about the mysterious businessman who suddenly
seemed to have taken over the club, too many people –
Martin Edwards, the United board, the media and the
supporters – were ready to accept the Knighton take-over
at face value without probing the inconsistencies. In a *Manchester Evening News* phone-in poll, supporters welcomed
Knighton by a margin of six to one. But gradually doubts
emerged.

Within a week the *Evening News* revealed that far from acting on his own, Knighton was being backed by two wealthy businessmen, Robert Thornton and Stanley Cohen, the chairman and deputy chairman of Betterware, the household goods conglomerate. The two men certainly belonged to a much higher bracket of millionaire than Knighton. Between them, for instance, they had made a profit of £34 million on selling the rejuvenated Schreiber kitchen furniture business in November 1988 – just eighteen months after buying it for £500,000.

Thornton, a former chairman of Debenham's stores, is described by Knighton as 'a very close personal friend', and lives only two miles from Killochan Castle in Ayrshire. The two men had enjoyed lunch together during Knighton's early negotiations with Martin Edwards. Thornton considered United a very attractive proposition at the price Knighton was getting, and offered to help both with financing and with contacts in the City. 'If you were to set up from scratch,' Thornton said later, 'a business like Manchester United would cost £60m or £70m.' Knighton agreed to sell his neighbour a forty per cent stake in MK Trafford Holdings. In turn Thornton provided Knighton with advisers – the American bankers, Citicorp, and the London solicitors, Forsyte Kerman. Thornton's son was a partner with Forsyte Kerman, and began working on the deal himself.

Martin Edwards had been told about Robert Thornton's involvement, but none of the other United directors knew about it until it became public. Knighton explains that he hadn't mentioned it earlier because Thornton didn't want any publicity. It seems extraordinary that he expected to keep it quiet, but then Knighton is the first to admit how 'very naïve' he was.

Stanley Cohen's role was less clear. Knighton says he hadn't yet met Cohen, and didn't even know about his proposed involvement. He insists it was purely a private agreement Cohen had made with Robert Thornton to buy part of his share in MK Trafford Holdings. Cohen says he saw the investment as one for 'prestige, not cash'.

Michael Knighton's arrival on the Old Trafford grass might have inspired victory over Arsenal, but United's form soon returned to the mediocrity of the previous season, despite £2,250,000 spent on acquiring Neil Webb from Nottingham Forest and Mike Phelan from Norwich. The financial constraints on Alex Ferguson had been eased by the £1,200,000 raised from selling Norman Whiteside and Paul McGrath, and the expected profit from 1988–9 of £1,433,000 – of which £780,000 came from the new television contract. But the two new midfield men did little to strengthen the side, particularly since Webb was injured for six months while playing for England in September.

Knighton's proposed investment seemed to loosen the purse strings still further. Alex Ferguson felt confident he could now bid again for two players he had failed to buy that summer. Middlesbrough had already rejected an offer of £2 million for their England centre back, Gary Pallister, and the deal finally settled at the end of August cost United £2.3 million – the highest fee ever paid by a British club. Middlesbrough drove a hard bargain, aware both of United's apparent new riches and the club's desperation after the Swedish centre back, Glenn Hysen, had unexpectedly gone to Anfield instead of Old Trafford.

Ferguson's other remaining target was the young West Ham midfield player, Paul Ince. Ince's agent, Ambrose Mendy, had been so eager for him to go to Old Trafford that he arranged for him to pose in a United shirt – a month before any deal had been agreed. But Ince's transfer was delayed first by West Ham needing a replacement and then the discovery that he had a pelvic injury. But Neil Webb's injury persuaded Ferguson to buy Ince on a pay-as-he-plays contract with West Ham. On top of United's £800,000 down-payment, West Ham would get £5,000 for every game Ince played over the next five years.

In addition Southampton's England winger, Danny Wallace, joined for £1,200,000. The three transfers took Fergu-

THE MAN WHO DIDN'T BUY UNITED

on's spending to almost £12 million in under three years,
while Martin Edwards had authorised payments of around
£21 million in almost a decade.

Michael Knighton, too, was talking of ambitious investment plans – and hoped to make United a £150 million
business within fifteen years. 'We are investing in the industry which has major pulling power that has not been
exploited,' he stated. In particular he wanted to make more
money from former stars such as Denis Law and Bobby
Charlton, though whether they themselves approved wasn't
clear. Marketing experts were to be brought in, and the
idea of a European Super League would be pursued vigor-
ously to obtain television rights that Knighton estimated
might be worth £10 million a season. The United name
would be used even more to endorse clothes, cosmetics and
holidays; there would be a chain of shops, a mail-order
catalogue and licensed goods; and printing and clothes firms
might be established. New sports such as tennis, boxing
and hockey would be staged at Old Trafford. A new club
magazine was envisaged. And, under the government's proposed compulsory membership scheme, Knighton believed
it would be possible to 'commercially exploit' United members by selling their names and addresses.

The only substantially new part of Knighton's plans,
however, was a five-star luxury hotel behind the Stretford
End, not exactly Manchester's most attractive location.
Knighton talked of getting an architectural design team
together and obtaining planning permission. The land
would be acquired from Manchester Council, by offering a
swap for one of United's car-parks on the other side of the
stadium.

Documents released later revealed that Knighton also
intended to axe Nigel Burrows and Amer Midani from the
United board. One of their replacements would be Barry
Chaytow, the man who had helped make it all possible.

Yet amidst all the ambitious plans both on and off the
pitch, everybody was forgetting that Knighton's agreement
with Edwards was only conditional. Though the document

they had signed was entitled 'Sale and Purchase Agreement', all it did was give Knighton the *option* to buy United. For some strange reason Martin Edwards had conceded this option for absolutely nothing in return. Whilst the property speculator could buy the club, he could also drop out of the deal altogether if he wished. Knighton had one month from the date of the original announcement – until Wednesday 20 September 1989 – to confirm the deal. In the meantime his accountants, Robson Rhodes, would carry out an audit of the club's affairs.

Seven days before Knighton was due to confirm the deal it began to unravel. His backers, Robert Thornton and Stanley Cohen, suddenly withdrew, taking with them their advisers, Forsyte Kerman and Citicorp. The two men decided not to make public their reasons for pulling out. All Robert Thornton will say is: 'a lot of people sat around a table and agreed to withdraw.' The phrase 'lot of people' implies there might well have been more investors than simply Thornton and Cohen, though he may just have been including their advisers.

Michael Knighton concedes that argument over the size of Thornton's and Cohen's stake in MK Trafford Holdings was certainly a factor in their pulling out. It seems that unless Knighton was prepared to back his own investment with hard cash instead of property assets, Thornton and Cohen now wanted at least a fifty per cent share, which would deprive Knighton of control. He was not prepared to concede this, partly because of his earlier public insistence that the takeover was 'his'. Knighton also says Thornton was worried they would not be able to fulfil their legal obligations within the necessary timetable – the 'due diligence' period.

Publicly Knighton seemed unperturbed by his partners' sudden withdrawal. 'I could do this deal all on my own without borrowing if I wanted to,' he insisted.

But help was at hand. On the very day Thornton and Cohen withdrew, Wednesday 13 September, Knighton had arranged to visit Glasgow Rangers, both to watch their

European Cup game against Bayern Munich, and to discuss possible business links with United. After watching Rangers lose 3–1, Knighton met their dynamic, young, new chairman, David Murray.

David Murray was one of a new aggressive breed of chairmen in Scottish football with whom Knighton identified closely; Wallace Mercer at Hearts and David Duff at Hibernian were two others. Knighton regarded Murray in particular as something of a model. The two men were both about the same age – 37 – and held similar views on the game. Both had suffered important injuries early in life – Murray had lost both legs in a car crash when he was only 22; and both turned to football after making millions in business.

'There was immediate personal empathy between us,' Murray said of their meeting, 'we sat down in the Blue Room at 11 o'clock that night and talked into the early hours of the morning.' Knighton wanted advice on how to arrange new financial backing. 'I thought Mr Knighton's heart was in the right place and decided to give him all the help I could,' Murray said.

Whilst denying any involvement in Knighton's deal at Old Trafford at the time it was announced, David Murray called it a 'mirror-image' of his own take-over of Rangers the previous year. One striking aspect of Murray's move at Ibrox had been how cheaply he had bought the Scottish club. Regular 40,000 attendances in the stadium that was largely all-seat, and Graeme Souness's big transfer deals involving English internationals, were indications that Rangers were now Britain's wealthiest soccer club. Yet Murray had managed to secure his majority holding for just £8 million. The soccer team alone was almost certainly worth more than that, while on paper the club's fixed assets were valued at £23 million. Murray's bargain was highlighted by the fact that within a year Rangers' shares were trading at three and a half times what he had paid – and he now considered Michael Knighton too was getting excellent value. 'The person who's kicking himself is Martin

Edwards,' Murray said later. 'By doing a deal behind everyone's back he has got much less for the club than he could have done.'

Football League rules prohibit anyone having a substantial involvement in more than one club within the British Isles, otherwise Murray might easily have been tempted to share Knighton's bargain. Instead the Rangers' chairman spent much of the next four working days with Knighton in Edinburgh, introducing him to legal and banking contacts. A finance package was set up, largely based on the Bank of Scotland. It meant that on Wednesday 20 September, just before United's Littlewoods Cup tie at Portsmouth, Knighton was able formally to sign the documents to confirm that his options to buy were being taken up. 'I am 95 per cent certain that without my involvement,' said David Murray at the time, 'he would have lost the deal, and that would have been tragic.'

'I've done it,' Knighton boasted. 'I've put together a £20 million package in three and a half days. . . . This was my own deal from day one and it remains so.' And he promised to fulfil his offer to United's other shareholders. So certain did it now look that Knighton would assume control that the *Manchester Evening News* even began calling him the 'new chairman'.

Within days, however, it had become clear Knighton wasn't happy with David Murray's Edinburgh package. 'He didn't fancy the colour of those deals,' Murray later explained. He would have had to put up personal assets as collateral and 'the terms were that he would have had a massive amount of debt to service'. Though the backing was technically feasible, Knighton would start repaying his substantial debt after only a year, and faced the penalty of forfeiting his property assets.

Knighton says his accountants, Robson Rhodes, advised him that rather than rely on the Scottish institutions, he should find new investors for MK Trafford Holdings, to replace Robert Thornton and Stanley Cohen. They suggested he contact some of the numerous people who had expressed interest since the deal was originally announced. Knighton again called on David Murray for help.

And from this arose the extraordinary situation of the chairman of Glasgow Rangers trying to sell Manchester United on behalf of a man who did not yet actually own it.

Among those contacted were two of the most flamboyant millionaires in North-west England, both of them prominent in the media industry: Eddie Shah, whose battles against the print unions had transformed the British newspaper industry; and Owen Oyston, the socialist radio station owner, former estate agent, and owner of Blackpool Football Club. Knighton insists, however, that in these and other cases, he was only 'approaching those who'd approached me'.

Eddie Shah confirms that someone in his office had indeed written to Knighton to explore possible financial opportunities. Having recently sold his newspapers for £25 million, Shah was looking for new investment possibilities, and says his staff often sent out letters to explore potential funding. 'I did not want to buy Manchester United,' he insists, meaning he wasn't interested in United as such, only whether Knighton's investment might be a good 'financing exercise'. Knighton says Shah's letter congratulated him on his 'coup' and that Shah claimed to be a great supporter of his.

When Michael Knighton first rang, Shah asked to be sent financial details that he might show to other members of a possible syndicate – among those he had in mind was Stephen Boler, a shareholder in Manchester City. Knighton sent Shah both information on his own finances, and Robson Rhodes' report on Manchester United. It proved to be a serious error.

While still considering these documents, Shah was rung up at about 5.30 one evening by a representative of Knighton. He asked if Shah was interested in buying the whole of Knighton's prospective majority share in United, for a premium of about six million pounds. Shah says he was told that Amer Midani had offered to pay a similar sum.

Worried that he might be being set up, Shah rang Midani
the next day, only to be informed that Midani's first discussions with Knighton about any purchase had only
occurred at 10.30 the previous evening, five hours after
Shah had been told about Midani's supposed offer. Shah
felt he was being used to play off against Midani, and
decided to leak everything to the local press. 'I don't like
the smell of this deal,' he said. 'I think I'm being set up
and I have no wish to take part in a Dutch auction. It is a
strange way to do business.' As a life-long Spurs supporter
he added that his children would never have allowed him
to get involved in United anyway.

Knighton says Owen Oyston, too, approached him first,
though a spokesman for Oyston denies this. The first public
sign of contact between the two men came when they were
spotted together watching Manchester City against Luton
Town – on a Saturday when United weren't playing.

With Shah's deliberate leaks, and Oyston's public
appearance with him, Knighton's attempts to sell some or
all of his prospective share in United produced big headlines. And Robert Maxwell's *Daily Mirror* revealed that
Knighton had offered the club to Maxwell too, though at
a lower price, which the publisher still wasn't interested
in. Much was made of the fact that Knighton had asking
for £16 or £17 million for shares he was buying from
Edwards for £10 million. By selling at a greatly undervalued
price, the United chairman had given Knighton the chance
to make a financial killing. David Murray was surprisingly
frank: 'Michael Knighton has the option to buy Manchester
United whether he is worth £2 million, £3 million, £4
million or whatever. He still has that option. If he could sell
the company that has that option – MK Trafford Holdings –
you can guarantee he would be worth three or four times
his present value.'

Martin Edwards was humiliated by the public disclosure
of Knighton's negotiations, and the implication that he had
undersold the club. The six other United directors were
furious with both men, yet until late September they had

llowed events to flow on around them. 'As a board we felt mpotent,' Bobby Charlton said later. One problem was hat the other directors had no independent advice of their wn. The rules of the Stock Exchange take-over panel say hat the director of any public company subject to a take-ver bid should appoint independent financial advisers to nake recommendations to the minority shareholders. For ome reason though, the United board waited six weeks to lo this. The City merchant bank, Henry Ansbacher, were lot appointed as advisers until almost the end of Sep-ember. Had the take-over rules been followed earlier by he board they might conceivably have avoided some of the ppalling mess that Manchester United got dragged into.

By the time Ansbacher's representative first met the Jnited board on Tuesday 3 October, most directors must lave wished Michael Knighton had never set foot inside)ld Trafford. There was surprise, indeed relief, when \nsbacher's adviser suggested there was a better-than-evens :hance of stopping the take-over. The original agreement igned by Michael Knighton had contained a confidentiality :lause, prohibiting him from disclosing anything about the :lub's financial affairs to outsiders. Bobby Charlton then nentioned a chance encounter with Eddie Shah at Mere ;olf club. Shah had told him about the copy of the Robson Rhodes report that he'd been sent by Knighton.

Moreover, the United board also feared a copy of the eport had been obtained by the directors of Manchester]ity, possibly through Stephen Boler the owner of Mere ;olf club, who is a friend of Eddie Shah and a powerful orce at Maine Road. They considered this to be particularly worrying since the document contained sensitive infor-nation about players' contracts, and details of sponsorship leals, which if they became public might damage United's elations with the sponsors. The thought that this infor-nation might now be floating around Maine Road only ntensified the United directors' anger with Knighton.

The problem for the United directors was that the impor-ant confidentiality clause was in the contract between

Michael Knighton and Martin Edwards, an agreement
Manchester United Football Club was not itself party to.
The only man who could take action was Edwards himself.
Though extremely worried about what Knighton was
doing, the United chairman was reluctant to jeopardise the
sale, even if it was now obvious he had badly underpriced
it.

The United board persuaded Edwards that Knighton had
to be stopped, and that legal action provided the only hope
of doing so.

On the evening of Wednesday 4 October 30,000 spectators were at Old Trafford watching the rugby league
world championship final between Widnes and Canberra.
Normally at such a prestigious, money-making occasion
Martin Edwards would be watching from the director's box
or patrolling the club suites. That night Edwards caught
only glimpses of the rugby from his office window, while a
Manchester QC sat by him at the conference table typing
up the necessary affidavit against Knighton on a portable
computer.

Edwards and his board needed hard evidence, however,
that Knighton had breached confidentiality. Bobby
Charlton and his fellow-director, Michael Edelson, went
round to Eddie Shah's home to retrieve the copy of the
Robson Rhodes report. Shah never signed an affidavit – he
says he wasn't asked – but a statement from Charlton and
Edelson saying they got the report from Shah was as good
as Shah giving evidence himself. Robson Rhodes, when
approached, were indignant that anyone might suggest their
report had been leaked. Only three copies had been sent
out, the accountants declared, each of them carefully num-
bered. Robson Rhodes said a figure '3' was written on the
report sent to Knighton; the same number appeared on the
photocopy retrieved from Shah.

The first Knighton knew of Martin Edwards' legal action
was when the United chairman appeared before a judge in
chambers in Manchester – a Mr Justice Judge, believe it
or not. An interim ruling was given in Edwards' favour,

pending a full hearing, and it stopped Knighton from disclosing any more confidential information. Knighton argued that he was only acting reasonably: 'If I have to advise potential investors,' he complained, 'how can I do so except by letting them see details of the company?'

The judge had made Knighton's search for new investors that much harder – indeed until the injunction was amended four days later not even his financial advisers could see the documents. But on paper he was still due to buy the club. By now Martin Edwards realised his deal had been a ghastly mistake, and sought counsel's advice on whether it could be stopped. The whole United board was bitterly opposed to a move that some members might once have privately hoped would bring handsome profits on their own shareholdings. The directors were 'all totally humiliated and embarrassed by the current position,' said Michael Edelson. Nigel Burrows called United 'the laughing stock of the world', while Bobby Charlton, describing events as 'disturbing and hurtful', offered to step in as chairman.

The six days following the judge's ruling were a period of frantic talks – between Michael Knighton and potential investors, to sell some or all of the holding he still did not own; and between Martin Edwards and Knighton to persuade him to withdraw. Knighton seemed to pursue both options simultaneously, unsure of what he really wanted to do. Involved in the discussions were not just the main parties themselves, but numerous legal and financial advisers as well.

The plan Knighton had originally, buying Manchester United and becoming chairman, seemed increasingly impractical. Even if he had the money to buy Edwards' shares and assume the chairmanship he would have faced numerous resignations from both directors and staff. This was something Knighton could not face. Moreover, there was the hostility of United fans, for whom Knighton was now an even more unpopular figure than Martin Edwards. A sign of that hostility occurred when Knighton visited his solicitor's office in Eccles. A group of United fans van-

dalised a Rolls-Royce outside the building wrongly thinking
it belonged to Knighton when it was actually owned by one
of his advisers. Nigel Burrows kept warning him just how
unpopular he now was with the fans.

On the other hand Knighton was determined to show
the world he could raise the money to buy the club. Owen
Oyston offered to invest up to £10 million, but there were
problems. Oyston couldn't take a share of more than ten
per cent in United without giving up his family's 75 per cent
stake in Blackpool Football Club. Rule 86 of the Football
League, instituted when Robert Maxwell became involved
in several different clubs at once, stipulates that no family
with a controlling interest in one team can own more than
ten per cent of another. In the end Knighton says he didn't
take the Oyston deal to a conclusion because he already
knew in his own mind that he would tear up the Edwards'
contract.

He was not prepared to do this, however, without compensation. The press talked of a million pounds, and
Knighton confirms that the total costs of his operation were
in the region of £750,000. This was mostly accounted for
by fees to his stockbrokers, Laing and Cruickshank, to the
accountants, Robson Rhodes, to his lawyer and to several
other advisers he had employed along the way, though large
sums of money had also been spent on hotel bills and, at
one point, on keeping a jet on permanent stand-by. It's not
clear if Edwards and Knighton ever did discuss financial
recompense – Knighton certainly denies it — but then a
new form of compensation emerged — a United directorship.

The Michael Knighton saga reached its climax on the
night of Tuesday 10 October – the day before he was legally
obliged to extend his purchase offer to the other United
shareholders. For days numerous rooms and suites had
been occupied at the Midland Hotel in Manchester by each
of the interested parties, and several more by interested
journalists. An official of the take-over panel was kept in
touch overnight by telephone. Michael Knighton was

accompanied by his wife Rosemary in these, the dying hours of his dreams. At one point he was so distraught that he had to leave the meeting.

Knighton claims that even at that late hour his financial advisers at the hotel, Laing and Cruickshank, were in contact with four 'very serious' separate parties willing to buy his option in United – two of them were well-known businessmen. One party, Knighton claims, was on the telephone 'all night, prepared with a bankers' draft, ready to fly to Manchester'.

Who these four parties were is not clear. One undoubtedly consisted of three Jewish businessmen from London – a property developer, a retailer and a financier. They had raised £20 million, and planned to float the club on the stock market at a valuation of £40 million, with the hope that Bobby Charlton would serve as chairman. Their bid probably failed because they were not, however, prepared to offer what Martin Edwards had already conceded, a place for Knighton on the United board. A second possibility centred around David Mond, a Manchester accountant who had long expressed his own interest in buying into the club. Mond had been advising Knighton since August, and was willing to put together for him a local package of financial support. And Knighton confirms that he was also in telephone contact with Sam Hashimi, an Iraqi businessman who later tried to buy Sheffield United. Hashimi was working on behalf of a wealthy Saudi from Jeddah.

Against the wishes of his legal and financial advisers, Knighton walked into the Henry Ansbacher suite and announced he would cancel his agreement and take Edwards' offer of a place on the board, providing the directors were unanimous in agreeing to elect him. Shortly after 1.00 a.m. on the Wednesday morning, the board met together at the hotel, with Amer Midani in contact by telephone. Knighton joined them in the room, and although Nigel Burrows felt so hostile towards him that he refused to sit at the same table, even he had formally to agree Knighton's election. The take-over panel representative was phoned at home and gave his assent to this rather unorthodox arrangement. It was a deal: or rather the deal was off.

The announcement the next day was held up for several hours. Michael Knighton insisted that the press release include a statement from his stockbrokers, Laing and Cruickshank, stating that he could have funded the take-over if he'd so wished. Whilst the firm's man in Manchester, Chris Yates, was happy to include this, Laing and Cruickshank's chairman, Ian Hay Davison, had reservations. In the end they were never resolved. The settlement was simply presented at another Old Trafford press conference. 'In the interests of Manchester United and the fans,' Knighton declared, 'I decided that control should return to Martin Edwards.' He justified the extraordinary series of events by saying he could not have known that his backers would not stay with him. Yet, he insisted, 'I could have done it all on my own. I could have made a huge amount by selling control on. . . . As a matter of honour it would have been wrong for me to do that.' Taking that option, he suggested, would have made him 'a very wealthy man indeed'. But that, surely, is what Mr Knighton was supposed to have been in the first place.

Few of the parties emerge well from the series of events that brought such ridicule upon Manchester United. The root of the problem is that, in practical terms, Michael Knighton could not go ahead with the take-over without substantial financial backing from other parties. He is clearly at fault for announcing the deal without firm arrangements with Robert Thornton, Stanley Cohen and anybody else who might have been involved with them; and then a month later for confirming the deal when it could only be funded with the Edinburgh package that would place an extreme strain on him financially.

Knighton himself issued an emotional tirade against the media, and blamed reporters for creating a 'circus'. But no wonder journalists distrusted him after the extremely misleading statements made at his initial press conference; he admits his 'credibility went out of the window' once the

Thornton–Cohen involvement was revealed. A little more 'glasnost' on Knighton's part might have helped everyone.

There seems little reason to doubt that Martin Edwards was guilty of serious misjudgement. He should have made much more stringent enquiries into Knighton's background and backing before announcing anything publicly. Had he done so he would have discovered that realistically it was most unlikely that Knighton could have funded the deal simply from his own resources; and Edwards should also have insisted that Robert Thornton's role in the take-over be made firm and public. Had Martin Edwards been more open with his fellow-directors they might at least have asked some of the questions he didn't. And Amer Midani could well have improved on Knighton's offer. Edwards perhaps feared that greater consultation with the board would have caused leaks to the press. He may be right, but it is hard to see how that could have been more damaging than the media coverage that actually occurred.

The other United directors also bear some responsibility. Had they acted in concert at a much earlier stage, and obtained outside specialist advice, some of the club's embarrassment might have been avoided.

Shortly after the deal was called off Michael Knighton was reprimanded by the Stock Exchange take-over panel for not announcing his deal 'after the most careful and responsible consideration', as their code requires. In particular they criticised him for confirming the take-over on September 20

> 'without adequate consideration of whether MK Trafford Holdings would, in fact, be able to conclude the transaction in the manner that it intended. It is understood that, at the time the statement was made, Mr Knighton did not have any independent corporate finance advisers, nor did he have any legal advisers advising him on the application of the Code. His previous advisers were no longer acting and Mr Knighton had not yet appointed replacements. He

must therefore take responsibility for this breach of
the Code and is criticised accordingly.'

The Panel decided, however, not to pursue further action
against Knighton.

Despite the personal humiliation, Martin Edwards now
at least knew that when it came to selling again he might
perhaps obtain five, six or seven million pounds more than
he had agreed with Knighton. Negotiations with Amer
Midani in December broke down when Edwards demanded
£15 million for his shares – fifty per cent more than the
Knighton price. Midani said it was wrong that he, a director, should have to pay £5 more per share than Edwards had
agreed with an outsider, whereupon the United chairman
declared he'd make no further moves until the end of the
season. United shares reached £24 by the end of 1989 in
anticipation of a new deal – compared with prices of only
seven and eight pounds in the days immediately before the
Knighton deal was first announced. The whole episode had
put a much firmer, higher price on the club, though valuing
football clubs is a particularly difficult business. When
Millwall carried out a public flotation in October 1989, the
London club was valued at £13 million, and the flotation
was thirty per cent oversubscribed. Given the respective
stature of Millwall and United, the £20 million value placed
on Manchester United in the Knighton deal was certainly
too low.

Amer Midani still remained favourite to buy the club
eventually, perhaps in conjunction with one or both of
his fellow directors, Nigel Burrows and Mike Edelson. In
November 1989 the three were part of a four-man 'consortium' which took a 29.6 per cent stake in Conrad Continental plc, a Manchester clothing firm chaired by Lord Barnett.
Apart from their association on the Old Trafford board, the
three had never acted together in business before. Edelson,
whose own textile firm, M. Edelson Ltd, went into receiver-
ship in January 1989, became executive director of Conrad,
and the company planned two new divisions covering Bur-

rows' and Midani's main British business interests, financial services and leisure. At the Manchester United AGM in December 1989 Martin Edwards promised to talk to Midani and Burrows if he did indeed decide once more to sell.

Michael Knighton's election to the board, meanwhile, was supported by just 20 or so shareholders in an AGM of 450 people, but Edwards swung his majority vote behind the new man, as obliged under the October settlement. After the events of that autumn, and United's disappointing playing form, the chairman perhaps escaped lightly from the assembled shareholders. 'You have abused the commitment and passion of the supporters of this club for too long,' warned one of them, however. 'If you cannot do anything about it then make way for someone who can.'

But there were increasing fears that Martin Edwards may have been so stung by events that next time he will go all out for the highest bid possible. Manchester United could then so easily fall into the wrong hands. An asset-stripper, for example, might sell off the players and the valuable Old Trafford site, situated in the promising Trafford Park development area. As the press speculated about who might next be interested in bidding for the club, Nigel Burrows warned that 'some of the people now making offers are interested only in stripping the club of its assets.'

Burrows joined his colleague Amer Midani in proposing that Manchester United ought to be floated publicly on the Stock Exchange, as Tottenham and Millwall have been. "Give Manchester United back to its people," said Midani, reflecting the views of ordinary United fans furious about millionaires haggling over the club. 'I believe it should be owned by a number of shareholders and solid institutions,' Midani argued, 'so that its future is safe for eternity.' And Midani promised there would be a public flotation if he ever gained control of the club: ten million shares would be issued at a value of £3 each. Burrows said that if he and Midani managed to buy the club they would only retain a 25 per cent share – the remaining 75 per cent would be floated.

The idea was supported also by Michael Edelson and
Bobby Charlton. 'I don't think any one person should have
charge of United,' said Charlton, 'and the best safeguard is
for the club to be floated on the market.' But the weightiest
support of all came from someone who had remained silent
throughout the Knighton affair, yet whose anguish must
have been acute: Sir Matt Busby. 'Recent events have dem-
onstrated only too clearly the problems that can arise from
private ownership when the time comes for the club to be
sold.' Mild though Sir Matt's comments were, they were
probably the strongest criticism he had ever voiced publicly
of the Edwards regime. 'I agree with the people who believe
we would get more stability and a better guarantee for the
future well-being of United if it were now to pass into the
control of a number of representative shareholders.'

But when the United board met in December to discuss
the idea of a public flotation the plan was firmly squashed
by Martin Edwards, though his reasons for doing so are
not clear.

Amidst all the wranglings over who might buy the club,
United's playing performance had that winter reached its
lowest point since the early 1970s. Alex Ferguson had been
granted a new three-year contract in September at a time
when United's inconsistent form had reached levels that
almost strained belief. A 5–1 win over Millwall, for
instance, was followed by the horror of defeat by the same
score at Manchester City. Other impressive high-scoring
victories over Coventry and Luton were quickly balanced
by the 3–0 loss at home to Spurs in the Littlewoods Cup,
a 2–0 defeat at Charlton, and home league defeats by Spurs,
Crystal Palace and Derby. As seemed to occur every Christmas, a creditable performance against Merseyside opposition – a 0–0 draw at Anfield, which United almost won –
was followed by another great setback – a 3–0 loss at Aston
Villa.

By January, relegation was a serious possibility as the
team struggled to keep out of the bottom three places.
Eleven league games went by without victory – the worst

uch run since 1972. Despite spending almost £12 million
pounds on some of Britain's most promising players, Alex
Ferguson's expensive imports did not operate as a team.
The supply of goals from Mark Hughes and Brian McClair
had dried up again, and at times only Gary Pallister held
the defence together.

Just as had happened in 1963, relief from the team's
relegation worries was provided by surprising success in
the FA Cup. A late goal by Mark Robins in a hard match
at Nottingham Forest led to a tricky tie at fourth-division
Hereford which United might easily have lost before Clayton Blackmore scored in the dying minutes. Rounds five
and six provided tough second division opposition in Sheffield United and Newcastle United in a cup run that had
been every tie played away from home, every game played
on a Sunday, and each victory achieved by a margin of one
goal. It was the ever-promising forward Mark Robins who
scored the winning goal in the exciting 3–2 win at Newcastle, and Robins again who finally produced the tickets for
a Wembley final against Steve Coppell's Crystal Palace.

In any other year a semi-final draw against Oldham Athletic would have produced hoots of delight: a side who had
lurked in the second division for longer than anyone could
remember, they were not feared as great cup-fighters. Not
until 1989 and 1990 that is, when aided by their plastic
pitch at Boundary Park, Oldham disposed of first-division
Southampton and Arsenal in a run to the Littlewoods Cup
final. And in the FA Cup Everton and Aston Villa had
already fallen to the Latics before the confrontation with
United at Maine Road. The first game was a ding-dong
battle in which the sides shared six goals, though the reds
were perhaps lucky to escape a side that simply wouldn't
let go. Oldham led first, but Manchester equalised quickly.
Then twice it was United's turn to have leads snatched
away. And in the replay three days later it seemed to be
happening all over again: the discarded United striker Andy
Ritchie wiped out McClair's opening goal, only for Mark

Robins to perform his remarkable act once more, with a winner in extra time.

As Alex Ferguson's men were bringing the club rich financial rewards in the FA Cup, Martin Edwards confirmed in February that it was his intention to sell United at the end of the season. By April he had received enquiries from more than a dozen different parties, quite apart from Amer Midani and Nigel Burrows' outstanding interest. A Manchester property developer, Gordon Bishop, a life-long United fan who had a box at Old Trafford, offered to pay £30 million for the club, and it's thought he also proposed a plan to buy half Edwards' shares and serve as joint chairman with him. News Corporation, the media empire owned by the Australian tycoon, Rupert Murdoch, confirmed that they had expressed interest. Sam Hashimi had pursued his enquiries beyond the collapse of Knighton's takeover; he visited Old Trafford and offered Edwards £15 million for his shares – £30 each; on getting no response he turned his attention to Sheffield United. Others thought to be interested included the rock group Genesis; the Manchester bookmaker, Fred Done; and the consortium of London businessmen that had been in touch with Knighton.

The independent United directors reappointed Henry Ansbacher to explore just how serious each bid was before consideration by the board. They were determined to prevent the problems that had arisen the previous year. Michael Knighton, the man at the centre of those problems, claimed that he too was still a 'serious contender', though after the events of 1989, few wanted to take his interest seriously.

The indication must be that Michael Knighton would probably have been a disastrous owner for United, even worse than the Edwards family. His inexperienced behaviour and self-confessed naïvety during the take-over period made many people believe he just wasn't up to the job of running such an important national institution. Moreover, it was clear from Knighton's talk about 'consultancy fees

hat, just like the Edwards family, he had expected to get
ome return on his investment in Manchester United.

The worry was, however, that if Manchester United went
imply to the highest bidder things could get far worse. As
he rival bids piled up on Martin Edwards' desk it looked
ncreasingly likely that the winner of the Old Trafford
uction would expect a quick and generous return on his
nvestment. The more the new owner has to pay for the
lub, the more Manchester United may have to pay him
ack.

Conclusion

Despite the successful 1990 FA cup run, the magic of Manchester United is fading rapidly. It is a hard thing for loyal supporters to admit, but arch-rivals Liverpool have now become what United were for more than a generation – the team with the aura and artistry, the side that everyone wants to watch.

Liverpool's phenomenal success – twenty-four major trophies since 1973 – had until recently failed to generate anything like the kind of worldwide affection enjoyed by Manchester United. For so long the Anfield team was mechanical rather than entertaining, scientific rather than artistic, and respected rather than loved. Despite winning championships and cups season after season, Liverpool's home crowds were until the late 1980s way below United's. In 1985–86, for instance, the year Liverpool won the league and cup double, attendances at Anfield were on average 11,000 below those at Old Trafford.

The turning point occurred perhaps in 1987 when Liverpool spent four million pounds on three new forwards – John Barnes, Peter Beardsley and John Aldridge. A new excitement was added to the Merseyside club's play, and it was rewarded immediately by a new level of popularity. Liverpool drew 28,095 spectators to Charlton Athletic in January 1988, for instance, an extraordinary crowd for the poorly supported South London club, and nearly four times the average for Charlton's other home matches that season. At one time only Manchester United could have boosted a London crowd like that, yet the reds' visit to Selhurst Park

he previous August had pulled in only 14,046, half the
Liverpool figure. And when United visited Wimbledon in
December 1989 the home club only found a match sponsor
t the last minute.

Meanwhile the Old Trafford crowd has lost its famous
ld roar, and ability to frighten opponents. Under the new
membership scheme large gaps have appeared on the most
ociferous side of the ground, the Stretford End. Away
supporters crammed into pens at the Scoreboard End often
eem to make more noise than the once-legendary Stretford
Enders. The home crowd only comes to life briefly to cel-
brate a United goal, or to rally the players if the opposition
cores. The large repertoire of witty United songs has given
vay to a handful of tedious chants – 'Here We Go', and
ncreasingly, 'What a Load of Rubbish'. And, impatient
or success, the fans seem ever more inclined to taunt indi-
ridual team-members such as Colin Gibson and Ralph
Milne. The heart has been torn from a once great club.

As Alex Feguson's side grappled with the threat of re-
egation in the 1989–90 season, media speculation inevitably
grew that he would become the sixth manager to be dismissed since Sir Matt Busby retired. Despite occasional
chants of 'Fergie Out!', few people associated with United
believed that another manager would solve the club's
roubles. If change was required, it was at the very top.

Even the world's most brilliant football manager could
not transform Manchester United, so long as the club is
un from the chairman's office in the way it has been.
United have been dragged into mediocrity by both adminis-
rative mismanagement and an obsession with money which
as infected the whole club.

The Edwards era, and its culmination in the Knighton
iasco have lessons for all football clubs. No longer can such
community institutions, dependent on thousands of local
supporters, be permitted to remain in the hands of single
ndividuals. Manchester United is not the first club to be
upset by boardroom squabbles over ownership. The Eng-
ish football authorities would do all fans a service by insist-

ing that no individual can own a majority of shares in one
club. Even such a mild reform as this is perhaps unrealistic
when it is those very same individuals who would have to
vote in such a rule change.

At Old Trafford the kind of public flotation recently
advocated by Sir Matt Busby and most of the board would
almost certainly be a turn for the better, but a public
flotation still cannot guarantee against one individual
accumulating a majority of the shares, or an effective
majority. The best solution would be for the majority shareholding to be transferred to a trust run by several supporters, on which no one person could predominate.

Of course it is only correct that football clubs in the 1990s
should apply a more stringent, entrepreneurial approach to
running the ailing national game. The two most successful
sides in the land, Liverpool and Everton, are both run on
good business lines. But neither the Liverpool chairman,
John Smith, nor his Everton counterpart, Philip Carter,
rewards himself with large dividends and salary bonuses.
At Anfield and Goodison the money generated by the teams'
success is almost all ploughed back into football.

The two Merseyside clubs have also reaped rewards from
perhaps the most important lesson of Sir Matt Busby –
family continuity – long after his own club rejected it. At
Old Trafford Sir Matt himself mistakenly abandoned such
continuity far too swiftly after the relative failure of the
inexperienced Wilf McGuinness. United has thus suffered
as each subsequent manager from outside has come, introduced his own ways, and taken the club in a new direction.

If anything can be salvaged from the dismal United
league results of 1988 and 1989, it may be the importance
of another major tenet of the Busby philosophy – nurturing
one's own talent through the youth teams. Even during the
rebuilding period between Munich in 1958 and the 1968
European Cup, Matt Busby bought fewer players than Alex
Ferguson in his first three years at Old Trafford. Yet often
Ferguson has achieved more commitment from youth players such as Russell Beardsmore and Mark Robins than

from established international stars who have cost the club millions in transfer fees and high wages.

One can only pray that Martin Edwards hands over control of Manchester United to an owner prepared to return to some of the Busby philosophy, rather than simply sell to some highest bidder with no feelings for the club. The magic of Manchester United will only be cast again if control of the club is restored to people prepared to represent those who inspired Sir Matt – the fans.

Postscript

They paraded the cup beneath the Wembley floodlights more with a sense of relief than triumph. The 1990 FA Cup final replay had been an undistinguished affair, notable not for any stylish play by the winners, but for the aggressive tactics used by the losing Crystal Palace team. United's 1–0 victory set several records: Bryan Robson became the first captain to lift three FA Cups at Wembley, and the club joined Aston Villa and Tottenham Hotspur in winning the trophy a record seven times.

In the first game the previous Saturday, Manchester United had also entered the history books as the most expensive club side ever seen at Wembley – assembled for almost twelve million pounds. Gary Pallister had cost £2.3 million; five others – Ince, Webb, Robson, McClair and Hughes – more than a million pounds each. Yet in the victorious Thursday night replay the most telling contributions came from the only two players to cost nothing.

Only hours before kick-off Alex Ferguson announced Jim Leighton was dropped: his poor goalkeeping the previous Saturday was blamed for at least two Palace goals in the 3–3 draw. Thrust into his place was an astonished Les Sealey, a 'keeper on loan from Luton Town who had appeared only twice before for United. Sealey survived an early, aggressive challenge by the Palace striker Mark Bright; high crosses Jim Leighton might have fumbled were collected confidently, and twice Sealey's legs foiled dangerous shots from Andy Gray.

The only creditable aspect of the replay was the quality

of United's winning goal. McClair and Wallace contributed
to the build-up. Webb swung the ball over into the penalty
area. Full back Lee Martin had timed his run down the
left perfectly; he chested the ball down, ran forward and
shot into the roof of the Palace net. A local boy from Hyde,
Martin had been on United's books for ten years, longer
than any other player. It was only his second first team
goal.

The original Wembley game the previous Saturday had
also lacked the high-class football once expected of Manchester United. But at least there was no shortage of tension
and drama. The 120 minutes game had been rendered all
the more nerve-racking by the desperate need shared by
both Alan Ferguson and thousands of United fans to salvage
the club's flagging reputation. Any United fan prone to
heart attacks should have kept well away.

The lead swung first south London's way, then to Manchester, and back south again. Steve Coppell reckoned Ian
Wright wasn't fit enough to start the match, but the forward's arrival as substitute after 69 minutes proved devas-
tating. A superb Palace equaliser came from almost his first
touch, and another Wright goal put his side ahead in the
second minute of extra time. Having fought back so well
Palace held the initiative, and several Manchester players
looked exhausted. United were heading for the kind of
humiliating defeat that would have outweighed any glory
in reaching Wembley in the first place. With eight minutes
left Danny Wallace pushed the ball through to Mark
Hughes, who quickly got the better of two Palace defenders
and the goalkeeper. His shot secured a replay worth several
hundred thousand pounds to the United balance sheet.

Sir Matt Busby, now 81, savoured the following
Thursday's replay from the Royal Box. It was the sixth
time Sir Matt had witnessed a Manchester United FA Cup
victory – twice as team manager, once as a director, and
three times as club president. Of all the six post-war cup-
winning teams, this United line-up may have been the most
expensive, yet it was probably the least impressive side, the

least in keeping with United's traditional class and style. They had finished the season thirteenth of the twenty first division clubs, a mere five points above relegated Sheffield Wednesday, and a colossal thirty-one behind the league champions, Liverpool. The silverware taken back to Manchester could not disguise the scale of the restoration job that lay ahead for whoever might soon take over the ownership of the club.

June 1990

Appendix A:
Match Attendances 1946–90

MANCHESTER UNITED ATTENDANCES 1946–1989

D2

— UNITED HOME AVERAGE
········· UNITED AWAY AVERAGE
‐ ‐ ‐ FIRST DIVISION AVERAGE

60.000, 55.000, 50.000, 45.000, 40.000, 35.000, 30.000, 25.000, 20.000

1947 1949 1952 1955 1958 1961 1964 1967 1970 1973 1976 1979 1982 1985 1988

The following table sets out United home and away attendances since the war, together with annual ratios between United's average attendance and the first division average.

Year	Home Average	Division One Average	Ratio	League Position	Away Average	Ratio
46–47	43,615	32,479	1.343	4	31,364	0.966
47–48	53,660	36,217	1.482	3	40,493	1.118
48–49	46,023	38,776	1.187	3	44,720	1.153
49–50	41,455	37,400	1.108	7	46,172	1.235
50–51	37,159	36,102	1.029	9	38,091	1.055
51–52	41,870	34,871	1.201	4	40,945	1.174
52–53	35,737	34,740	1.029	8	37,068	1.067
53–54	33,637	34,967	0.962	10	37,096	1.061
54–55	34,077	32,656	1.044	9	35,865	1.098
55–56	38,880	30,539	1.273	3	32,872	1.076
56–57	45,192	29,877	1.513	1	39,772	1.332
57–58	45,583	31,317	1.456	1	45,352	1.448
58–59	53,258	31,878	1.671	1	44,028	1.381
59–60	47,288	31,150	1.518	2	41,026	1.317
60–61	37,807	27,980	1.351	3	34,139	1.220
61–62	33,490	26,106	1.283	5	33,964	1.301
62–63	40,317	27,035	1.491	4	34,894	1.291
63–64	43,753	27,027	1.618	3	38,697	1.432
64–65	45,990	27,508	1.672	1	41,377	1.504
65–66	38,456	27,014	1.424	3	38,171	1.413
66–67	53,984	30,828	1.751	1	45,577	1.478
67–68	57,759	33,094	1.745	1	45,802	1.384
68–69	51,121	31,569	1.619	1	44,295	1.403
69–70	51,115	32,183	1.588	1	43,997	1.367
70–71	44,754	30,204	1.481	2	41,695	1.380
71–72	45,999	31,352	1.467	2	44,085	1.406
72–73	48,623	30,299	1.605	1	41,171	1.359
73–74	42,721	28,292	1.510	1	35,337	1.249
74–75	48,388	27,301	1.772*	1	25,556	0.936*
75–76	54,750	28,331	1.932	1	37,037	1.307
76–77	53,710	29,540	1.818	1	35,357	1.197
77–78	51,938	28,692	1.810	1	30,424	1.060
78–79	46,687	27,499	1.697	1	30,498	1.109
79–80	51,562	26,327	1.958	1	34,101	1.295
80–81	45,055	24,660	1.827	1	29,849	1.210
81–82	44,685	22,556	1.981	1	27,214	1.207
82–83	41,583	20,120	2.066	1	25,294	1.257
83–84	42,534	18,856	2.256	1	24,936	1.322
84–85	43,010	21,129	2.035	1	27,884	1.320
85–86	44,422	19,562	2.270	1	28,204	1.442

Year	Home Average	Division One Average	Ratio	League Position	Away Average	Ratio
86–87	40,625	19,794	2.052	1	25,221	1.274
87–88	39,155	19,272	2.031	2	23,041	1.196
88–89	36,488	20,552	1.773	2	23,713	1.154
89–90	39,078	20,745	1.884	1	26,666	1.285

* Second division season – ratios compared with first division average.

NOTES

1. All official attendance figures are extremely unreliable. Clubs often understate their crowds for financial reasons, though this is probably less prevalent since clubs stopped paying away teams a percentage of gate receipts. Unlike many clubs, Manchester United include season ticket and league match book holders at Old Trafford for matches even if they do not turn up. Most clubs include only people who are at the game. During periods of disillusionment, or lack of interest at the end of a dull season, when season ticket holders often do not use their tickets, the Old Trafford figures are overstated significantly.

2. Figures since 1983 are also distorted by live television games. United played one live home league game in the 1983–84, 1984–85 and 1985–86 seasons, two home TV games in the 1986–87 season, one in 1987–88, three in 1988–89 and two in 1989–90.

Appendix B:
Player Transfers 1945–90

Transfer fees quoted in the press are usually only rough estimates, based on information supplied by the club. Most of the figures below, however, are the actual fee. They do not include VAT or the additional 5 per cent levy payable to the Football League when players are signed.

SIR MATT BUSBY (1945–71)

Arrivals			*Departures*		
1945–46					
J. Delaney	Celtic	£4,000	J. Smith	Blackburn	£3,000
1946–47					
J. Dale	Witton	£1,130	T. Breen	Glentoran	£600
			N. Tapken	Darlington	£530
1947–48					
J. Ball	Wigan	£2,000	J. Walton	Preston	£12,000
			J. Dale	Port Vale	£1,000
			H. Worrall	Swindon	£1,000
1948–49					
J. Downie	Bradford PA	£20,000	J. Hanlon	Bury	£5,500
B. Stenson	Altrincham	£500	J. Morris	Derby	£25,000
			R. Burke	Huddersfield	£15,500
1949–50					
T. Bogan	Preston	£3,500	J. Anderson	Nott'm Forest	£8,000
R. Wood	Darlington	£6,000	E. Buckle	Everton	£6,500
R. Allen	QPR	£11,000	H. Williams	Witton	£500
T. Ritchie	Bangor	£750	R. McMorran	Walsall	£1,000

1950–51

E. McIlvenny	Philadelphia £1,700	I. Feehan	Northampton £525
H. McShane	Bolton £5,000	J. Ball	Bolton *exchange*
	(& J. Ball *exchange*)	C. Hughes	Leeds £1,250
		J. Delaney	Aberdeen £3,100
		S. Lynn	Bradford PA £3,500
		T. Bogan	Aberdeen £8,000
		T. Lowrie	
		J. Warner	Oldham £150

1951–52

J. Berry	Birmingham £25,000	C. Mitten	Fulham £16,200
E. Bond	Leyland M £250	L. Cassidy	Oldham £450
		B. Birch	Wolves £6,000

1952–53

T. Taylor	Barnsley £29,999	W. McGlen	Lincoln £3,000
		H. Killin	Lincoln £1,250
		E. Bond	Carlisle £5,000
		T. Ritchie	Reading £3,250
		F. Clempson	Stockport £2,000
		R. Hampson	Reading £300

1953–54

J. Downie	Luton £9,500
S. Pearson	Bury £4,000
F. Mooney	Blackburn £600
H. McShane	Oldham £750
T. McNulty	Liverpool £6,000

1954–55

H. Cockburn	Bury £1,250

1955–56

D. Gibson	Sheff Weds £8,000
E. Lewis	Preston £9,000
J. Scott	Grimsby £1,500

1956–57

P. Kennedy	Blackburn £2,000
W. Whitehurst	Chesterfield £750

1957–58

H. Gregg	Doncaster £23,000	T. Barrett	Plymouth £1,000
S. Crowther	Aston Villa £23,000	J. Doherty	Leicester £6,500
E. Taylor	Blackpool £8,000	J. Whitefoot	Grimsby £8,000
T. Heron	Portadown £7,000		

NB: Jimmy Murphy was responsible for signing Stan Crowther and Ernie Taylor immediately after Munich.

1958–59

A. Quixall	Sheff Weds £45,000	C. Webster	Swansea £6,000
W. Bradley	Bishop Auk £100	R. Wood	Huddersfield £1,500
		E. Taylor	Sunderland £9,000
		S. Crowther	Chelsea £10,000

1959–60

K. McDowall	Rhyl £1,000	R. Harrop	Tranmere £4,000
M. Setters	West Bromwich	G. Clayton	
	£30,000	E. Holland	Wrexham £1,750
T. Dunne	Shelbourne £6,000	F. Goodwin	Leeds £15,000
		E. Jones	Wrexham £2,250

1960–61

N. Cantwell	West Ham £29,500	A. Scanlon	Newcastle £17,500
		J. Carolan	Brighton £9,000
		I. Greaves	Lincoln £2,000
		T. Spratt	Bradford PA £1,750
		K. Morgans	Swansea £2,000

1961–62

D. Herd	Arsenal £40,000	R. Cope	Luton £10,000
D. Law	Torino £115,000	D. Viollet	Stoke £24,000
		A. Dawson	Preston £20,000
		W. Bradley	Bury £2,500

1962–63

D. Sadler	Maidstone £750	N. Lawton	Preston £11,500
P. Crerand	Celtic £56,000		

1963–64

G. Moore	Chelsea £35,000	F. Haydock	Charlton £10,000
J. Connelly	Burnley £56,000	J. Giles	Leeds £34,000
P. Dunne	Shamrock £10,000	M. Pearson	Sheff Weds £17,000
		S. McMillan	Wrexham £6,000
		P. Chisnall	Liverpool £25,000

1964–65

		A. Quixall	Oldham £3,300
		M. Setters	Stoke £30,000
		J. Nicholson	Huddersfield £1,000
		I. Moir	Blackpool £10,000
		R. Smith	Scunthorpe £3,000

1965–66

		E. Dunphy	York £4,000
		G. Moore	Northampton
			£15,000

1966–67

A. Stepney	Chelsea £52,000	J. Connelly	Blackburn £40,000

966–67 (cont.)

| | | | W. Anderson | Aston Villa | £20,000 |
| | | | P. Dunne | Plymouth | £4,000 |

968–69

| W. Morgan | Burnley | £105,000 | F. Kopel | Blackburn | £9,000 |

969–70

| . Ure | Arsenal | £80,000 | J. Ryan | Luton | £20,000 |
| | | | D. Givens | Luton | £15,000 |

970–71

| | | | N. Stiles | Middlesbrough | £22,500 |

NB: Wilf McGuinness neither bought nor sold any players during his six months as team manager in 1970.

FRANK O'FARRELL (1971–72)

Arrivals   Departures

1971–72

| M. Buchan | Aberdeen | £125,000 | F. Burns | Southampton | £40,000 |
| . Moore | Nott'm Forest | £180,000 | A. Gowling | Huddersfield | £60,000 |

1972–73

W. Davies	Manchester C	£60,000	J. Aston	Luton Town	£30,000
. MacDougall	B'rnem'th	£200,000	J. Connaughton	Sheff Utd	£15,000
T. Anderson	Portadown	£20,000			

TOMMY DOCHERTY (1972–77)

Arrivals   Departures

1972–73

G. Graham	Arsenal	£120,000	E. MacDougall	West Ham	£170,000
A. Forsyth	Partick T	£100,000	P. Edwards	Oldham	£13,000
L. Macari	Celtic	£190,000	C. Sartori	Bologna	£45,000
J. Holton	Shrewsbury	£91,000	W. Davies	Blackpool	£14,000
M. Martin	Bohemians	£25,000			
R. O'Brien	Shelbourne	£20,000			
G. Daly	Bohemians	£22,000			

1973–74

P. Roche	Shelbourne £15,000	D. Sadler	Preston £20,000
S. Houston	Brentford £45,000	J. Rimmer	Arsenal £36,750
J. McCalliog	Wolves £60,000	R. O'Brien	Notts County
S. Pearson	Hull £200,000		£40,000
		P. Fletcher	Hull £33,000

1974–75

R. Davies	Portsmouth £43,000	G. Buchan	Bury £10,000
S. Coppell	Tranmere £60,000	B. Kidd	Arsenal £85,000
		G. Graham	Portsmouth £35,000
		T. Anderson	Swindon £25,000
		J. McCalliog	Southampton
			£40,000
		W. Morgan	Burnley £30,000

1975–76

| G. Hill | Mlllwall £85,000 | M. Martin | West Brom £20,000 |

1976–77

A. Foggon	Middlesbro £25,000	A. Foggon	Sunderland £30,000
C. McGrath	Tottenham £30,000	J. Holton	Sunderland £64,000
J. Greenhoff	Stoke £100,000	G. Daly	Derby £170,000
A. Grimes	Bohemians £40,000		

DAVE SEXTON (1977–81)

Arrivals   *Departures*

| J. Jordan | Leeds £350,000 | G. Hill | Derby £275,000 |
| G. McQueen | Leeds £450,000 | | |

1978–79

T. Connell	Coleraine £20,000	D. Bradley	Doncaster £5,000
T. Sloan	Ballymena £32,500	J. Clark	Derby £50,000
M. Thomas	Wrexham £300,000		

1979–80

R. Wilkins	Chelsea £700,000	M. Rogers	QPR £5,000
N. Jovanovic	RS Belgrade £350,000	S. Pearson	West Ham £200,000
		D. McCreery	QPR £170,000
		B. Greenhoff	Leeds £350,000

1980–81

| A. Whelan | Bohemians £30,000 | A. Ritchie | Brighton £500,000 |
| G. Birtles | Nott'm Forest £1,2500,000 | C. McGrath | Tulsa £30,000 |

RON ATKINSON (1981–86)

Arrivals			*Departures*		
1981–82					
T. Gidman	Everton	£355,000	J. Jordan	AC Milan	£250,000
F. Stapleton	Aresenal	£900,000	M. Thomas	Everton	£450,000
R. Moses	West Brom	£500,000	S. McIlroy	Stoke	£350,000
B. Robson	West Brom		J. Nicholl	Toronto	£235,000
		£1,500,000	T. Connell	Glentoran	£37,000
P. McGrath	St Patrick's	£60,000			
1982–83					
P. Beardsley	Vancouver	£250,000	P. Roche	Brentford	£15,000
			G. Birtles	Nott'm Forest	
					£275,000
			P. Beardsley	Vancouver	£250,000
1983–84					
A. Brazil	Tottenham	£700,000	A. Grimes	Coventry	£200,000
A. Graham	Leeds	£65,000	S. McGarvey	Portsmouth	£85,000
J. Olsen	Ajax	£800,000	R. Wilkins	AC Milan	£1,400,000
1984–85					
G. Strachan	Aberdeen	£600,000	D. Platt	Crewe	£50,000
			A. Graham	Bradford C	£10,000
1985–86					
C. Turner	Sunderland	£275,000	S. Pears	Middlesbro	£85,000
C. Gibson	Aston Villa	£312,000	A. Davies	Newcastle	£65,000
P. Barnes	Coventry	£55,000	A. Brazil	Coventry	£280,000
T. Gibson	Coventry	£630,000	M. Hughes	Barcelona	£1,800,000
P. Davenport	Nott'm Forest				
		£600,000			
J. Sivebaek	Vejle	£285,000			
J. Hanrahan	UC Dublin	£30,000			
M. Higgins	Everton	£58,500			
1986–87					
L. O'Brien	Bohemians	£72,500	M. Dempsey	Sheff Utd	£4,500

ALEX FERGUSON (1986–)

Arrivals			*Departures*		
1986–87					
			F. Digby	Swindon	£25,000
			P. Barnes	Manchester C	
					£15,000

Arrivals   *Departures*

1986–87

| | | | M. Higgins | Bury | £10,000 |
| | | | M. Russell | Norwich | £25,000 |

1987–88

V. Anderson	Arsenal	£250,000	S. Ratcliffe	Norwich	£40,000
B. McClair	Celtic	£850,000	T. Gibson	Wimbledon	£200,000
S. Bruce	Norwich	£825,000	J. Sivebaek	St Etienne	£227,000
P. Dalton	Brandon	£5,000			
L. Sharpe	Torquay	£185,000			
J. Leighton	Aberdeen	£450,000			
M. Hughes	Barcelona	£1,600,000			

1988–89

M. Donaghy	Luton	£650,000	G. Hogg	Portsmouth	£150,000
R. Milne	Bristol C	£170,000	C. Turner	Sheff Weds	£175,000
G. Maiorana	Histon	£30,000*	P. Davenport	Middlesbro	£700,000
Neil Webb	Nott'm Forest		J. Olsen	Bordeaux	£375,000
		£1,500,000	L. O'Brien	Newcastle	£275,000
M. Phelan	Norwich	£750,000	G. Strachan	Leeds United	
					£300,000

1989–90

B. Carey	Cork City	£55,000	P. McGrath	Aston Villa	£400,000
G. Pallister	Middlesbrough		N. Whiteside	Everton	£750,000
		£2,300,000			
P. Ince	West Ham	£800,000*	W. Heseltine	Oldham Athletic	
					£40,000
D. Wallace	Southampton		S. Goater	Rotherham	£30,000
		£1,200,000			
A. Rammell	Atherstone	£20,000			
D. Irwin	Oldham	£625,000			
N. Whitworth	Wigan	£45,000			

* plus £5,000 per game

A breakdown of the transfer dealings of United's managers since the war is as follows:

	£ Purchases	£ Sales	£ Loss
Sir Matt Busby	833,179	631,505	201,674
Frank O'Farrell	585,000	145,000	440,000
Tommy Docherty	1,249,000	902,750	346,250
Dave Sexton	3,482,500	1,585,000	1,897,500
Ron Atkinson	8,048,000	5,841,000	2,207,000
Alex Ferguson	12,250,000	3,737,000	8,513,000
Totals	26,447,679	12,842,255	13,605,424

Although no United manager has made a transfer profit during his period in charge, the Busby era must rank as the most impressive in terms of the number of years involved and the success achieved.

Appendix C

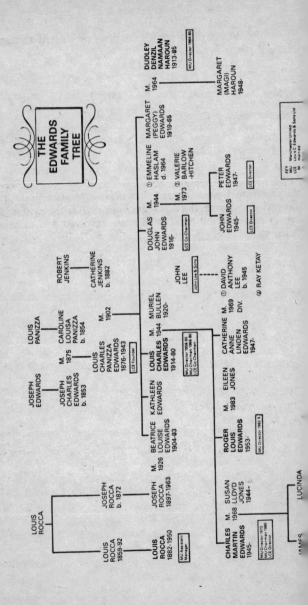

THE EDWARDS FAMILY TREE

LOUIS ROCCA

LOUIS ROCCA 1859-92

LOUIS ROCCA 1882-1950
MU Assistant Manager

JOSEPH ROCCA b. 1872

JOSEPH ROCCA 1897-1963

JOSEPH EDWARDS

JOSEPH CHARLES EDWARDS b. 1853

LOUIS PANIZZA

CAROLINE LOUISA PANIZZA b. 1854

M. 1875

LOUIS CHARLES PANIZZA EDWARDS 1876-1943
LCE Founder

ROBERT JENKINS

CATHERINE JENKINS b. 1882

M. 1902

BEATRICE LOUISE EDWARDS 1904-83

M. 1926

KATHLEEN EDWARDS

LOUIS CHARLES EDWARDS 1914-80
MU Director 1958-80
MU Chairman 1965-80
LCE Co-Chairman

MURIEL BULLEN 1920-

M. 1944

JOHN LEE
John Lee & Sons

DOUGLAS JOHN EDWARDS 1916-
LCE Co-Chairman

EMMELINE HASLAM

①

VALERIE BARLOW-HITCHEN

②

M. 1973

MARGARET (PEGGY) EDWARDS 1919-65

M. 1944

DUDLEY DENZIL NAMAAN HAROUN 1913-85
MU Director 1964-85

MARGARET (MAGI) HAROUN 1948-

CHARLES MARTIN EDWARDS 1945-
MU Director 1970
MU Chairman 1980
LCE Director

SUSAN LLOYD JONES 1944-

M. 1968

ROGER LOUIS EDWARDS 1953-
MU Director 1982-5

EILEEN JONES

M. 1983

CATHERINE ANNE LINDEN EDWARDS 1947-

DAVID ANTHONY LEE b. 1945

①

RAY KETAY

②

M. 1969
DIV.

PETER EDWARDS 1947-
LCE Director

JOHN EDWARDS 1945-
LCE Director

LUCINDA

JAMES

KEY
MU Manchester United
LCE Louis C Edwards & Sons Ltd
M. married

Bibliography

Arthur, Max, *The Manchester United Aircrash* (Aquarius, London, 1983).

Atkinson, Ron, *United To Win* (Sidgwick & Jackson, London, 1984).

Ball, Peter, and Shaw, Phil, *The Book of Football Quotations* (Stanley Paul, London, 1984).

Beardsley, Peter, with Cairns, Andy, *Beardsley* (Stanley Paul, London, 1988).

Best, George, *Where Do I Go From Here?* (Queen Anne Press, London, 1981).

Best, George, *Best of Both Worlds* (Pelham Books, London, 1968).

Bird, Alex, *The Life and Secrets of a Professional Punter* (Queen Anne Press, London, 1985).

Busby, Matt, *Matt Busby's Manchester United Scrapbook* (Souvenir Press, London, 1980).

Busby, Matt, *My Story* (Souvenir Press, London, 1957).

Busby, Matt, *Soccer at the Top* (Weidenfeld and Nicolson, London, 1973).

Cantwell, Noel, *United We Stand* (Stanley Paul, London, 1965).

Charlton, Bobby, *Bobby Charlton's Most Memorable Matches* (Stanley Paul, London, 1984).

Clarke, Alf, *Manchester United FC* (Convoy, London, 1951).

Coppell, Steve, *Touch and Go* (Collins Willow, London, 1985).

Crerand, Pat, *On Top With United* (Stanley Paul, London, 1969).

Docherty, Tommy, *Call the Doc* (Hamlyn, London, 1981).

Dunphy, Eamon, *Only a Game? The Diary of a Professional Footballer* (Kestrel Books, London, 1976).

Ferguson, Alex, *A Light in the North: Seven Years with Aberdeen* (Mainstream, Edinburgh, 1985).

Finn, Ralph, *Champions Again: Manchester United 1957 and 1965* (Robert Hale, London, 1965).

Fitton, Peter, and Keith, John, *Manchester United FC Official Annual 1978* (Circle Publications, Ilford, 1977).

Fitton, Peter, and Keith, John, *Manchester United FC Official Annual 1979* (Circle Publications, Ilford, 1978).

Foulkes, Bill, *Back at the Top* (Pelham Books, London, 1965).

Fynn, Alex, and Guest, Lynton, *The Secret Life of Football* (Macdonald Queen Anne Press, London, 1989).

Gallacher, Ken, *Jock Stein: The Authorised Biography* (Stanley Paul, London, 1981).

Gowling, Alan, *Football Inside Out* (Souvenir Press, London, 1977).

Greaves, Jimmy, *Taking Sides* (Sidgwick & Jackson, London, 1984).

Green, Geoffrey, *There's Only One United* (Hodder & Stoughton, London, 1978).

Gregg, Harry, *Wild About Football* (Souvenir Press, London, 1961).

Harris, Norman, *The Charlton Brothers* (Stanley Paul, London, 1971).

Hodgson, Derek, *The Manchester United Story* (Arthur Barker, London, 1979).

Hugman, Barry, *Rothmans Football League Players' Records* (Queen Anne Press, London, 1981).

Hughes, Mark, with Fitton, Peter, *Sparky, Barcelona, Bayern and Back* (Cockerel Books, London, 1989).

Inglis, Simon, *League Football and The Men Who Made It* (Collins, London, 1988).

Inglis, Simon, *The Football Grounds of England and Wales* (Collins Willow, London, 1983).

Keith, John, *Manchester United FC Official Annual 1981* (Circle Publications, Ilford, 1980).

Law, Denis, *An Autobiography* (Queen Anne Press, London, 1979).

Law, Denis, *Living for Kicks* (Stanley Paul, London, 1963).

Liversedge, Stan, and Keith, John, *Manchester United FC Official Annual 1980* (Circle Publications, Ilford, 1979).

Liversedge, Stan, and Keith, John, *Manchester United FC Official Annual 1982* (Circle Publications, Ilford, 1981).

Longmore, Andrew, Viv Anderson (Heinemann, London, 1988).

Macari, Lou, *United – We Shall Not Be Moved* (Souvenir Press, London, 1976).

McCartney, Iain, and Cavanagh, Roy, *Duncan Edwards: A Biography* (Temple Nostalgia Press, Nottingham, 1988).

Macdonald, Roger, *Manchester United in Europe* (Pelham Books, London, 1968).

McIlroy, Sammy, *Manchester United: My Team* (Souvenir Press, London, 1980).

Matthews, Tony, *Manchester United's Who's Who 1945–85* (Breedon Books, Derby, 1985).

Meek, David, *Anatomy of a Football Star: George Best* (Arthur Barker, London, 1970).

Meek, David, *The Manchester United Football Book, Nos 1–15*, (Stanley Paul, London, 1966–80).

Meek, David, *Manchester United Football Book No. 16 and Official Annual 1983* (Circle Sports, Ilford, 1982).

Meek, David, *Manchester United Greats* (Sportsprint, Edinburgh, 1989).

Meek, David, *Red Devils in Europe* (Cockerel Books, London, 1988).

Meek, David, and Tyrrell, Tom, *Manchester United: An Official History* (Hamlyn, London, 1988).

Mellor, Keith, *Heathens and Red Devils: Pictorial Milestones of Manchester United* (Temple Nostalgia Press, Nottingham, 1987).

Miller, David, *Father of Football: The Story of Sir Matt Busby* (Stanley Paul, London, 1970).

Morrison, Ian, and Shury, Alan, *Manchester United: A Complete Record 1878–1986* (Breedon Books, Derby, 1986).

Murphy, Jimmy, *Matt . . . United . . . and Me* (Souvenir Press, London, 1968).

Manchester United Supporters' Yearbooks (Manchester United Supporters' Club, Manchester, 1972–1989).

Neill, Terry, *Revelations of a Football Manager* (Sidgwick & Jackson, London, 1985).

Parkinson, Michael, *Best: An Intimate Biography* (Hutchinson, London, 1975).

Ponting, Ivan, *Manchester United: Player by Player* (Crowood Press, Marlborough, 1989).

Radford, Brian, *Through Open Doors* (Harrap, London, 1984).

Reed, Al, *It's All in the Book* (W. H. Allen, London, 1985).

Roberts, John, *George Best: Fall of a Superstar* (Manchester, 1973).

Roberts, John, *The Team that Wouldn't Die* (Arthur Barker, London, 1975).

Robson, Bryan, *United I Stand* (Pelham Books, London, 1984).

Rogan, Johnny, *The Football Managers* (Macdonald Queen Anne Press, London, 1989).

Rothmans Football Yearbooks 1970–1990 (Rothmans/Queen Anne Press, London, 1969–89).

Stepney, Alex, *Alex Stepney* (Arthur Barker, London, 1978).

Stepney, Alex, *In Safe Keeping* (Pelham Books, London, 1969).

Stiles, Nobby, *Soccer My Battlefield* (Stanley Paul, London, 1968).

Taylor, Frank, *The Day a Team Died* (Souvenir Press, London, 1983).

Thornton, Eric, *Manchester United: Barson to Busby* (Robert Hale, London, 1971).

Tyrrell, Tom, *Manchester United* (Hamlyn, Feltham, 1984).

Tyrrell, Tom, *The Manchester United Annual 1989* (Hamlyn, London, 1988).

Tyrrell, Tom, *The Red Devils Disciples* (Kaye and Ward, London, 1970).

Williamson, Stanley, *The Munich Air Disaster* (Cassirer, London, 1972).

Young, Percy, *Manchester United* (Heinemann, London, 1960).

Index

Index

In the following index, 'Manchester United' is abbreviated to 'MU'.

Aberdeen 99, 235, 240, 243
AC Milan 70, 85, 156, 223, 230
Accrington Stanley 198
Adam, Hugh 214
Adidas 264–6
Admiral kit suppliers 264
advertising, ground 77, 262–3
agents 226, 227, 228, 230–1
air travel 39–41, 44, 45–6
Ajax, Amsterdam 230
Albiston, Arthur 116
alcohol, and violence 159, 267
Aldridge, John 302
All Football 27
Allen, Reg 72
Allison, Malcolm 179
Altrincham 13
AMM Group of Companies Ltd 192
Analysis Financial Services 195
Anderlecht 36, 37–8
Andersen, Arthur 144–5
Anderson, a shareholder 255
Anderson, John 19, 24
Anderson, Viv 241, 242, 245
Anfield 16
Annual General Meetings, MU 29, 141, 179, 186, 200–1, 269, 297
Ansbacher, Henry 289, 293, 300

Appleby, Tommy 53–4, 55, 56, 57
Ardiles, Osvaldo 229
Argyll Foods 143–4, 173, 190, 196
Aris Salonika 92
Armstrong, Joe 22, 28
Arsenal 11, 25, 27, 37, 43, 44, 45, 73, 89, 91, 97, 105, 113, 153, 176, 201, 220, 229–30, 237, 241, 261, 279–80, 282, 299
ASK Vorwaerts 79
Association of Former Manchester United Players 166–7
Association of Manchester United Supporters 154–5
Aston, John Jr 81, 83, 89
Aston, John Sr 14, 20, 27, 56, 76, 86, 103
Aston Villa 11, 42, 43, 49, 75, 90–1, 118, 177, 245, 274, 299
Atherden, Ernest 251–2
Atkinson, Ron 165, 175, 186, 190, 193, 227, 230, 235, 237–40, 242, 248, 261, 268
Atletico Bilbao 39–40, 41
attendance figures 11, 24–7, 37, 38, 49, 71, 150–4, 158, 176–7, 178, 231, 273, 302–3, 311
Australian tour, 1975 115–16

Austrian clubs 74
Ayr United 16

Bacuzzi, Dave 149
Bailey, Gary 145, 226
Baldwin, Nicholas 199
Ball, Alan 81, 97
Barcelona 223–4, 225, 238, 252–3, 256
Barnes, John 302
Barnes, Peter 242
Barnett, Joel, Lord 189
basketball 247–52, 254–7
Bayern Munich 74, 224, 285
BBC 202, 203
BEA airline 72, 77
Beardsley, Peter 239, 300
Beardsmore, Russell 246, 304
Behan, Billy 22
Belgian clubs 36, 37–8
Benfica 74, 79, 80, 82
Bent, Geoff 47
Bermitz Farmer Ltd 263
Bernabeu, Santiago 73, 74
Berry, Johnny 31, 33, 38, 42, 45, 46, 47, 50, 72
Best, George 76, 78–81, 83, 89, 96, 122
   and attendance figures 152–3
   behaviour of 90, 98–100, 102, 108–9
   business interests of 98
   retirement plans of 99
   threats to 97–8
Betting and Gaming Board 215–16, 217–18
Biddle and Co. 187
'Big Five' football clubs 201–4
Birmingham City 42
Birtles, Garry 177, 179, 230, 234
Bishop, Bob 22
Bishop, Gordon 300
Blackburn 81
Blackmore, Clayton 233, 241, 245, 299
Blackpool 24, 32, 107, 292

Blanchflower, Jackie 31, 33, 42, 43, 50, 56, 72
Blyth, Jim 145
board of MU 17–18, 52–5, 57–9, 62, 65–6, 77, 101–2, 119–22, 133, 135–40, 160–1, 171–2, 180–2, 189–96, 198, 239, 289–90, 295–8
Bobroff, Paul 183
Boler, Stephen 287, 289
Bolton Wanderers 51, 112, 276
Bond, John 179
bonuses for players 24, 39, 228, 229, 231–2
Bordeaux 231, 242
Borussia Dortmund 38–9
Bournemouth 42, 101, 106
boxes, private 209–10, 220–1
Brady, Liam 227, 229–30, 244
Brazil, Alan 239, 242
Brennan, Shay 49, 51, 86, 87, 89
Brighton 177, 183, 237–8
Bristol City 245
Bristol Rovers 101
British Aerospace 130, 220
British Gas 262
British Rail 157
Brook, Eric 13
Brown, Laurie 119, 120–1, 123
Brown, Mary 119–20, 121, 166
Brown, Mick 235, 240
Bruce, Steve 241, 245, 279
BSB (British Satellite Broadcasting) 202, 203
Buchan, Martin 99, 109, 113, 118, 121, 166, 176, 234
Buckley, Eddie 227, 270
Burke, Bill 161, 174, 207–9, 211–13, 218, 219, 221, 262, 264
Burnley 112
Burrows, Nigel 195, 277–8, 283, 291, 292, 293, 295–7, 300
Busby, Jean 16, 47, 54, 69, 80, 121
Busby, Sandy 47, 137–8, 168, 269–71

Busby, Sheena 47, 54, 137
Busby, Sir Matt 6, 13, 131, 205,
  258, 298
  ambitions for Old Trafford 206
  and Dave Sexton 179
  and European Cup 35–8, 42, 43,
  69, 70, 73, 78–83, 85
  and Frank O'Farrell 102, 103–4
  and George Best 102
  and idea of MU flotation 298
  and Jock Stein 93–4, 95
  and Louis Edwards 8, 53, 56,
  67, 137, 138
  and Manchester City 15–16, 18,
  37, 75
  and MU board 17–18, 54–5,
  57–8, 77
  and Munich air disaster 47,
  50–1, 69
  and Red Devils Souvenir
  Shop 84, 269
  and rights issue 136, 137, 138
  and Tommy Docherty 104–5,
  109–10, 114
  and transfers 20, 27–8, 29,
  74–6, 81
  and Wilf McGuinness 86, 91
  as possible successor to Louis
  Edwards 168
  background of 15
  character of 17, 22–3
  honours of 70, 83
  joins MU 16–17
  MU shares of 133, 144
  resignation from MU
  board 180–1
  retirement from managing
  MU 84–5, 303
  salary/bonuses of 25, 70, 76, 78,
  83
  style of management 17–19, 22,
  25, 76–7, 304–5
  youth policies of 27–33
Busby Babes 6, 31–3, 86, 111,
  151, 153
Business magazine 190

Butcher, Terry 239
Butlin, Sir Billy 128
Butlin's executives, bribes to 128
Byrd, Alton 254, 256
Byrne, Roger 29, 31, 32, 33, 47,
  51, 100, 153

Canon 261
cantilever stands 209, 213, 277
Cantwell, Noel 73
Carey, Johnny 14, 18, 19–20, 21,
  27, 31, 138
Carman, George 146–7
Carter, Philip 202, 267, 304
Case, Jimmy 118
catering operations, MU 219–20;
  see also meat business
Cavanagh, Tommy 113, 115, 176
Cee-N-Cee 172
Celtic see Glasgow Celtic
Central League Cup 33
Chaplin, Fred 128
Charles, Mel 48
Charlie Bubbles 210
Charlton, Bobby 32, 45, 50, 51,
  70, 76, 80, 86, 87, 89, 96, 99,
  152, 153, 214, 252, 278, 283, 293
  and European Cup 82–3
  and George Best 100
  and inconsistency of MU 78
  and Munich air disaster 83
  and Wilf McGuinness 87, 88
  attitude to other players 100–1,
  102
  business interests of 181, 193,
  217
  early successes of 43–4
  election to MU board 181–2,
  193
  FA Cup debut 42
  in 1959 season 71
  on MU board 239, 289, 290–91,
  296–8
  retirement from playing 107
Charlton, Norma 83
Charlton Athletic 44, 298, 302

Chataway, Chris 203
Chaytow, Barry 276, 283
Cheeseman, Keith 122
Chelsea 35, 75, 78, 153, 164
Chilton, Allenby 14, 21, 27
Christmas hampers 217
Circle Sports Promotions
  Ltd 227, 270
Clarke, Colin 241
Clayton, Gordon 152
Clemence, Ray 118
Clough, Brian 99
coaches to football matches 149
Cockburn, Henry 19, 21, 27, 31
Cockney reds 148
Cohen, Stanley 281-2, 284, 286,
  294-5
Collins, Tony 193
Colman, Eddie 30, 33, 42, 47,
  100
commercialism of MU 4, 6-7,
  145-6, 161, 163-4, 165, 178-9,
  189, 203-4, 219-21, 258, 259-71
Connelly, John 78, 81
Conrad Continental plc 296
contracts with players 228-9
Coopers and Lybrand 185
Cope, Ron 49
Coppell, Steve 112, 114-15, 116,
  117, 118, 175, 176, 230, 234, 299
corporate hospitality
  packages 263-4
corrupt business methods 126-9,
  146
Coventry City 75, 239, 274, 298
Cowan, Sam 13
Crerand, Pat 73, 75, 77-8, 80,
  81, 89, 91, 92, 94, 96, 99, 100,
  106, 108, 110, 113, 116, 122, 123,
  149, 166, 168, 263
Crick, Michael 8
Crickmer, Walter 11-15, 17, 19,
  20, 27, 47, 53, 134, 151-2
Croker, Ted 137
Crompton, Jack 19, 27, 76, 86,
  137

Crook, Winnie 207
crowds see attendance figures
Crowther, Stan 49
Cruyff, Johann 227
Crystal Palace 103, 104, 298, 299
Cullis, Stan 44
Curry, Tom 21-2, 47
Czech clubs 44

Daily Express 104, 185
Daily Mirror 187, 279, 288
Dalton, Paul 236
Daly, Gerry 109, 117
Danish clubs 236
Davenport, Peter 226, 239, 241,
  245
Davies, J. H. 196
Davies, Ron 87, 89
Davies, Wyn 101, 106-7
Davison, Ian Hay 294
Dawn Print 216
Dawson, Alex 49, 50
debts of MU 11, 24
Delaney, Jimmy 20, 24
Delta Group 198
Delta Sports Ltd 195, 262, 263
Derby County 27, 101, 117, 119,
  121, 187, 274, 298
Development Association see
  Manchester United Development
  Association (MUDA/MUDL)
Distillers 190
dividend payments by MU 59,
  137, 139, 179-80, 186-7, 200-1
Docherty, Agnes 119
Docherty, Tommy (Thomas
  Henderson) 93, 158, 166, 179,
  205
  affair with Mary Brown 119-21
  and football tactics 165-6
  and Louis Edwards 114, 119
  and Matt Busby 109-10, 114
  and transfers 105-6, 107
  character of 105, 113
  discarding of players 106-8,
    111, 114

dismissal of 119–22
dispute with Willie
Morgan 111–13, 122–3
financial dealings of 115, 122–3
joins MU as manager 104–5
on tour in Australia,
1975 115–16
unpopularity of 110, 111, 112,
113–14, 115–16, 121
Doherty, Johnny 33
Donaghy, Mal 245
Donald, Dick 240
Done, Fred 300
Drinkell, Kevin 241
Duff, David 285
Dukla Prague 44
Duncan, Scott 12, 17
Dunfermline Athletic 94
Dunne, Tony 73, 89, 92, 166
Dunstable Town 122
Dutch clubs 230
Duxbury, Mike 241
Dyke, Greg 202–3

Eadie, Gerard 278
Edelson, Michael 142, 180–1,
278, 290–91, 295, 296, 297
Edgbaston 205, 206
Edwards, Beatrice 56
Edwards, (Charles) Martin 53,
56, 62, 147, 274
and 'activity centre' 251–2
and Alex Ferguson 240, 242–3,
244, 283
and Amer Midani 191–3, 250,
252
and basketball 247, 248–9,
250–1, 252, 254–7
and 'Big Five' clubs 201–4
and Bobby Charlton 181–2,
193, 239
and Dave Sexton 178
and deal with Michael
Knighton 272–3, 276–81,
283–4, 287, 288–301
and decline of MU 300–1

and Dennis Roach 226
and Exclusive Cleaning 196–8
and illegal dividend
payment 200–1
and Inland Revenue 234
and James Gulliver 189–91
and membership scheme 1–5, 6,
163–4
and MU
shares/shareholders 134–5,
136, 140–2, 182–4, 192, 194,
195, 254–5
and Robert Maxwell's bid for
MU 184–6
and transfers 199–200, 225–6,
229, 231, 242–5
background of 2, 169–70
commercialism of 177, 179–80,
182–7, 189, 198, 225–6
election as MU chairman, 168–9,
173
election to MU board 133, 171
in family meat business 170–1,
172–3
income of 6, 173–4, 179, 181,
186, 189, 199–200
office of 188–9
on MU board 171–2
sporting interests of 171, 172,
252–3
tightens grip on MU 174–5,
177, 180–1
treatment of David Smith 4–7
Edwards, Douglas 55, 62–3, 64,
66, 125, 128, 129, 130, 142, 143,
147, 170, 199
Edwards, Duncan 6, 30–3, 45,
47, 50, 51, 58, 100, 153
Edwards, Emmeline 55
Edwards, Louis Charles 8, 52,
102, 105, 168, 169, 170, 172,
205, 210
acquires control of MU 65–8
and commercialization of
MU 145–6
and Matt Busby 56, 137, 138

and MU shares/shareholders 58, 59–68, 131–7, 146
and Munich air disaster 58
and rights issue 131–3, 135–7, 138–40
and Tommy Docherty 114, 119
and *World in Action* allegations 126–7, 146–7
background of 55, 124–5
character of 175
corrupt business methods of 126–9, 146
death of 147
election to MU board 53, 58
in meat business 125–30, 142–4, 146
insider trading by 134–5
Edwards, Louis Charles Panizza 124–5
Edwards, Martin *see* Edwards, (Charles) Martin
Edwards, Muriel 55, 56, 121, 134, 169, 199
Edwards, Roger 135, 138, 180, 181, 194
Edwards, Susan 190, 192–3, 278
Elder, Stephen 201
England, Mike 81
English Basketball Association 249
Equipe, L' 34
Estudiantes 85
European Cup (European Champion Clubs Cup Competition) 34–43, 69–71, 73, 94, 203
1957 36–43
1958 44–6
1966 78–81
1968 82–3, 85, 150, 154, 259
1969 156
1977 118
European Cup-Winners Cup 76, 77–8, 79, 89, 95, 160, 238
Eusebio 82
Evans, David 197

Everton 42, 81, 86, 87, 97, 174, 201, 202, 212, 238, 245, 259, 267, 273, 299, 304
Exclusive Cleaning and Maintenance Ltd 196–8
Executive Suite 219, 260
expenses, MU directors' 103, 196
ex-United players 166–7

FA Cup
1909 10
1934 13
1948 23–4, 26, 27, 151
1949 25
1957 41–2, 43
1958 48–51, 69
1963 75–6
1964 77
1970 89–90
1976 116–18, 121
1977 118
1979 144, 176
1981 177
1983 183, 237–8
1985 222, 225, 236, 237
1988 241
1989 246, 273
1990 299
FA Youth Cup
1953 30
1954 32
1955 32
1957 71
1964 76
fans *see* supporters, MU
Farrington, Frank 60–1, 134
Ferencvaros 78
Ferguson, Alex 222, 231, 235, 237, 298, 299, 303–4
and Martin Edwards 242–3, 244
and transfers 241–5, 282
joins MU as manager 240–1
second season at MU 245–6
FIFA 226
Financial Times 141
Finney, Albert 210

first division 12, 236–7
First Vienna 74
Flashman, Stan 122
Fletcher, John 140, 145
flotation of MU, proposed 297, 304
Football Association 30, 34, 48, 70, 137, 139, 156, 186, 206, 226, 244
'Football in the Community' 253
Football League 10, 36, 39, 40, 41, 70, 129, 138, 184, 202–3, 235, 251, 267, 286, 292
  Management Committee 35–6, 137, 201
Football League Championship see league championship
football pools 205–8, 211–13, 217
'football specials' (trains) 157–8
foreign transfers 229
Forsyth, Alex 105
Foulkes, Bill 31, 32, 34, 49, 71, 76, 82, 83, 86, 87, 89, 101, 107
  on air travel 39–41
Francis, Trevor 227
French clubs 231
friendly games 236
Fry, Barry 122
FSO Manchester United Basketball Club 249
Fulham 50, 153

Gallacher, Ken 95
Garton, Billy 233, 240
Gascoigne, Paul 193, 226, 241, 242, 243–5
Gaskell, David 71
gate receipts 66; see also attendance figures
General Electric Co. 37
Gibson, Alan 52, 54, 58, 59, 62, 65–7, 131, 133–5, 141, 169, 180, 181, 190
Gibson, Anne 59, 62
Gibson, Colin 303
Gibson, Don 137

Gibson, Gordon 67
Gibson, James W. 11–14, 16, 18, 19, 26, 27, 52, 54, 59, 169, 196
Gibson, Terry 239, 242
Giles, Johnny 224
Gill, Tony 246
Gillette 115
Glasgow Celtic 15, 75, 93, 94, 95, 106, 149, 215, 233
Glasgow Rangers 149, 174, 213–15, 219, 250, 284–5, 286–7
G-Mex Centre 249
Goldstein, Oscar 194–5, 234
Goldstone, Michael 155
Goodman, Derrick and Co. 147
Goodwin, Freddie 49
Gorna, John 146
Gornik 82
Gowling, Alan 92, 96
Graham, Deiniol 246
Graham, George 105
Granada TV 43, 112, 123, 126–7, 128, 140, 146–7
Greaves, Ian 49–50
Green, Geoffrey 7, 55–6, 154
Greengrass, Paul 146
Greenhoff, Brian 109, 114, 115, 117, 145, 146
Greenhoff, Jimmy 118
Greenhough, supporters' club founder 11, 150–1, 152
Greenwood, Richard 256, 257
Gregg, Harry 49, 51, 67, 71, 72, 101, 106, 124, 184, 237
Gulliver, James 168, 169, 180, 185, 189, 192
  buys Edwards' meat business 142–4, 172–3
  joins MU board 144–5
  resignation from MU board 189–91

Halifax Town 276
Hanrahan, Joe 225
Hardaker, Alan 39, 129
Hardman, Elizabeth 134, 135

Hardman, Harold 18, 26, 52, 54, 57–9, 65–7, 133, 134, 205, 207
Haroun, Denzil 7, 63–4, 65–6, 121, 136, 160–1, 174, 180, 193
Haroun, Peggy (née Edwards) 63
Harper, Bob 22
Harrington Kilbride & Partners Ltd 174
Harrison Baldwin 199
Hartlepool 42
Hashimi, Sam 293, 300
Hassall, Harold 262
Hayes, Steve 121
Hayters 266
head-tennis tournament in Australia 115, 116
Herd, Alec 13
Herd, David 73, 75, 78, 153
Heysel disaster 251
Hibernian 35, 285
Hibernians of Malta 82
Higgins, Mark 242
Hilditch, Clarence 64–5
Hill, Gordon 115, 116, 117, 175–6
Hill, Jimmy 206
Hillsborough disaster 150
HJK Helsingin 79
Hogg, Graeme 245
Holton, Jim 106, 107, 109, 166
Honved 39
hooliganism see violence, football
House of Fraser 131
Houston, Stewart 109
Howell, Denis 159
Huddersfield 44, 75
Hughes, Mark 189, 222–6, 229, 233, 241, 244, 245, 279, 299
Hull City 111
Humphreys, Alex 172
Hungarian clubs 35, 39, 78
Hysen, Glenn 282

ICI executives, bribes to 128
Icke, David 274
identity card scheme 2, 4, 163–4

Ince, Paul 282
Inland Revenue 147, 234–5
insider trading by Edwards family 134–5
insurance for Munich air disaster 71–2
Inter-Cities Fairs Cup 78, 81, 93
International Sports Travel 149
Ipswich Town 12, 176
Ireland 213
Irish supporters 148–9
Italian clubs 39, 70, 85, 156, 223, 225–6, 230, 238
ITV 202–3

James Chapman and Co. 181
Jardine, Sandy 214
John, Elton 169, 187
John Lee and Sons 130, 219
Johnson, Anton 184
Johnson, Peter 197
Johnston, Craig 241
Jones, Cliff 48
Jones, Mark 31, 33, 42, 47
Jordan, Joe 223, 229, 230
Jovanovic, Nikola 226–7, 229
Judge, Mr Justice 290
Juventus 225–6, 230, 238

Kay, David 256, 257
Kearns, Ernie 196
Kelly, Michael 278
Kennedy, Alan 118
Kershaw, Les 194
Kidd, Brian 83, 89, 253
Killochan Castle 272, 273, 277, 280, 281
Kilmarnock 30–1
Kingstonian 138
kits, football see strips/kits, football
Kleinwort Benson 131, 132, 135, 183, 185, 186
Knighton, Albert 274
Knighton, Mark 275

Knighton, Michael
  background of 274–6
  bid for MU 272–3, 276–8,
    279–81, 282–94, 297–8
  character of 297–8
  flamboyant style of 278–9
  in property business 275
Kopa 43

Ladbrokes 212
Laing and Cruickshank 291–2
Lancashire & Yorkshire Nominees
  Ltd 187
Law, Denis 58, 67, 75–8, 80, 81,
  87, 89–91, 96, 99, 100, 105,
  107–8, 110–11, 123, 152, 153,
  156, 166, 214, 215, 283
Lawlor, John 140
Lawton, James 104
Layton, William 274
league championship 34, 238
  1949 25
  1952 27
  1956 32, 151
  1957 41–2, 43
  1958 44
  1959 71
  1963 75
  1964 77
  1965 78, 231
  1966 80, 81–2
  1967 81–2, 153–4
  1969 84–5
  1970 89
  1971 90–1
  1972 96–7
  1973 101
  1976 117
  1977 118, 122
  1983 261
  1986 222–3
  1989 245–6
Lee, Catherine (née
  Edwards) 130
Lee, David 130, 219

Leeds United 78, 90, 93, 95, 97,
  101, 118, 145, 164, 174, 242
Leicester City 12, 75, 96, 101
Leighton, Jim 235, 241, 245
leisurewear 270
Lillie, John 161, 163, 174, 198,
  218
Lineker, Gary 224
Littlewoods Cup 239, 240, 298,
  299
Littlewoods Organisation 125
Littlewoods Pools 208, 212
Liverpool 16, 18–19, 23, 48, 77,
  79, 80, 93, 117, 118, 161, 174,
  176, 201, 202, 225, 238, 241, 243,
  259, 267, 279, 302, 303, 304
Lofthouse, Nat 51
London fans of MU 148, 153–4
lotteries 211, 212–13, 215–17,
  218
Lotteries and Amusements Act
  1976 212
Luton Town 197, 245, 298
Lyle, Ron 170

Macari, Lou 106, 117, 118, 123,
  234
McCalliog, Jim 109, 118
McClair, Brian 189, 224, 231,
  233, 241, 245, 279, 299
McCreery, David 112, 145
Macdonald, Malcolm 89
McDougal, Jimmy 19
MacDougall, Ted 101, 102, 106,
  123
McGrath, Chris 177
McGrath, Paddy 49, 57, 168
McGrath, Paul 226, 233, 236,
  240–2, 244, 245, 282
McGregor, Danny 198, 252, 266,
  267
McGuinness, Wilf 73, 152, 179,
  239, 304
  becomes chief coach 86–7
  becomes manager 90
  dismissal of 91–2

playing career of 86
style of coaching 87–8, 90
McHutchon, Andrew 184
McIlroy, Sammy 109, 114, 115, 117, 176, 234
McKeown, Thomas 62, 63, 134
McLean, Dr 54
McMenemy, Lawrie 178, 237
MacParland, Peter 43
McQueen, Gordon 176
Maine Road stadium 15, 19, 23, 25, 37
Manchester City 12, 13, 15–16, 18, 23, 26, 29, 37, 65, 75, 89, 90, 95, 101, 107, 110, 113, 172, 179, 227–8, 244, 288, 289, 298
Manchester Evening News 67, 101–2, 178, 204, 280, 286
Manchester Giants 191, 192, 247–8, 250, 252, 257
Manchester Guardian 9–10, 57
Manchester Opera House 53–4
Manchester Senior Cup 15
Manchester United Action Group '78 140
Manchester United Basketball Ltd 249
Manchester United Club-Call 268
Manchester United Development Association (MUDA/MUDL) 6, 139, 163, 207–13, 216–19, 221, 250, 262
Manchester United Diary 266–7
Manchester United Junior Athletic Club (MUJACs) 13–14, 28
Manchester United Lottery 213
Manchester United Social Club 154–5
Manchester United Supporters' Association (MUSA) 155–6
Manchester United Supporters' Club
and ban on attending away games 159
and ban on overseas travel 160
and football violence 156–7, 158, 159–60
and Scanlite fan club 161–3
history of 150–2, 154–6
membership of 158–9, 163
obtain office at Old Trafford 158
rejection by MU 2–7, 163, 164
special trains by 157–8
Manchester United Supporters' Yearbook 156
Manchester University 14
Man-U-News 266
Marbella Club 193, 244
Martin, Lee 232, 246
match sponsors 263
Mather and Nutter (architects) 209
Matthews, Stanley 24
Maxwell, Robert 184–6, 187, 278, 288, 292
meat business 125–30, 142–4, 146, 170–1, 172–3
Mee, Bertie 226
Meek, David 67, 101–2, 178, 240
membership scheme for football clubs 1–5, 6, 163–4, 221
Mendy, Ambrose 282
Mercer, Joe 30
Mercer, Wallace 285
Meredith, Billy 64
Meredith, Winifred 64
Midani, Amer Mouaffac 191–3, 248, 250, 252, 276–7, 283, 287–8, 292–300
Midani, Mouaffac Al 191–2
Middlesbrough 245, 282
Milk Cup 161, 237
Mills, Mick 89
Millwall 12, 116, 164, 296, 297, 298
Milne, Ralph 245, 303
Miss Manchester United contest 152, 156
Mitsuda, Toshi 261
Mitten, Charlie 19, 20

MK Trafford Holdings Ltd 280, 281, 284, 286, 288, 295
Mond, David 293
Moorhouse, Barry 218
Moran, Kevin 232–3, 238, 240
Morgan, Willie 81, 89, 91, 92, 96, 105, 108, 116, 122
dispute with Tommy Docherty 111–13, 122–3
Morgans, Jimmy 71
Morgans, Ken 50
Morris, Johnny 19, 20, 24, 27
Mortensen, Stan 24
Mortimer, Dennis 274
Moses, Remi 237, 239–40
Muhren, Arnold 229, 234
Munich air disaster 7–8, 34, 46–8, 50–1, 52–3, 58, 69, 71–2, 83
Murdoch, Rupert 300
Murphy, Jimmy 31, 50–1, 106
and Munich air disaster 46–7, 48
joins MU 21
on European Cup 44–5
purchases of players after Munich air disaster 48–9
Murray, David 285–8
Musgrove, Malcolm 97, 99, 100, 103

National Basketball League 248
National Federation of Football Clubs 161
National Union of Journalists 178
National Westminster Bank 141, 142
Newcastle United 149, 226, 242, 243, 299
Nice 42
Nicholl, Jimmy 117, 234
Nicklin, Frank 266
Nish, David 101
Noble, Bobby 81
Norman, Beryl 134, 135, 146

Norwich City 82, 245, 282
Nottingham Forest 48, 99, 177, 230, 239, 273, 282, 299
Nou Camp stadium, Spain 206

Oblitas, Juan 227
O'Brien, Liam 233
O'Farrell, Frank 179
and George Best 97, 98, 100
and Matt Busby 102, 103–4
and MU board 101–2
and transfers 97, 99, 101
dismissal of 102–3, 104, 128–9
joins MU as manager 96
style of management 97, 99
Official History of Manchester United FC, The (video) 266
'Official Manchester United Fan Club' 161–3
O'Hora, Thomas 126–8, 129, 146
Oldham Athletic 299
Old Trafford
as venue for FA Cup semi-finals 14
bombing of 9–10
boxes at 209–10, 220–1
cantilever stands at 209, 213, 277
catering facilities at 219–20
Executive Suite at 219, 260
floodlights at 36–7, 42–3
Matt Busby's ambitions for 206–7
post-war return to 26
safety of 164, 165
size of crowds at 150, 151; see also attendance figures
Olive, Les 19, 22–3, 53, 62, 74, 86, 119, 121, 155–6, 175, 179, 186–7, 194, 195, 205, 207
and rights issue 138–40
Olsen, Jesper 226, 229, 230, 233, 239, 241, 242
Orme, Stan 189
Oxford United 184, 185, 222
Oxo 258–9

Oyston, Owen 287, 288, 292

Pallister, Gary 241, 282, 299
Parkes 117
Parkinson, Michael 98
Partick Thistle 105
Partizan Belgrade 80
Paterson, Steve 177
Peacock, Arthur 170
Pearson, Mark 49, 51
Pearson, Stan 14, 20, 21, 24, 27, 31
Pearson, Stuart 111, 117, 118, 145
Pegg, David 30, 33, 38, 47
People Management Ltd 256
perks for players 233–5, 244
Peruvian clubs 227
Peters, Martin 101
Petherbridge, William 54
Phelan, Mike 282
Philen Establishment 192–3
Polish clubs 82
Pontin's executives, bribes to 128
Pool Competitions Act 1971 212
pools competitions see football pools
Portsmouth 25, 245, 257, 286
Portuguese clubs 74, 77–8, 79, 80, 82
Potter, Derek 185
preference shares 59
Preston North End 41–2, 181
Price Waterhouse 194, 234
Priestley, Roy 155
Professional Footballers' Association 206, 235, 253
  Player of the Year award 245
Professional Representation Organisation Ltd (PRO) 226, 227, 228
profits of MU 24–5, 26

Queen's Park Rangers 84–5, 108, 117, 118, 145
Quixall, Albert 58, 72

Rangerman Promotions Ltd 214–15
Rangers see Glasgow Rangers
Raymond, Peter 185, 186
Read, Al 258
Read, Herbert Henry 258
Reagan, Ronald 191–2
Real Madrid 34, 39, 41, 42–3, 73–4, 80, 82, 252, 256
Reaney, Paul 101
Red Devil lager 267–8
Red Devils Souvenir Shop 84, 268–71
Red Star Belgrade 45–6, 226
Redfern, Norman 129, 130
relegation of MU to second division, 1974 109–10
Revie, Don 78, 101
rights issue of MU shares 131–3, 135–7, 138–40, 141, 145
Ritchie, Andy 177, 299
Rix, Graham 176
Roach, Dennis 225–8, 230–1, 236, 248, 257
Robins, Mark 246, 299, 304
Robson, Bobby 237
Robson, Bryan 189, 224–5, 230, 233, 237, 242, 244
Robson Rhodes 284, 286, 287, 289, 290, 292
Rocca, Louis 12, 14, 15, 16, 22, 55–6
Roden, Nigel 248
Rojas, Percy 227
Rose, Nat 61
Rossi, Paolo 238
Rous, Sir Stanley 34
Rover Group 130
Rowbotham, Alice 60–1
Rowbotham, Norman 60–1
Rowland, 'Tiny' 131
Rowley, Jack 14, 20, 24, 27, 31
Roxburgh, Andy 231
Ryder Brow junior club 29

Sadler, David 73, 81, 87, 89, 166

salaries/wages of players 24, 223, 224, 228, 229–30, 232–3, 244
Salford City Council 253–4
Sarajevo 82
Satinoff, Willie 57–8
Saunders, Ron 237
Scanlite Co. 161–3
Scanlon, Albert 30, 50, 71
Scholar, Irving 183, 202
school meals 125, 126
Scottish Cup 94
scouting/scouts 22, 28, 55
second division 12
Second World War 9–10, 15
sending off players 81, 85
Setters, Maurice 72
Sexton, Dave 95, 175–9, 227
and transfers 145, 177, 226, 229
dismissal of 178–9, 232, 237
style of management 166, 175, 177–8, 266
Shah, Eddie 287–90
Shamrock Rovers 44
Shankly, Bill 77, 79
shares/shareholders, MU 58, 59–68, 131–7, 138–42, 146, 182–4, 200–1, 254–5, 277, 289, 304–5
Sharp Electronics 174, 249, 250, 252, 254, 255, 256, 259, 260–2, 266
Sharpe, Lee 235–6, 246
Shaw, Richard 64
Sheffield United 177, 293, 299, 300
Sheffield Wednesday 12, 40, 48–50, 58, 72, 242, 274
Shelbourne 72
Shilton, Peter 101
shirt advertising 174, 260, 261–2
Shrewsbury Town 106
signing-on fees 230, 231, 244
Simmons, Alan 130, 131
Singette Ltd and others v. Martin 211

Sivebaek, John 226, 229, 236, 242
Smart, Jim 134
Smith, Anne (née Gilliland) 5, 155–6, 157
Smith, David 1–8, 155
and football violence 159–60
and MU membership scheme 4–5, 163–4
and rejection of supporters' club by MU 3–4, 5, 6, 163, 164
and Scanlite fan club 161–3
and special trains to Manchester 157–8
photographic work of 5, 160, 163
Smith, John 203, 267, 304
Smith, Prof. Roland 130–2, 184, 189, 220
Souness, Graeme 285
Southampton 75, 86–7, 89, 117–18, 178, 238, 282, 299
Spaceshot contest 214–15, 250
Spanish clubs 39–40, 41, 42–3, 73–4, 80, 82, 223–4, 225, 238, 252–3, 256
sponsorship 174, 249, 250, 252, 254, 255, 256, 259–62
Sporting Cristal 227
Sporting Lisbon 77–8
Sports Council 267
spot-the-ball competitions 212, 214
Spurs see Tottenham Hotspur (Spurs)
Spycatcher (Wright) 146
St David's School 275, 280
Stade de Rheims 34
Stapleton, Frank 230, 234, 237
Stefano, Di 42, 43
Stein, George 94–5
Stein, Jean 94
Stein, Jock 93–5
Stephens, Joe 183
Stepney, Alex 81, 82, 88–9, 90, 92, 108, 109, 113, 116, 123

Steven, Trevor 241
Stewart, Paul 241
Stiles, Nobby 80, 89, 101
Stoke City 172
Stokes, Bobby 117–18
Storey-Moore, Ian 99
Strachan, Gordon 233, 239, 240, 242
Stretford Leisure Centre 249, 251, 256
strips/kits, football 264–5
Summerbee, Mike 172
Sunday Mirror 104
Sunday People 120
Sunday Telegraph 100–1
Sunday Times 110
Sunderland 43, 149, 154
Sunderland, Alan 176
'Super League' proposal 202, 203–4
Supercall, British Telecom 268
Superga disaster 72
supporters, MU 148–67
  and football violence 156–7, 158, 159–60, 164–5
  and Knighton takeover bid 291–2
  attendance figures 150, 151, 152–3; *see also* attendance figures
  ban on attending away games 159
  disillusionment of 302–3
  early supporters' clubs 150–1, 152, 154–5
  fanaticism of 165–7
  journeys to Manchester on Saturday mornings 148–9
  London-based 148, 153–4
  Manchester United Supporters' Association (MUSA) 155–6; *see also* Manchester United Supporters' Club
  number of 148–50, 165
  revolt in 1930 11
  special trains for 157–8

Swales, Peter 179
Swift, Frank 13
Swiss clubs 70
Sydenham, John 86–7

Tabner, John 140
tactics, football 109, 110, 165–6, 175
Tara Travel 149
tax investigations *see* Inland Revenue
Taylor, Ernie 48, 49
Taylor, Rick 247, 252, 254, 255
Taylor, Tommy 31, 32, 33, 37–8, 40, 41, 43, 45, 47, 51, 72, 153
Taylor Report (1989) 150
Team Advance 267
television/television advertising 115, 202–3, 251–2, 260
Thatcher, Margaret 2
Thomas, Mickey 234
Thornhill, Archie 140
Thornton, Robert 281, 284, 286, 294–5
Thorpe, Jeremy 147
ticket-dealing, black-market 122–3
Tillmanns, Mr 234
Tilson, Fred 13
Todd, Colin 89
Torino 39, 58, 72, 75
Torquay 235–6
Tottenham Hotspur (Spurs) 25, 42, 43, 48, 79, 81, 101, 182, 183, 193, 201–2, 220, 226, 229, 239, 242, 244–5, 257, 265, 288, 298
Tracey, Richard 253
Trafford Park 9
Tranmere Rovers 112
transfers of players 20, 27–9, 48–9, 74–6, 81, 97, 99, 101, 105–7, 145, 177, 199–200, 222–6, 229–31, 235–7, 239, 241–5, 282–3, 298, 314–21
Tulsa Roughnecks 177

Turner, Chris 241, 242
Tyrrell, Tom 240

UEFA 70, 160
 multiplier system 223, 230
UEFA Cup 176
Umbro International 264
United Review 3, 148, 160, 162, 266
University of Manchester Institute of Science and Technology (UMIST) 130, 131
Unlisted Securities Market (USM) 183
Ure, Ian 89

Vejle Boldklub 236
Venables, Terry 224, 242
Vernons pools 208
video tapes of MU games 266
Villa, Ricky 229
Villa Park 24
violence, football 3, 156-7, 158, 159-60, 164-5
Viollet, Dennis 31, 33, 37, 38, 40, 41, 45, 50, 51, 71, 73, 152

wages of players *see* salaries/wages of players
Wall, Derek 183
Wallace, Danny 282
Walsall 118
Walsh, Gary 233
Warrington Vikings Basketball Club 191, 248, 249
Warwickshire Cricket Club 205-6
Watford 187
Watkins, Maurice 5, 181, 183, 185, 194, 201, 229, 240, 248, 278
Webb, Neil 279, 282
Webster, Colin 49, 50
West Bromwich Albion 12, 32, 50, 72, 237
West German clubs 38-9, 74, 224

West Ham United 72, 79, 81, 82, 106, 145, 164, 282
Whalley, Bert 21, 47
Wharton, 'Tiny' 214
Whelan, Billy 30, 33, 38, 40, 47
Whiteside, Norman 149, 225, 226, 233, 238, 240-2, 244, 245, 282
Whittaker, George 52, 53, 54, 59-60, 62
Whittaker, Mabel 59, 62
Whittaker, Sidney Hilton 126-7
Widzew Lodz 176
Wigan Athletic 181
Wilkins, Ray 145, 229, 235, 237
Wilmslow 171
Wilson, Bob 226
Wilson, David 246
Wimbledon 273, 303
Wolves 11, 30, 31-2, 42, 44, 46, 70, 71, 116-17, 177
Wood, Ray 32, 33, 43, 50, 71, 72
Woodward, Tony 163, 218
Woolworths 125, 128
World Cup 35, 51, 77, 79, 86, 89, 181, 209, 210
World Cup Championship (unofficial) 85
World in Action programme 126-7, 146-7
Wrexham 42
Wright, Peter 146

Yates, Chris 294
York City 92
Young, Bill 58, 65, 135-6, 169, 180, 181, 190
Young Boys Berne 70
youth policies of MU 27-33, 71
Yugoslav clubs 45-6, 79-80, 82, 226

Index compiled by Peva Keane

All Pan books are available at your local bookshop or newsagent, or can be ordered direct from the publisher. Indicate the number of copies required and fill in the form below.

Send to: **CS Department, Pan Books Ltd., P.O. Box 40, Basingstoke, Hants. RG21 2YT.**

or phone: 0256 469551 (Ansaphone), quoting title, author and Credit Card number.

Please enclose a remittance* to the value of the cover price plus: 60p for the first book plus 30p per copy for each additional book ordered to a maximum charge of £2.40 to cover postage and packing.

*Payment may be made in sterling by UK personal cheque, postal order, sterling draft or international money order, made payable to Pan Books Ltd.

Alternatively by Barclaycard/Access:

Card No. ☐☐☐☐☐☐☐☐☐☐☐☐☐☐☐☐☐☐☐

Signature:

Applicable only in the UK and Republic of Ireland.

While every effort is made to keep prices low, it is sometimes necessary to increase prices at short notice. Pan Books reserve the right to show on covers and charge new retail prices which may differ from those advertised in the text or elsewhere.

NAME AND ADDRESS IN BLOCK LETTERS PLEASE:

....

Name ————————————————————————

Address ————————————————————————

————————————————————————————

————————————————————————————

————————————————————————————

3/87